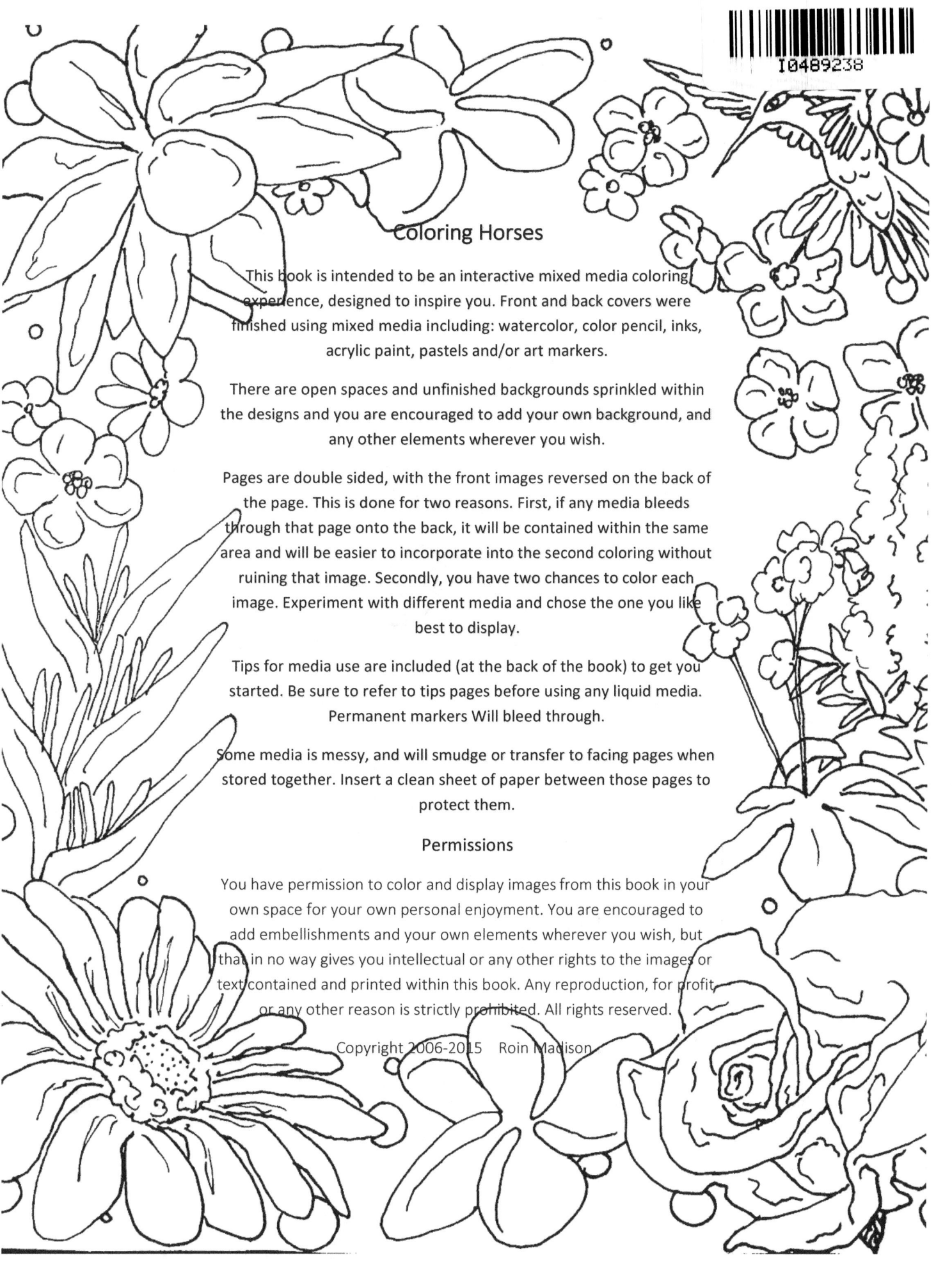

Coloring Horses

This book is intended to be an interactive mixed media coloring experience, designed to inspire you. Front and back covers were finished using mixed media including: watercolor, color pencil, inks, acrylic paint, pastels and/or art markers.

There are open spaces and unfinished backgrounds sprinkled within the designs and you are encouraged to add your own background, and any other elements wherever you wish.

Pages are double sided, with the front images reversed on the back of the page. This is done for two reasons. First, if any media bleeds through that page onto the back, it will be contained within the same area and will be easier to incorporate into the second coloring without ruining that image. Secondly, you have two chances to color each image. Experiment with different media and chose the one you like best to display.

Tips for media use are included (at the back of the book) to get you started. Be sure to refer to tips pages before using any liquid media. Permanent markers Will bleed through.

Some media is messy, and will smudge or transfer to facing pages when stored together. Insert a clean sheet of paper between those pages to protect them.

Permissions

You have permission to color and display images from this book in your own space for your own personal enjoyment. You are encouraged to add embellishments and your own elements wherever you wish, but that in no way gives you intellectual or any other rights to the images or text contained and printed within this book. Any reproduction, for profit, or any other reason is strictly prohibited. All rights reserved.

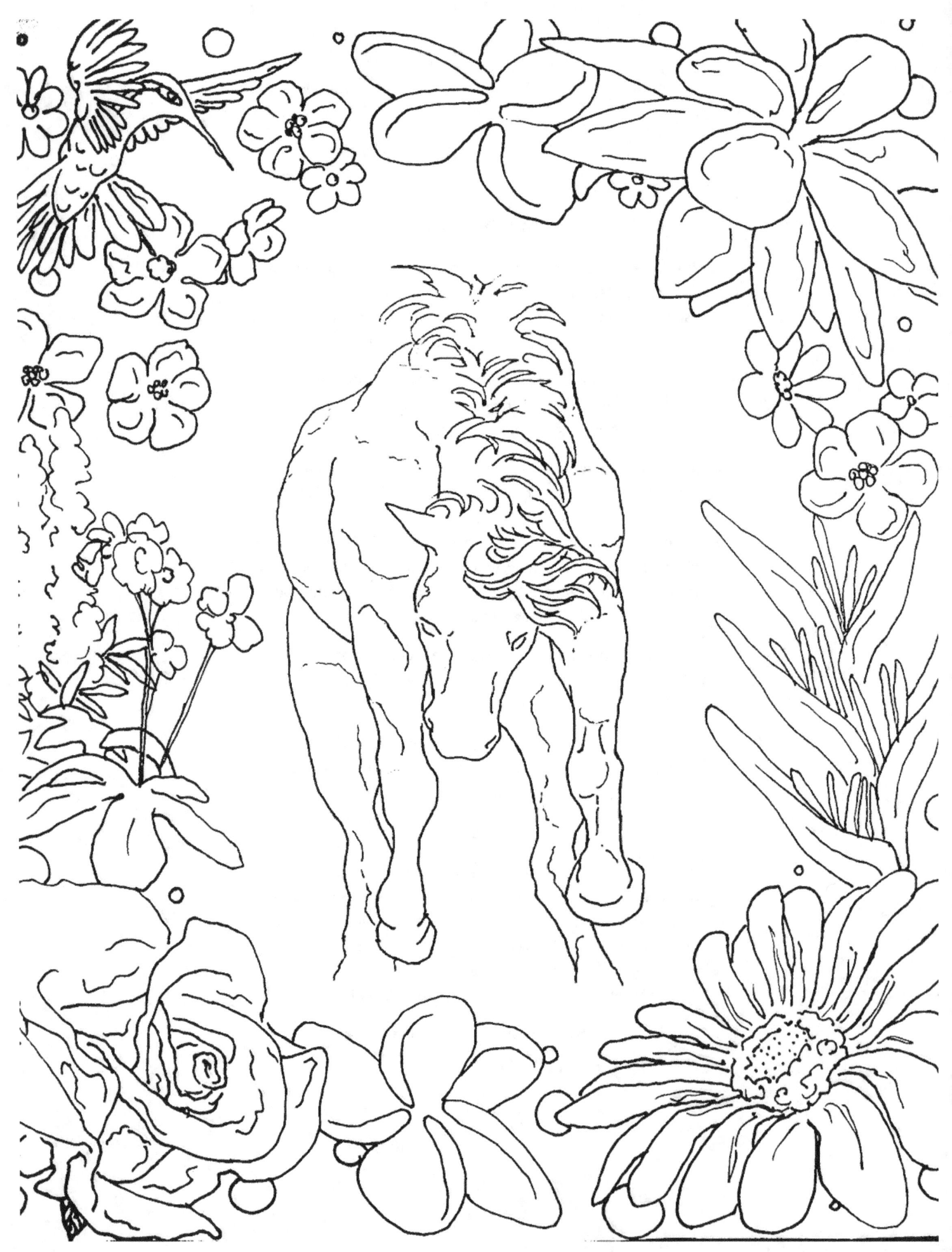

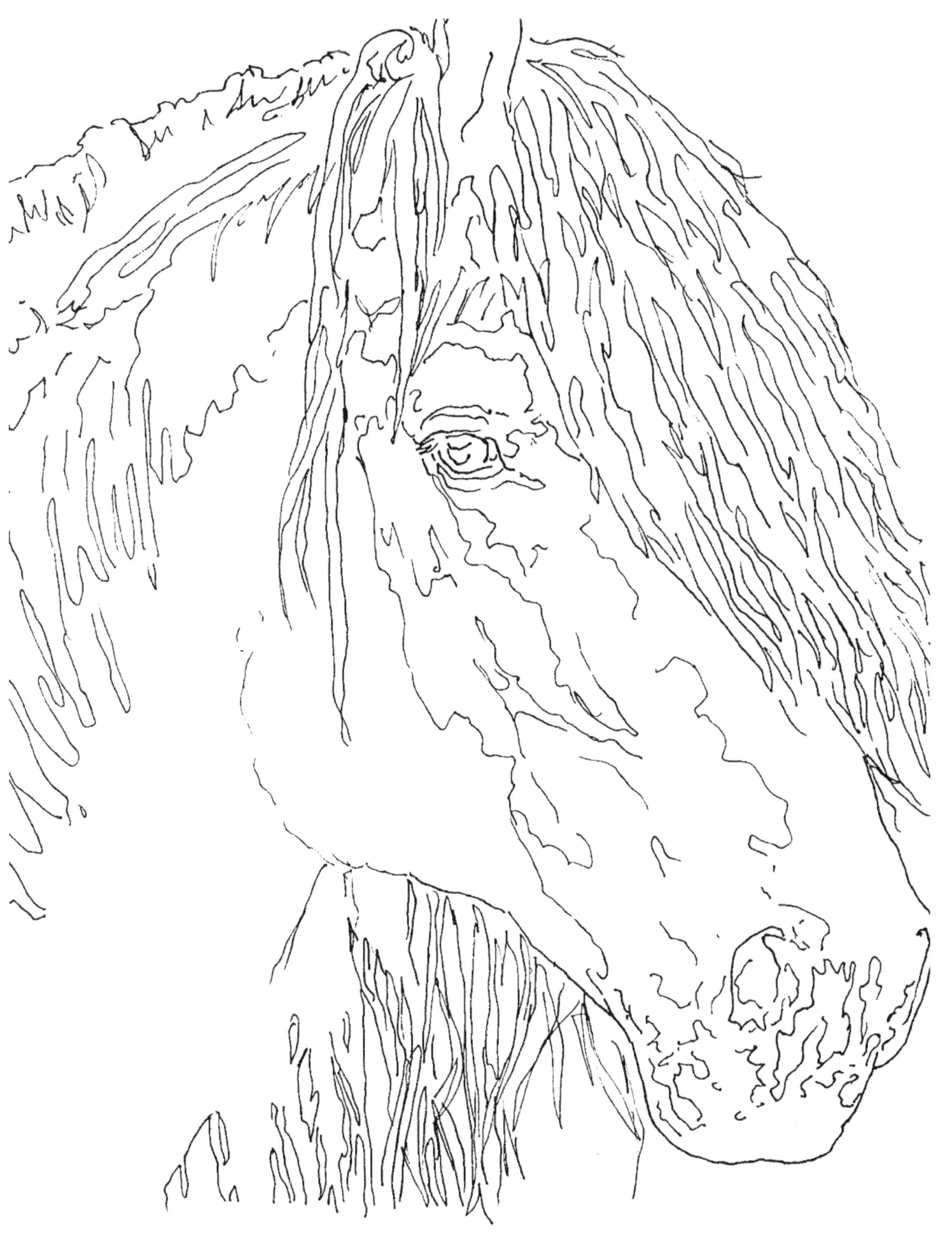

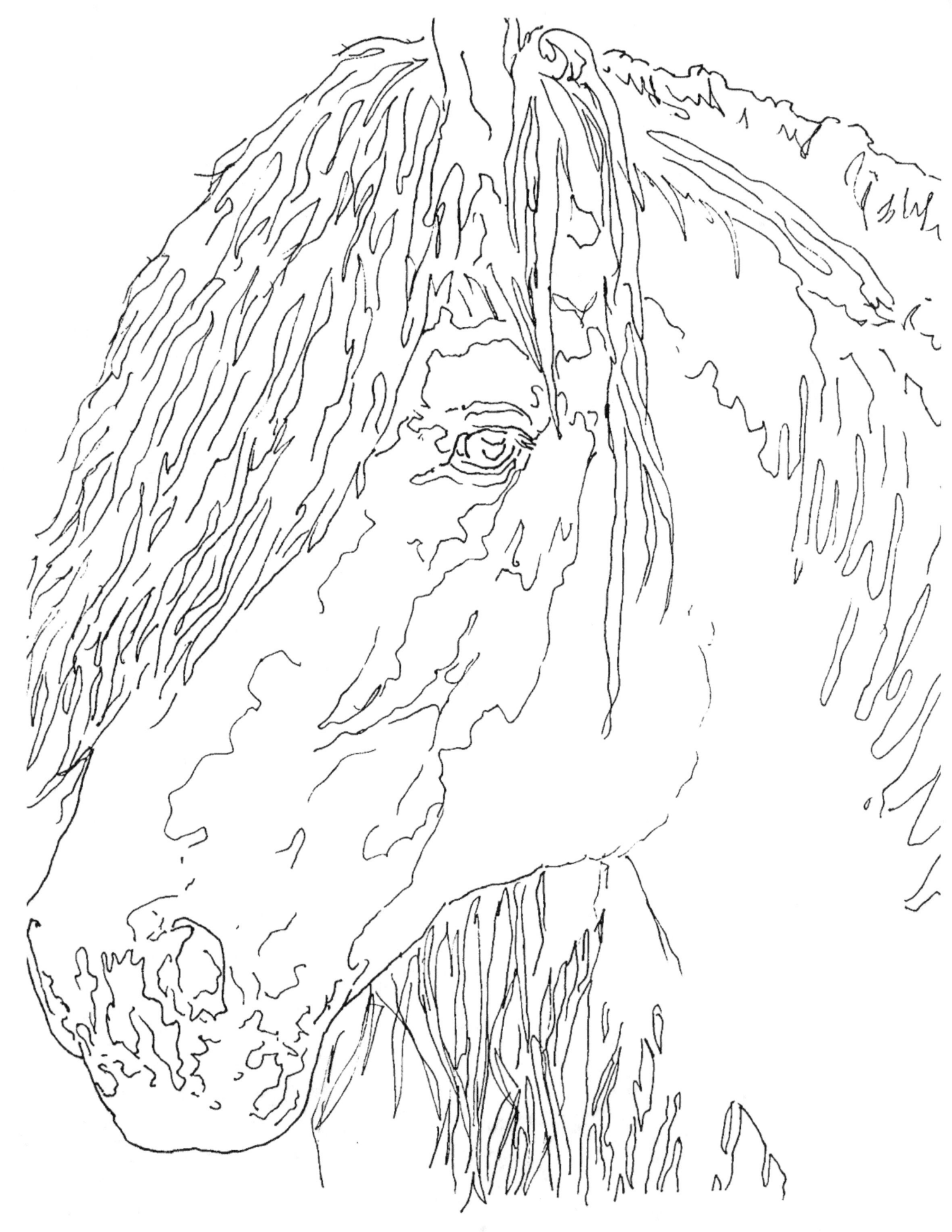

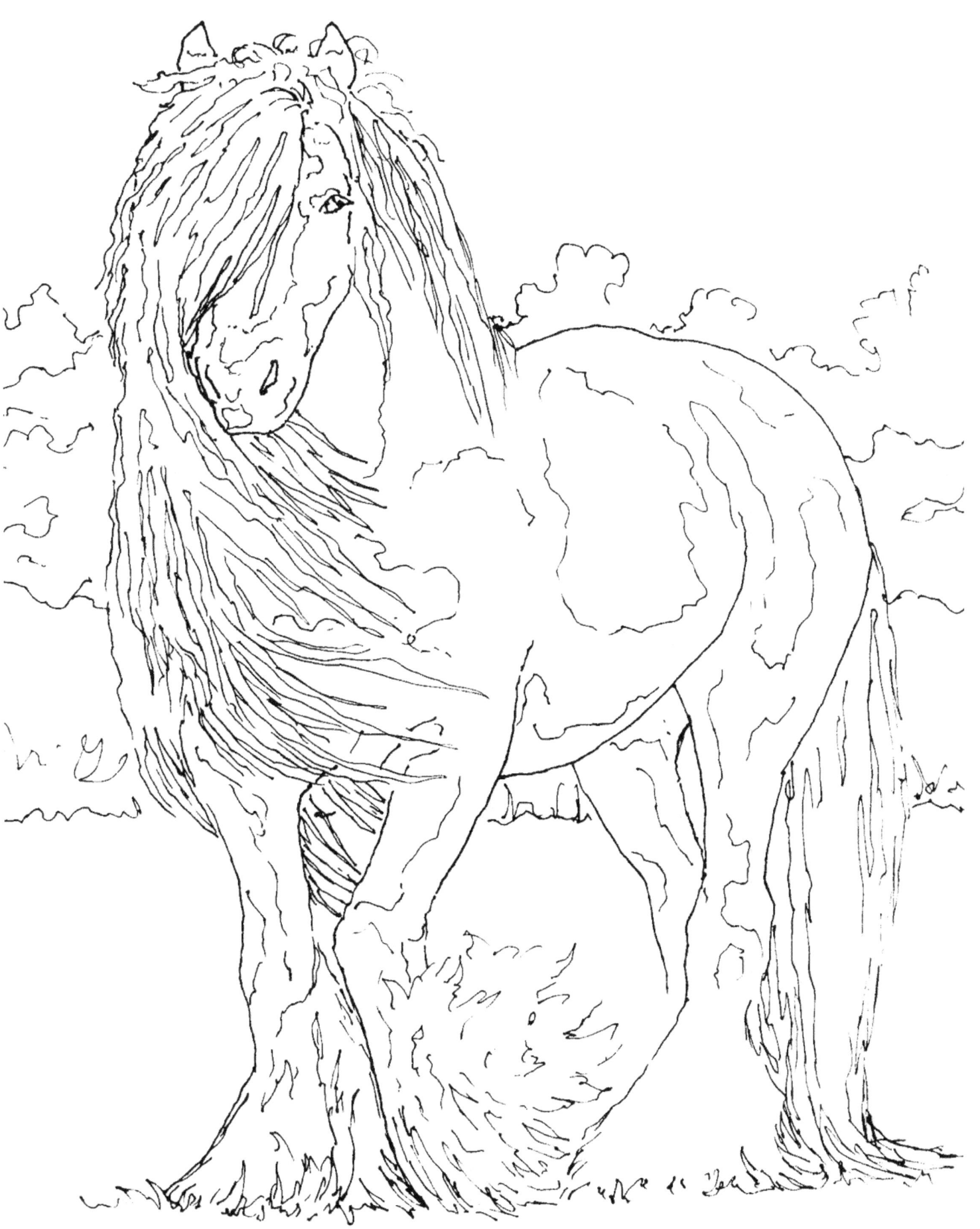

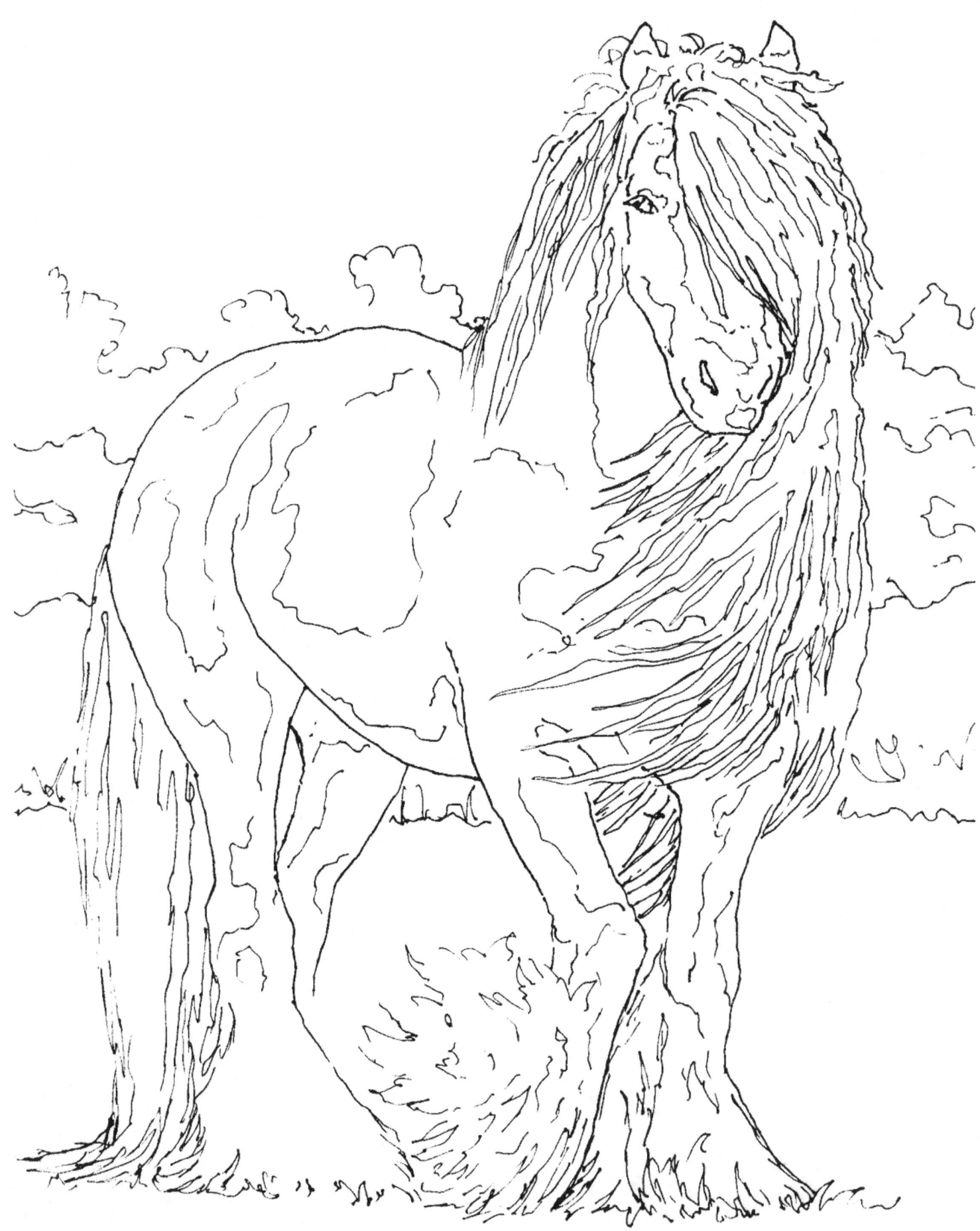

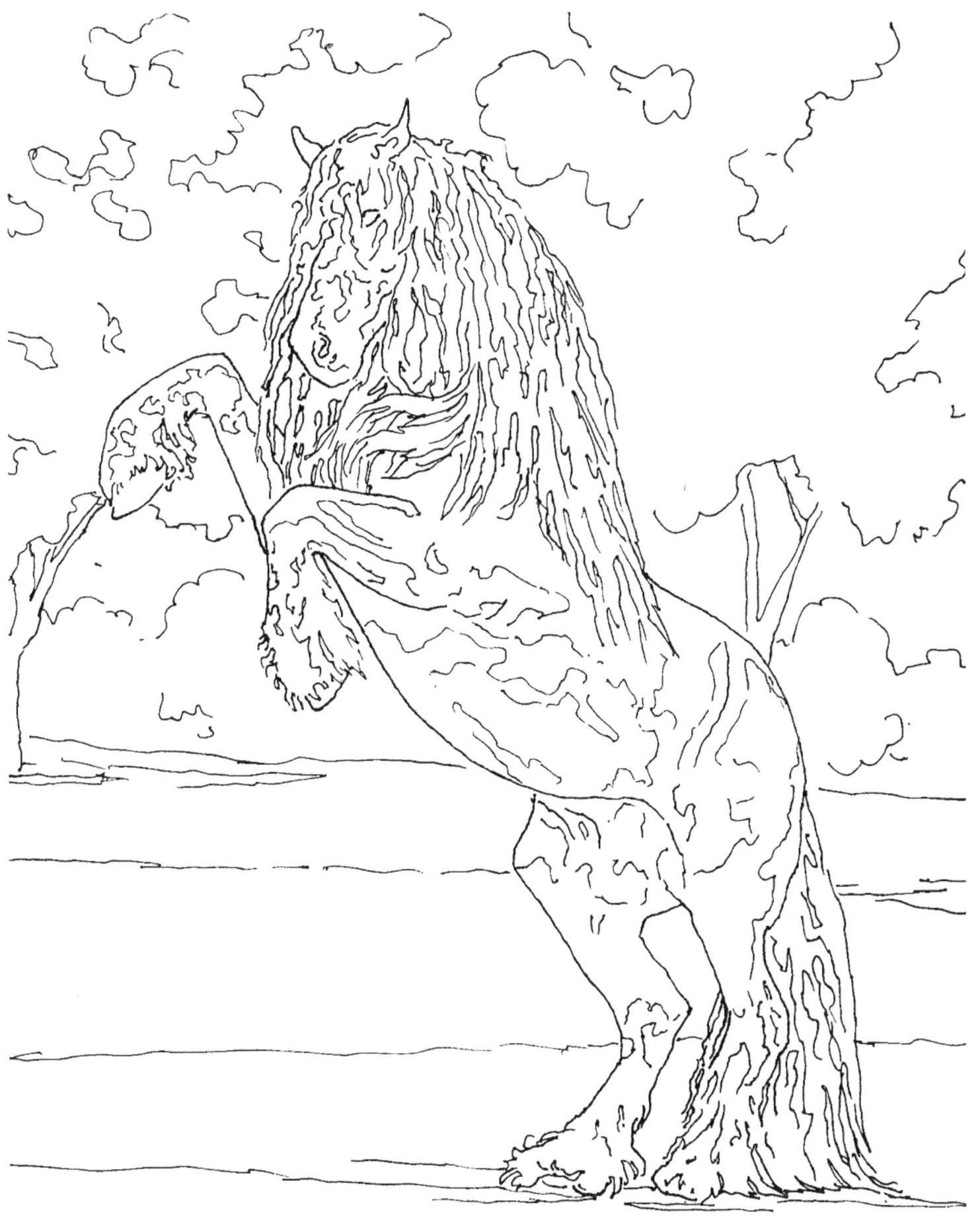

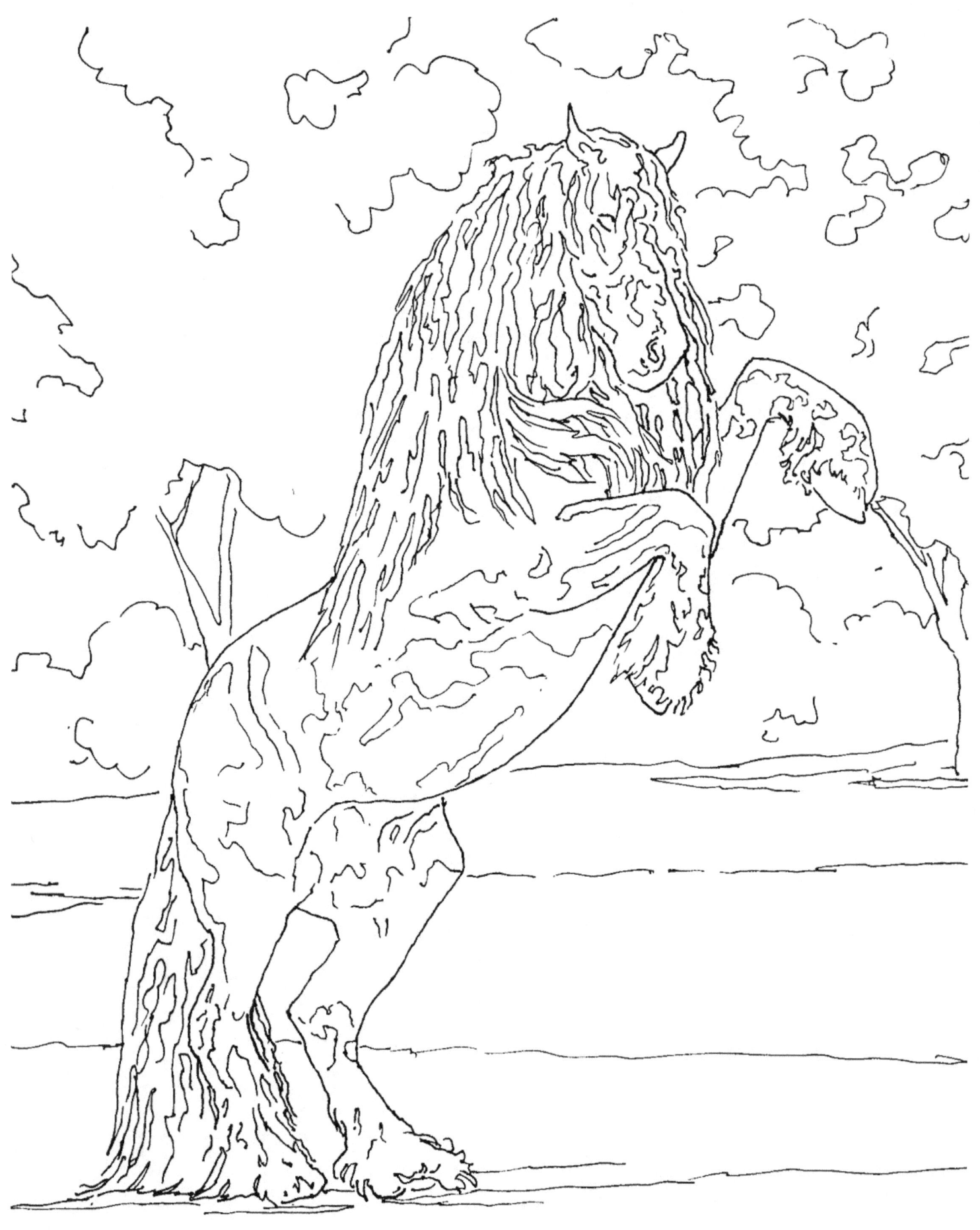

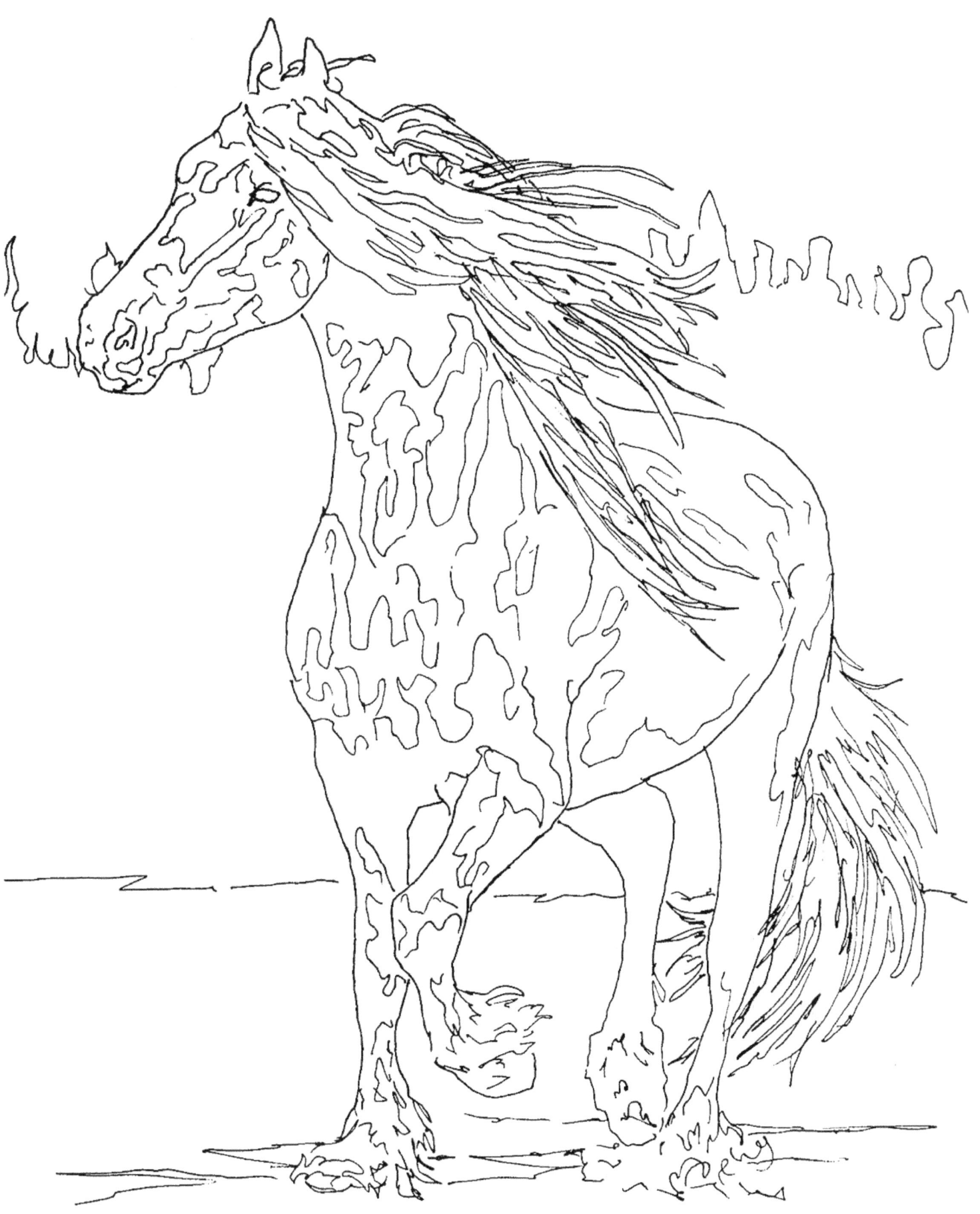

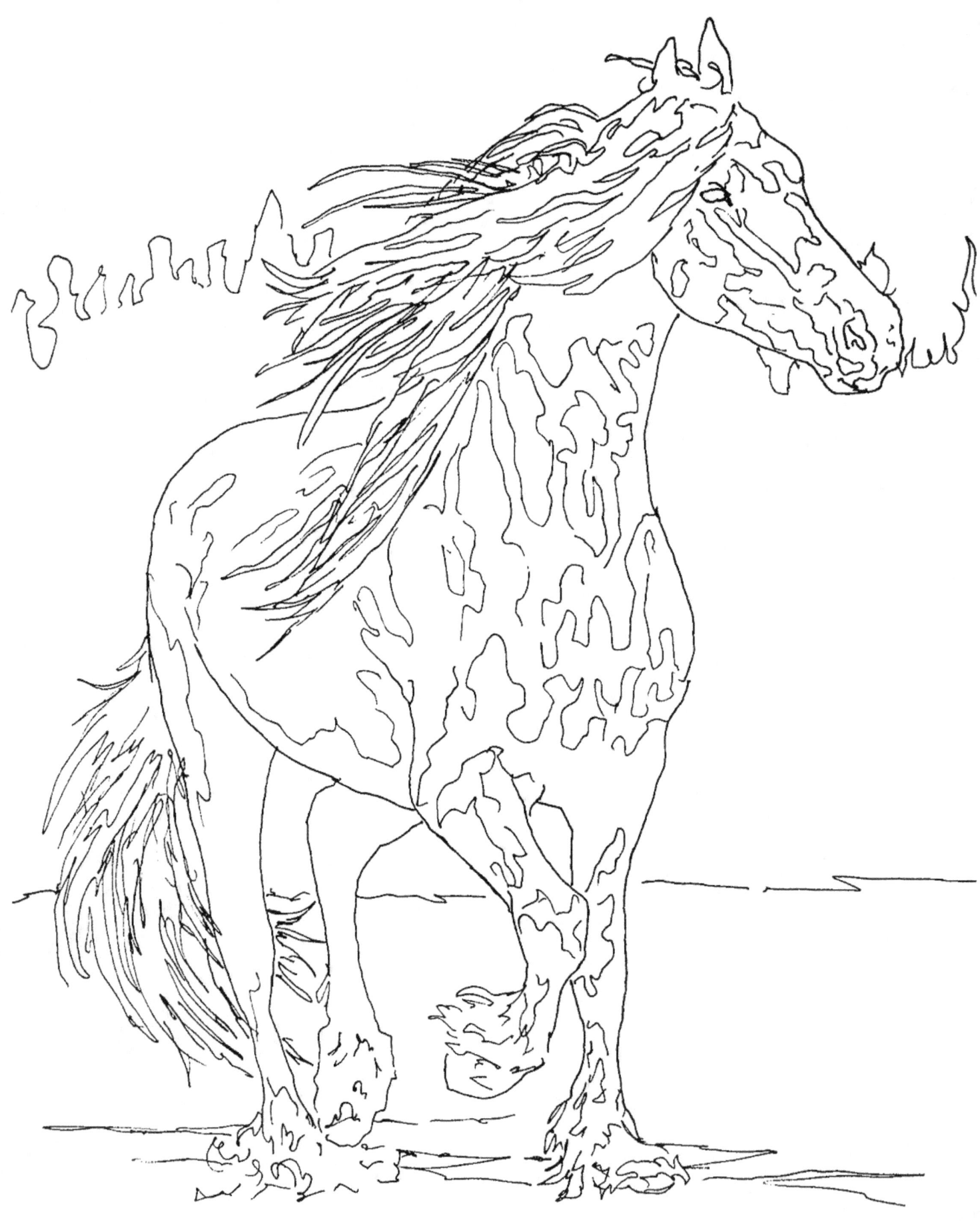

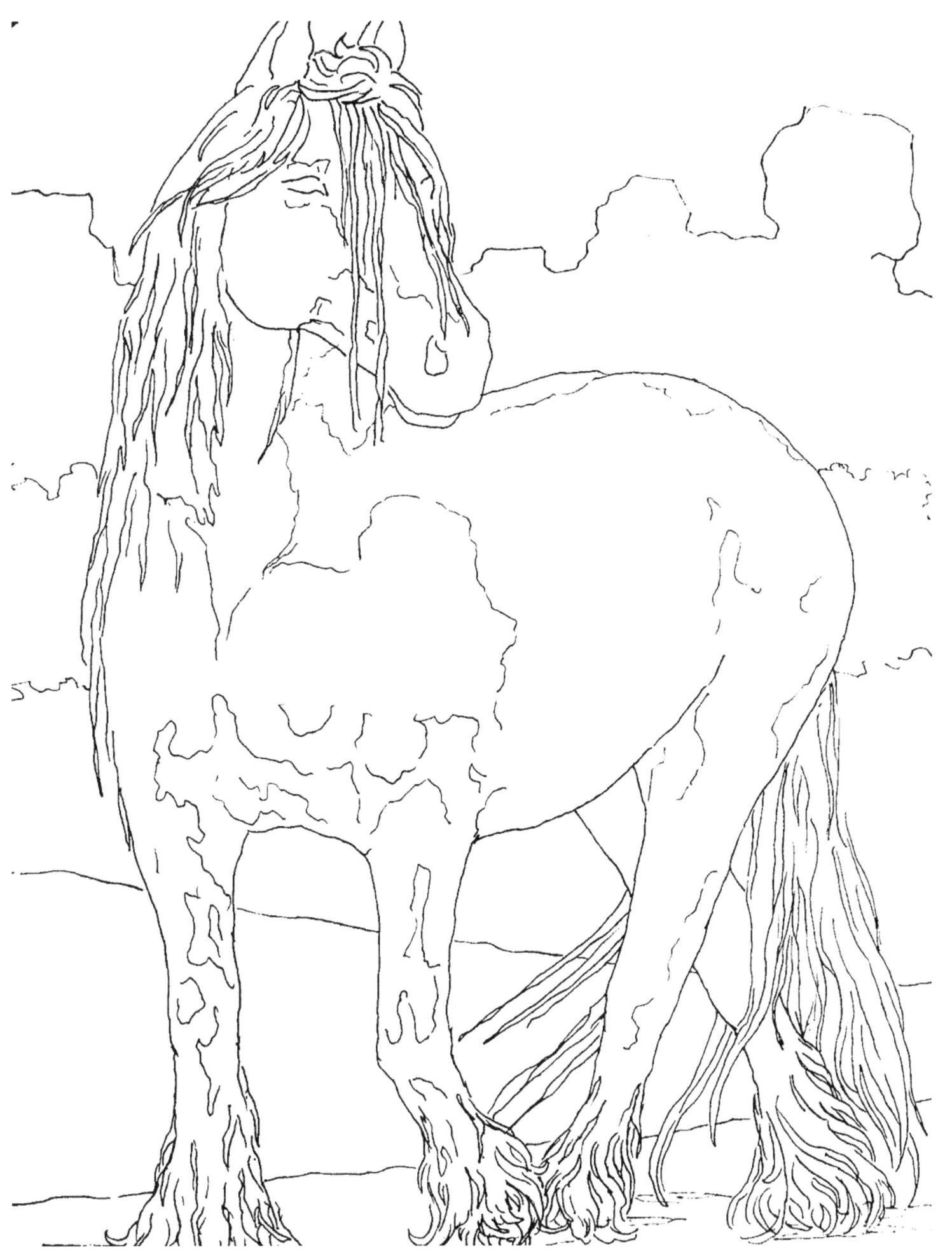

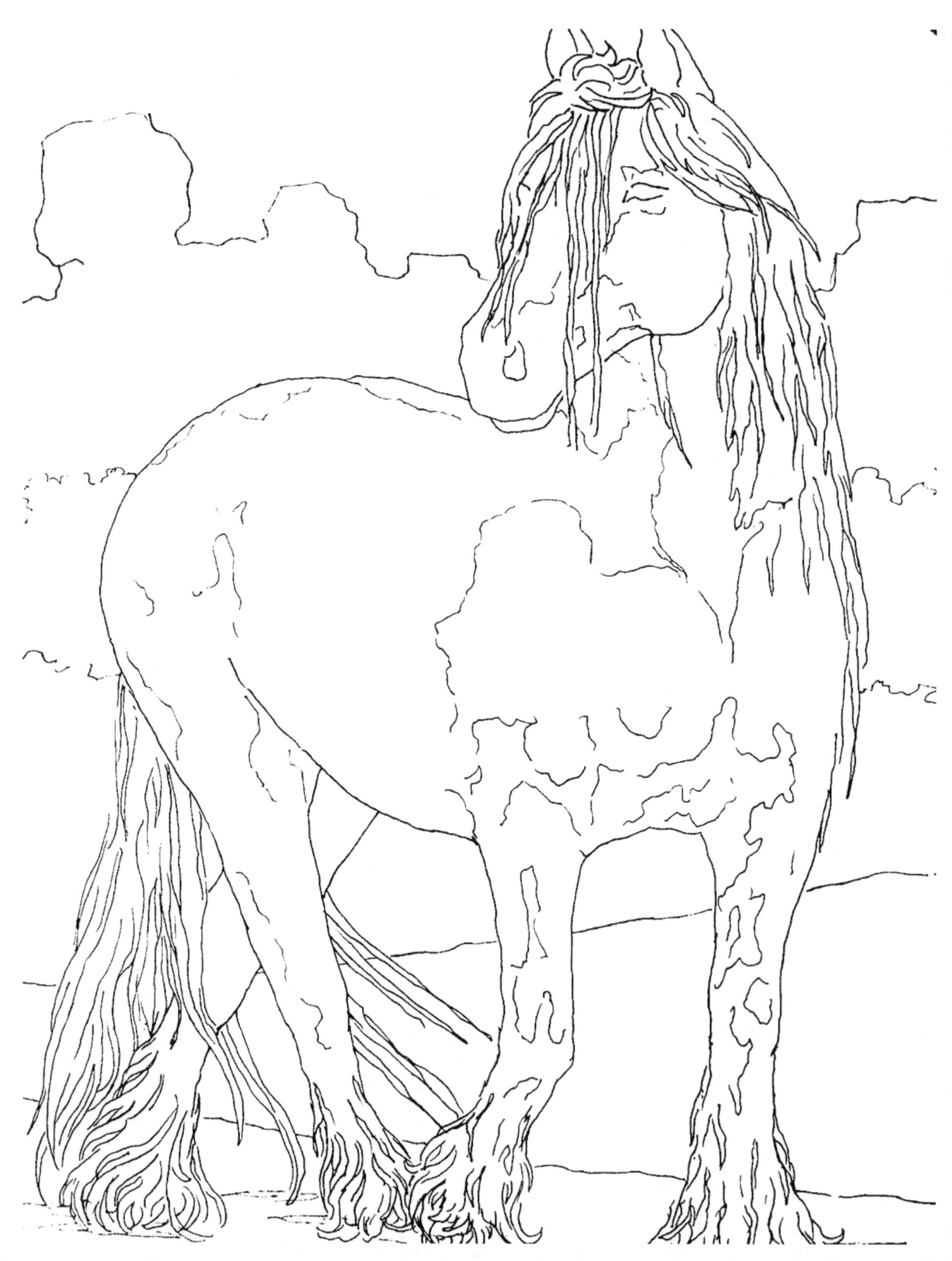

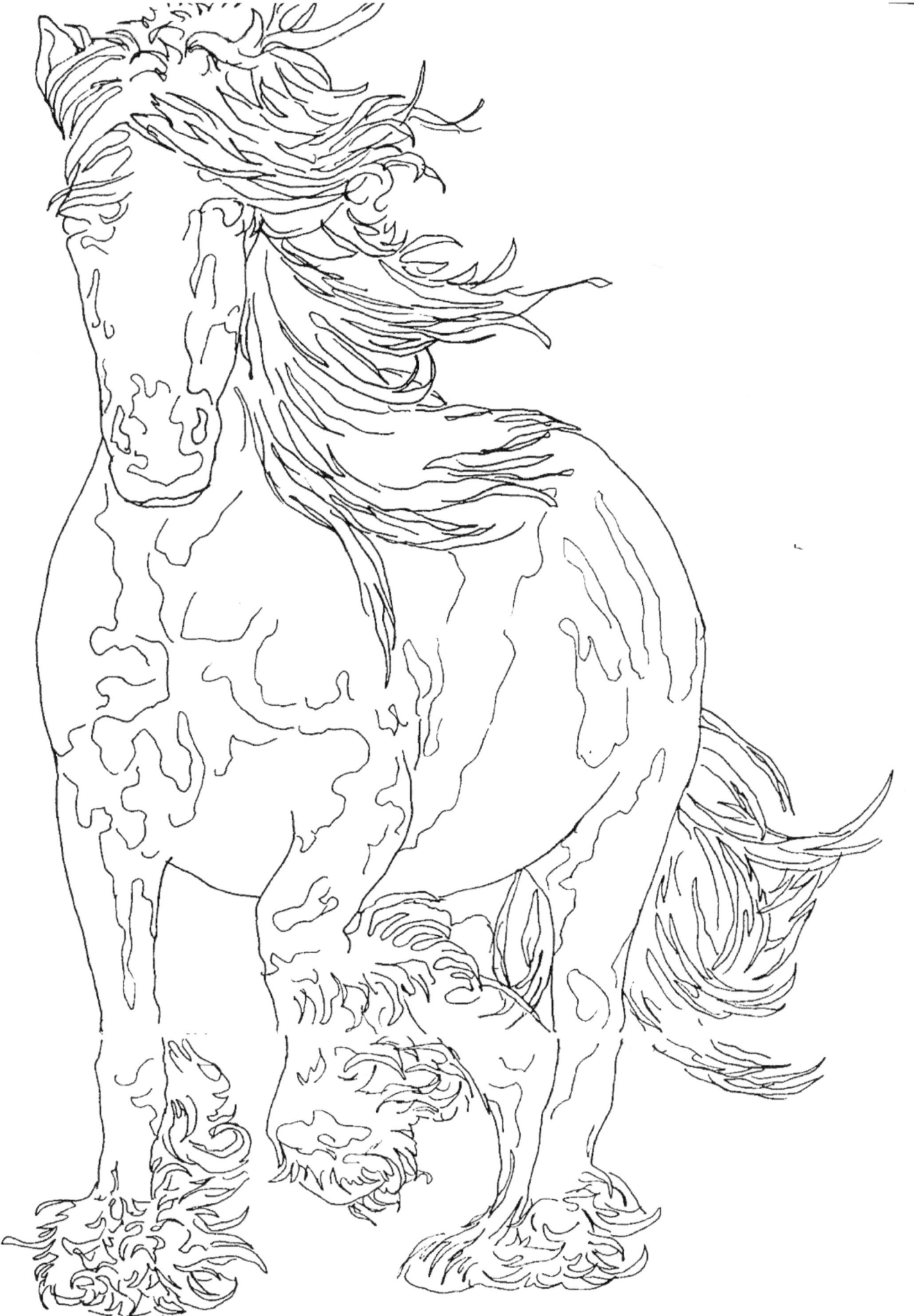

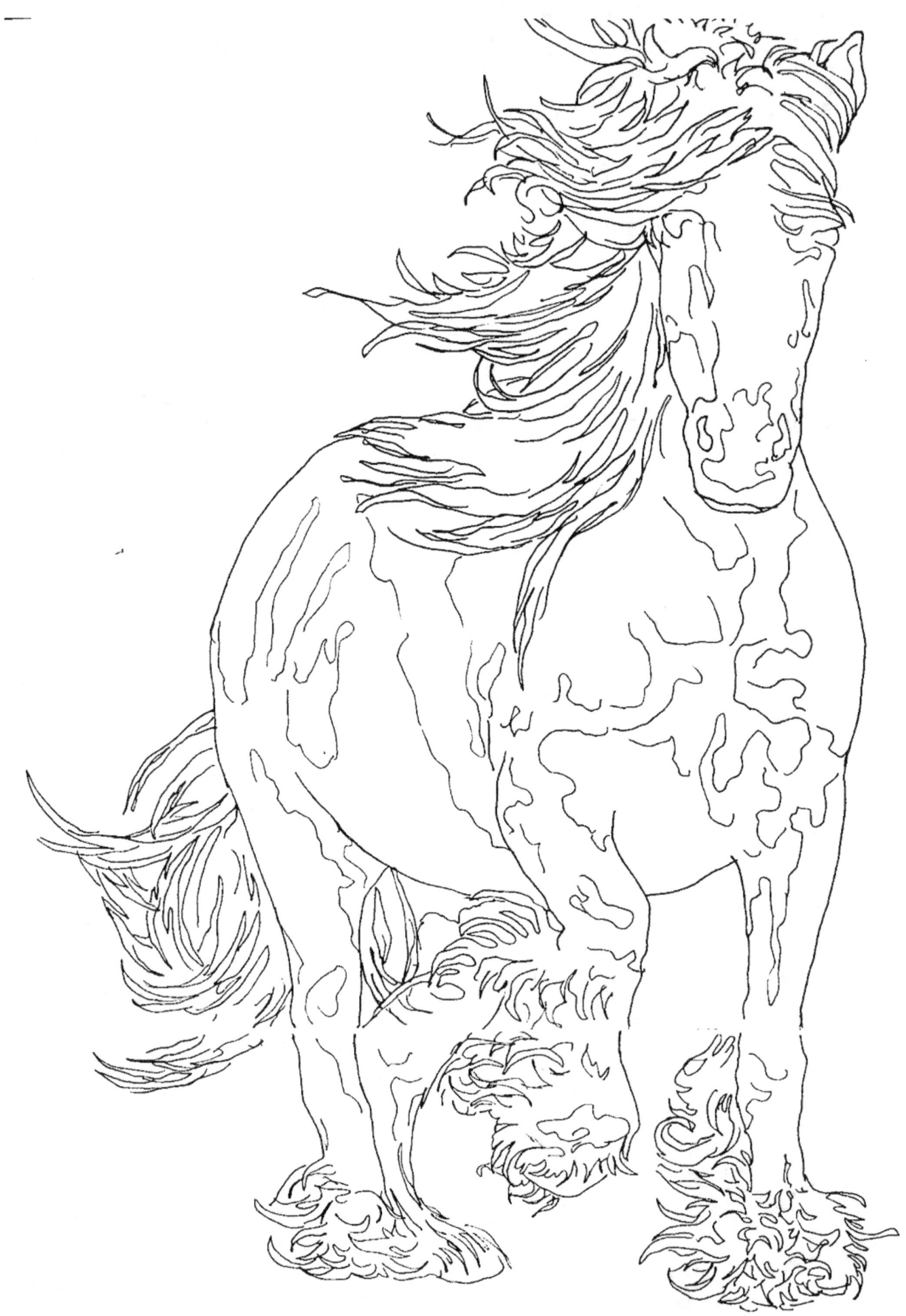

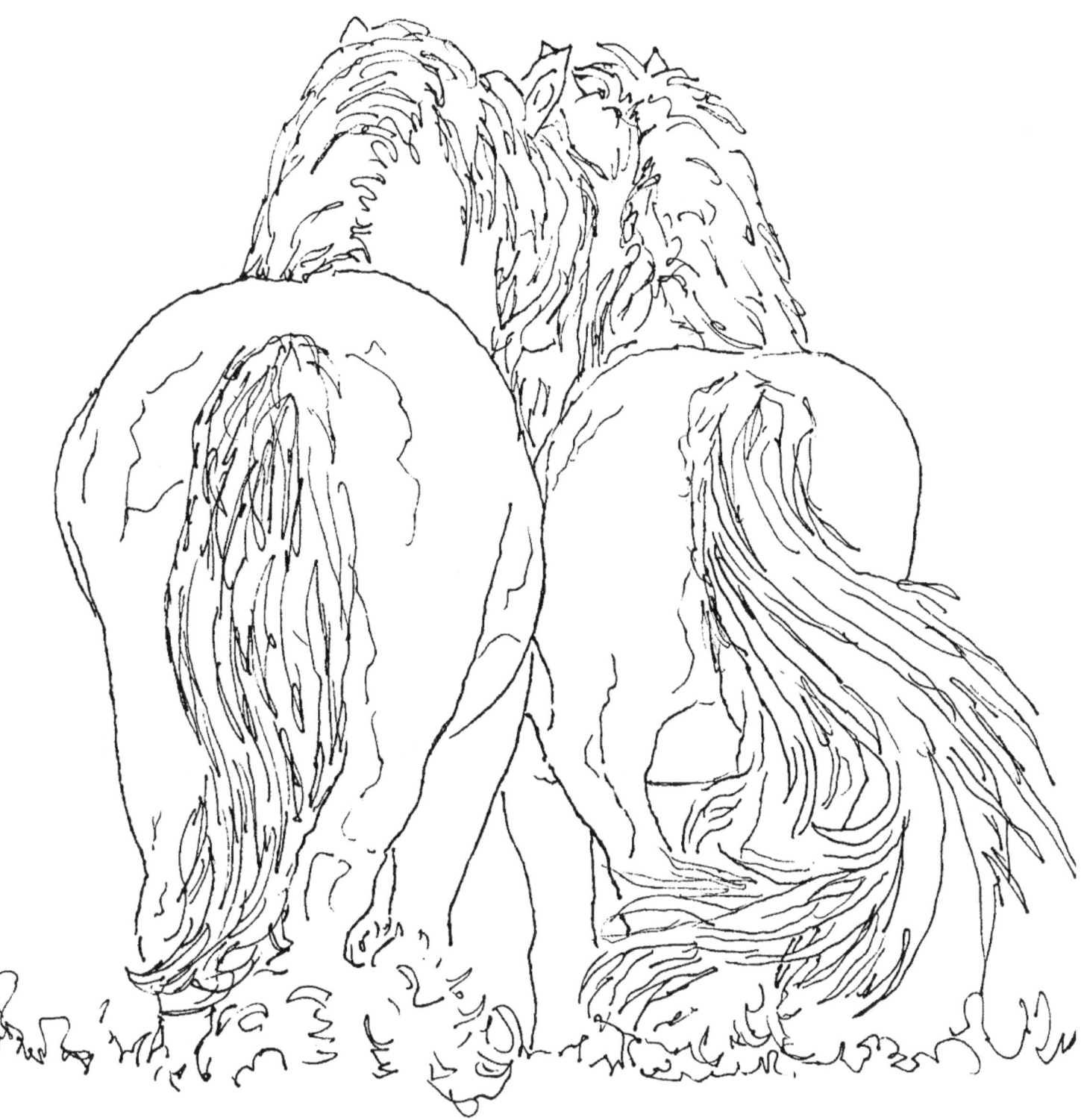

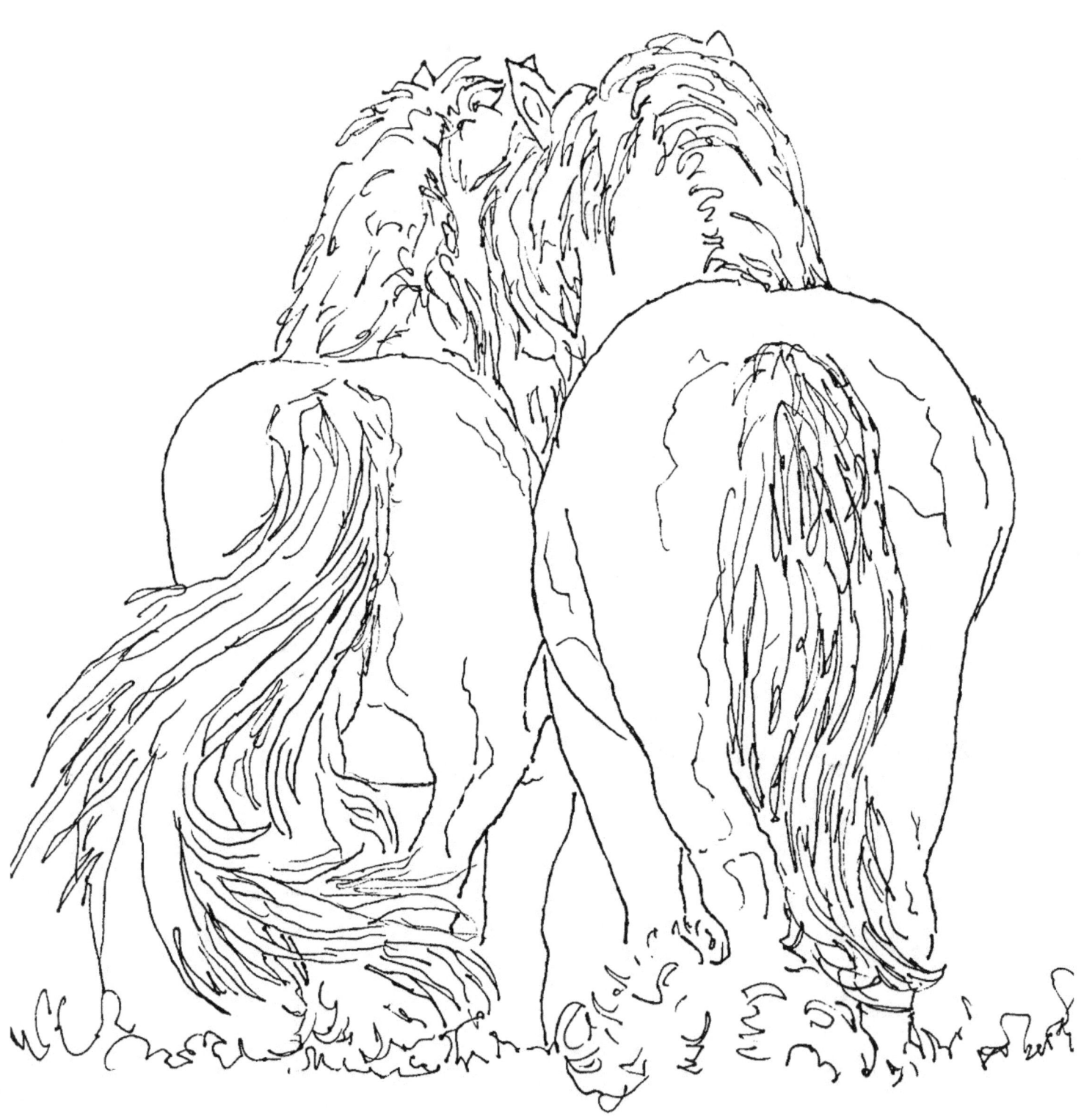

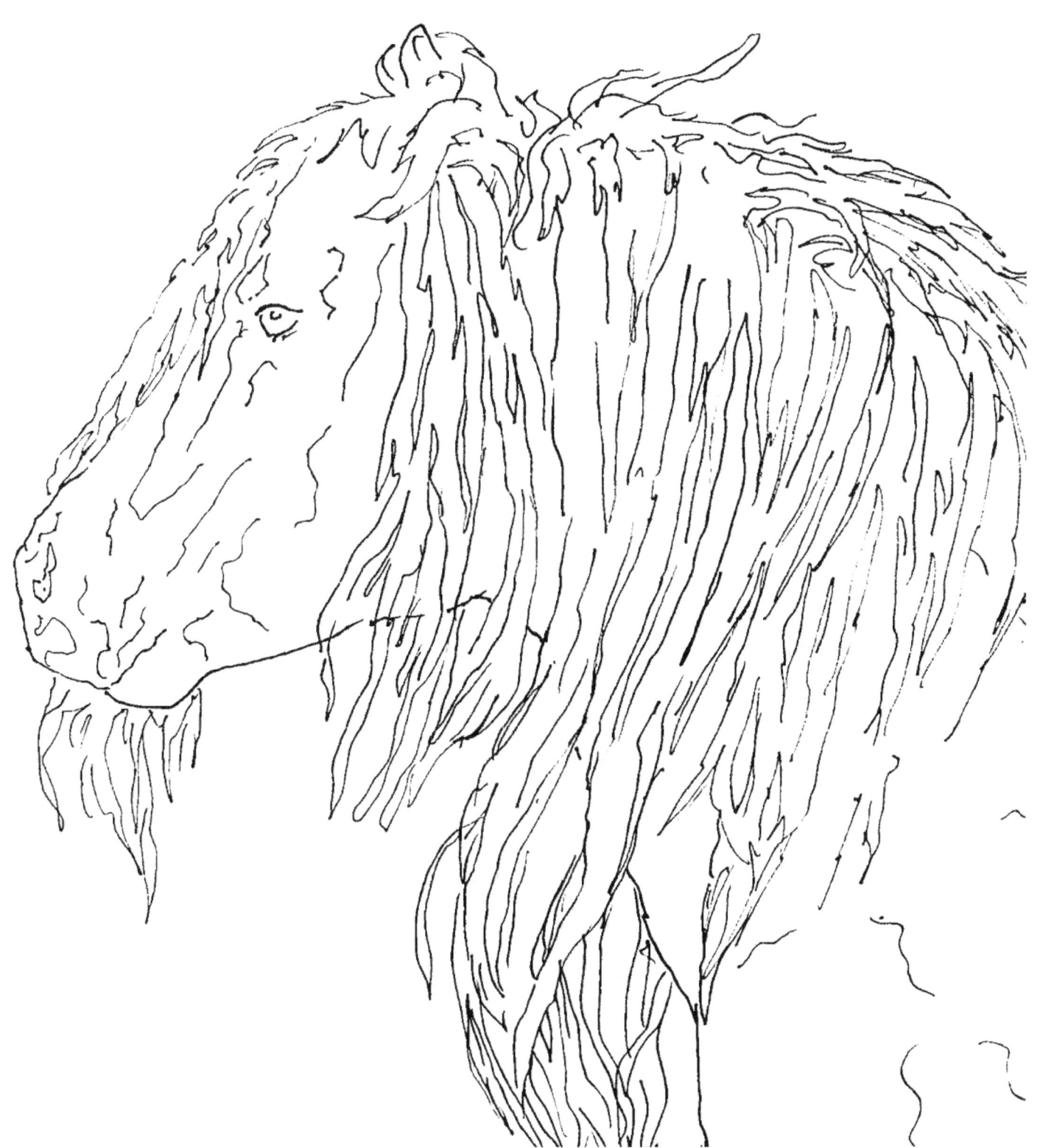

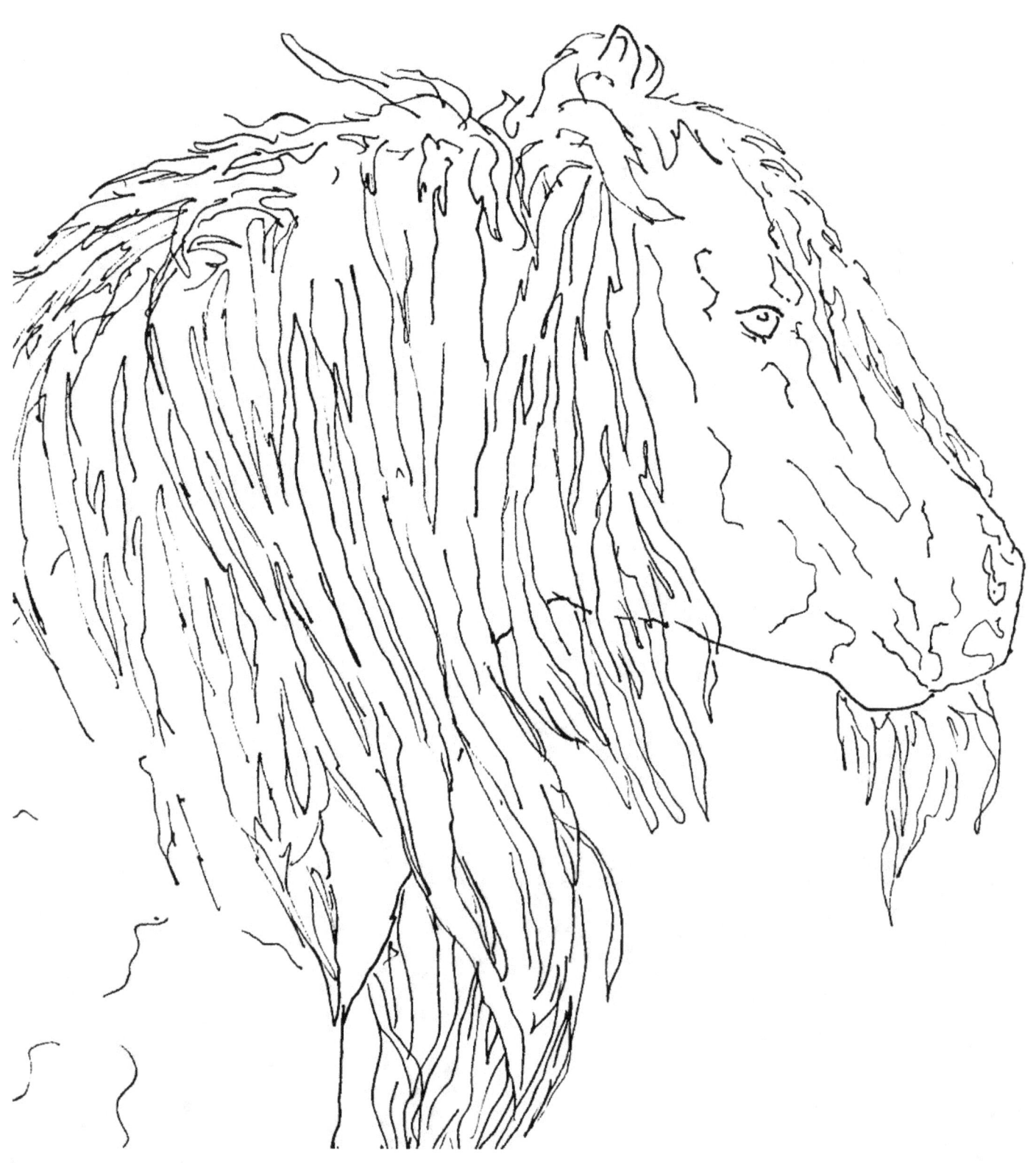

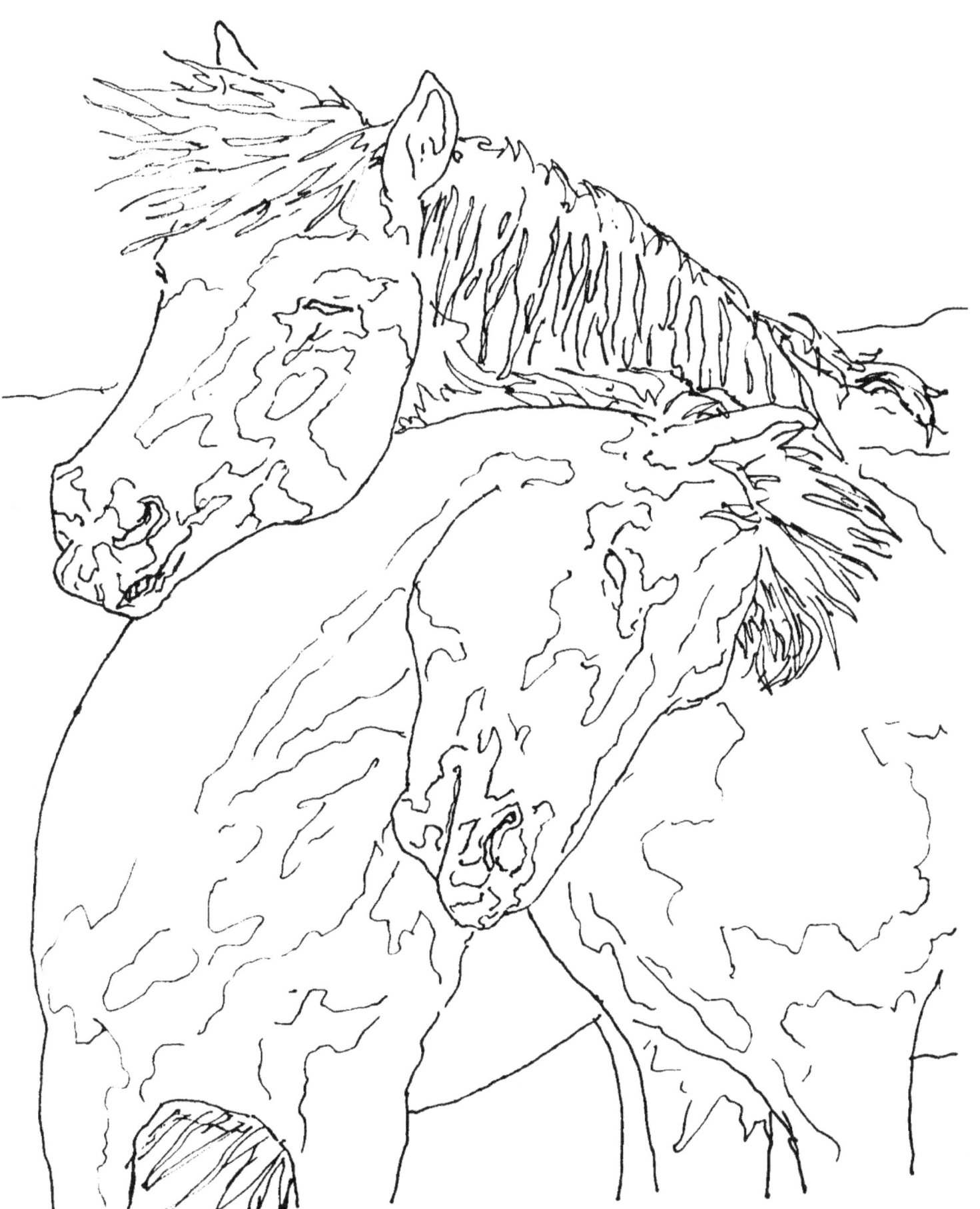

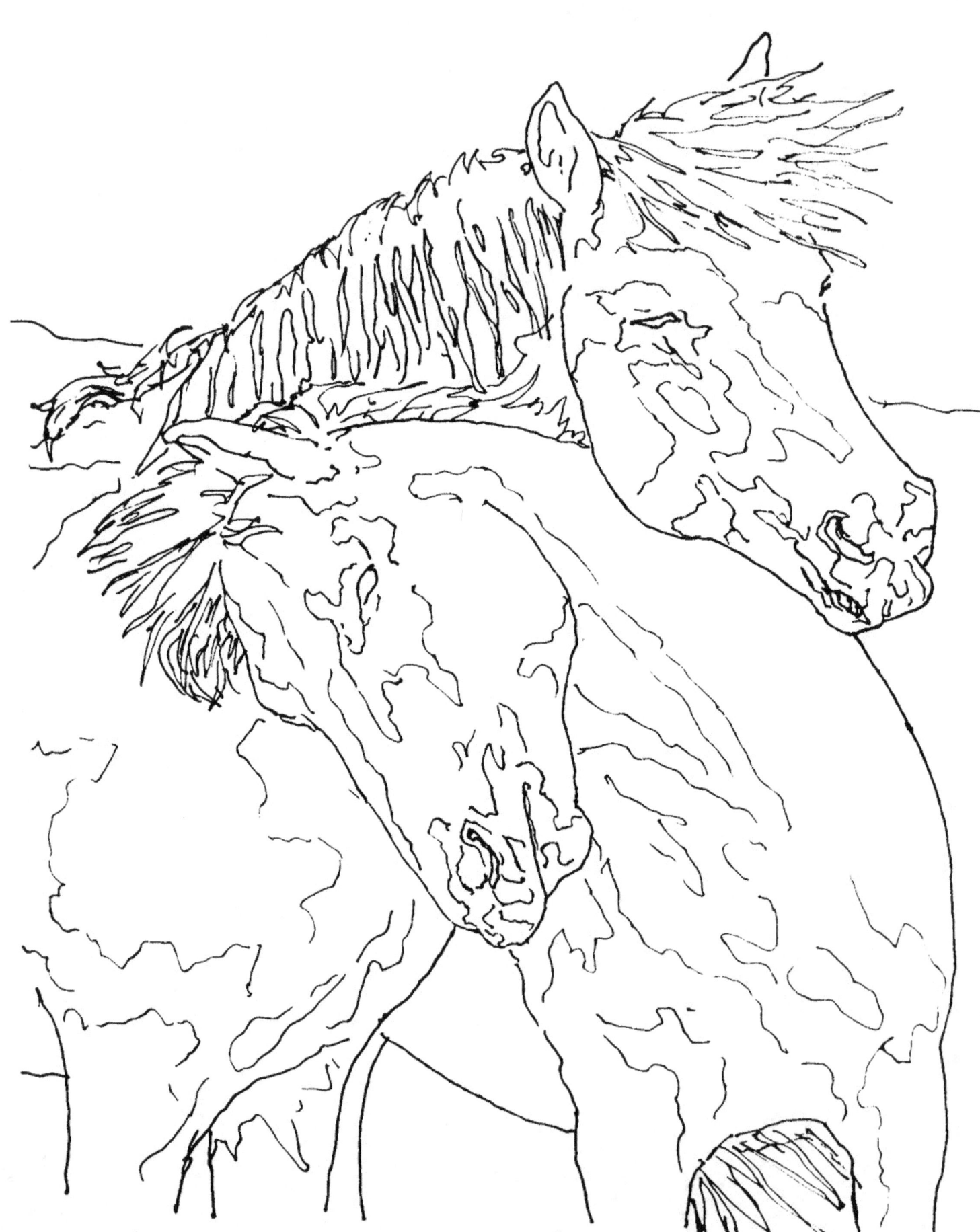

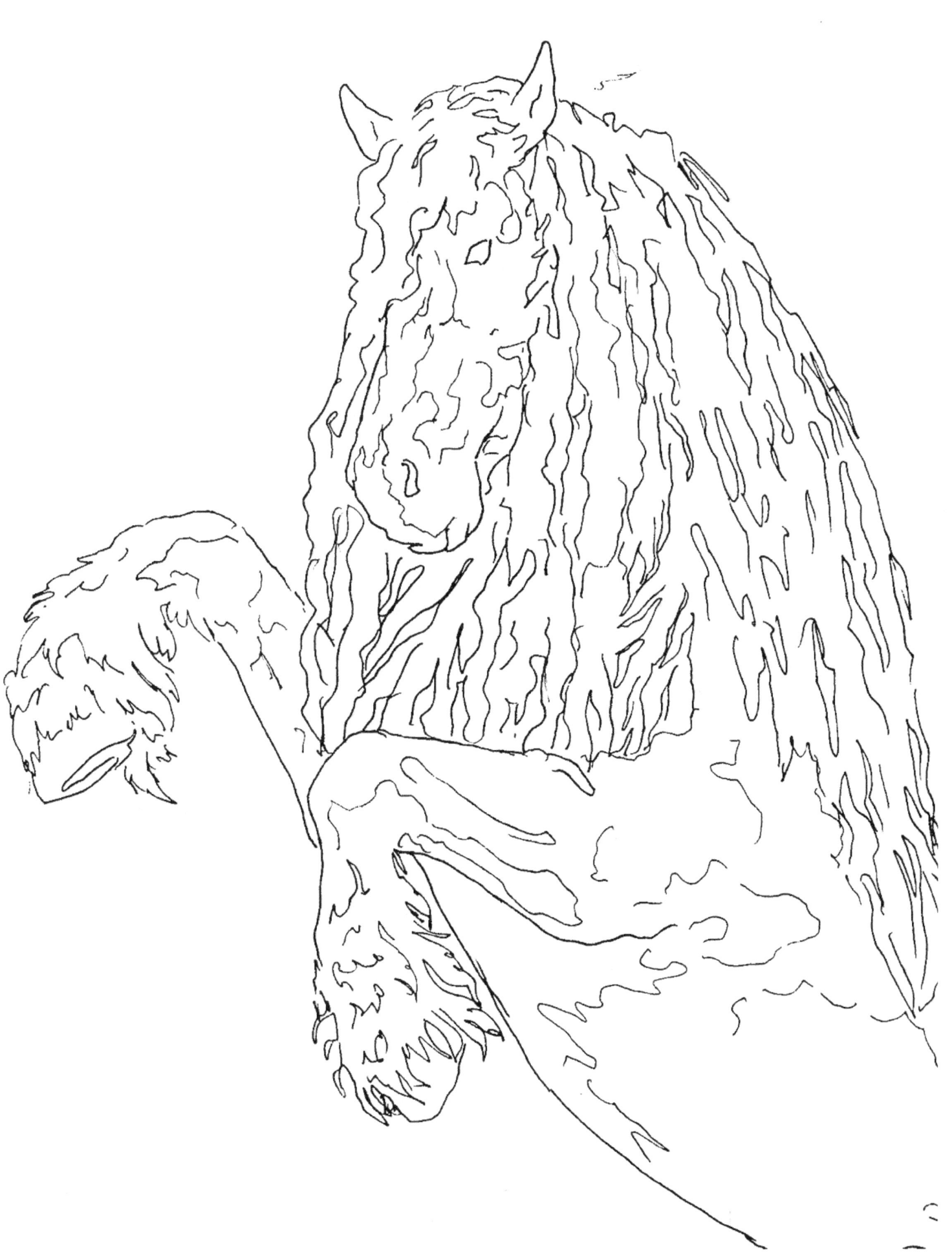

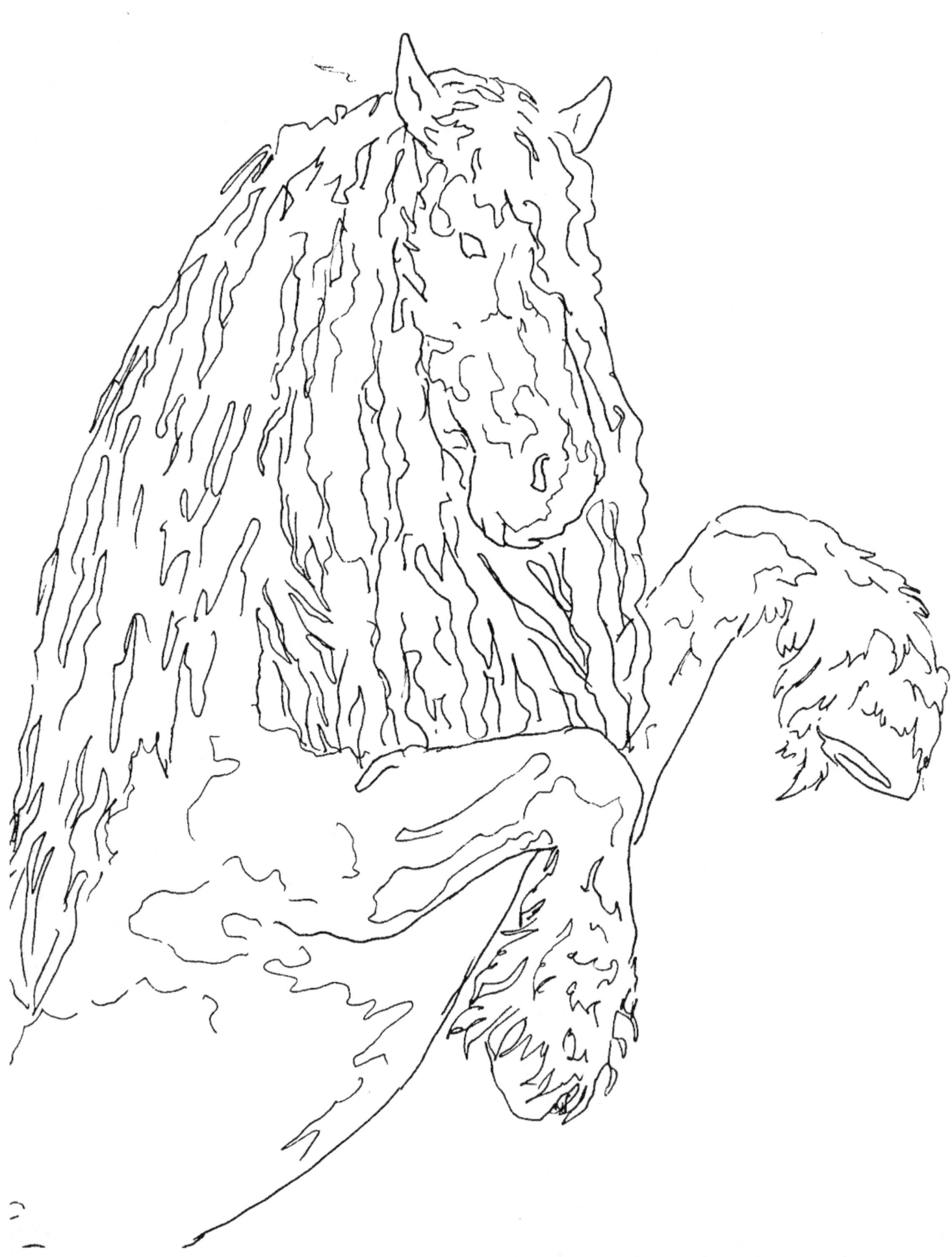

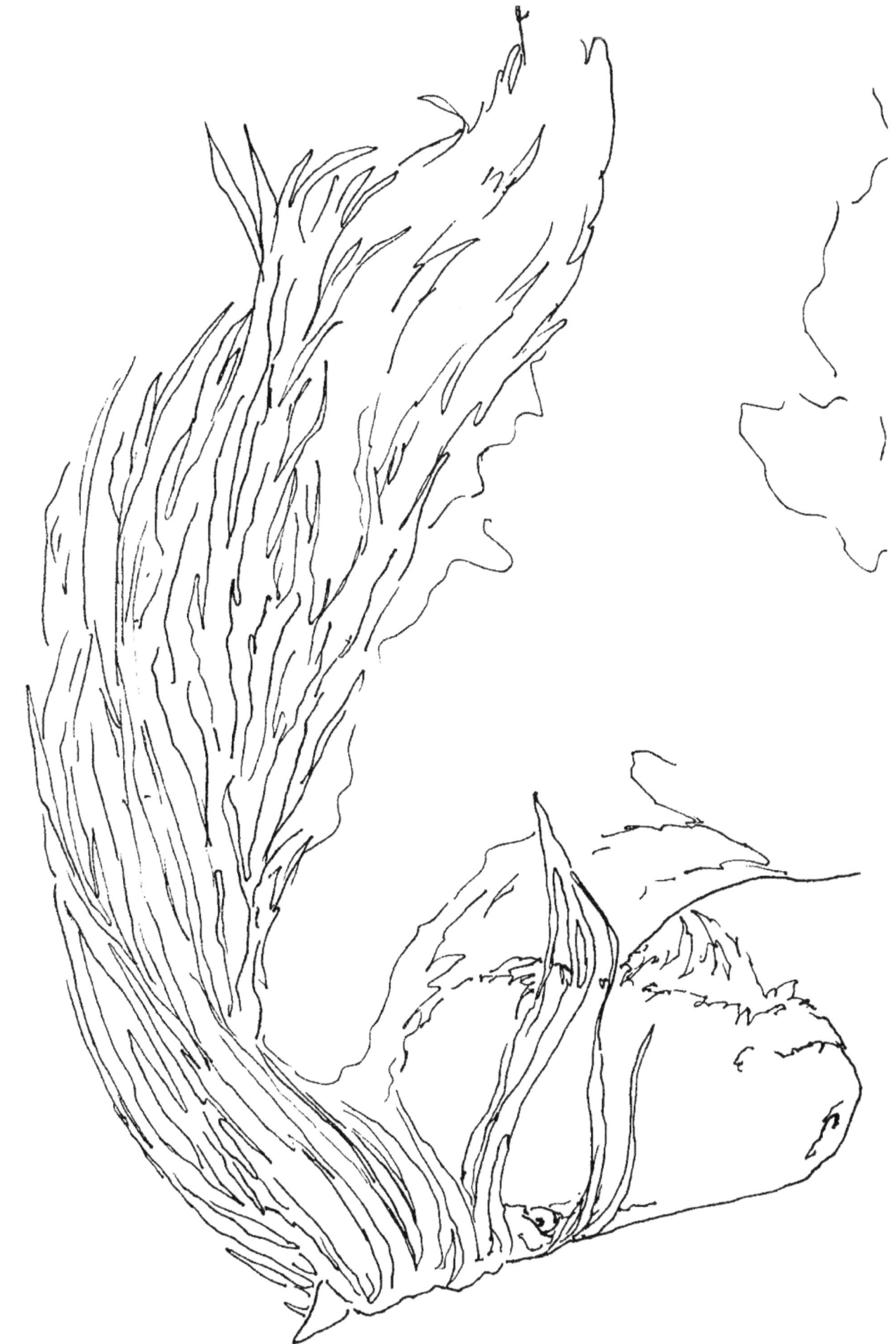

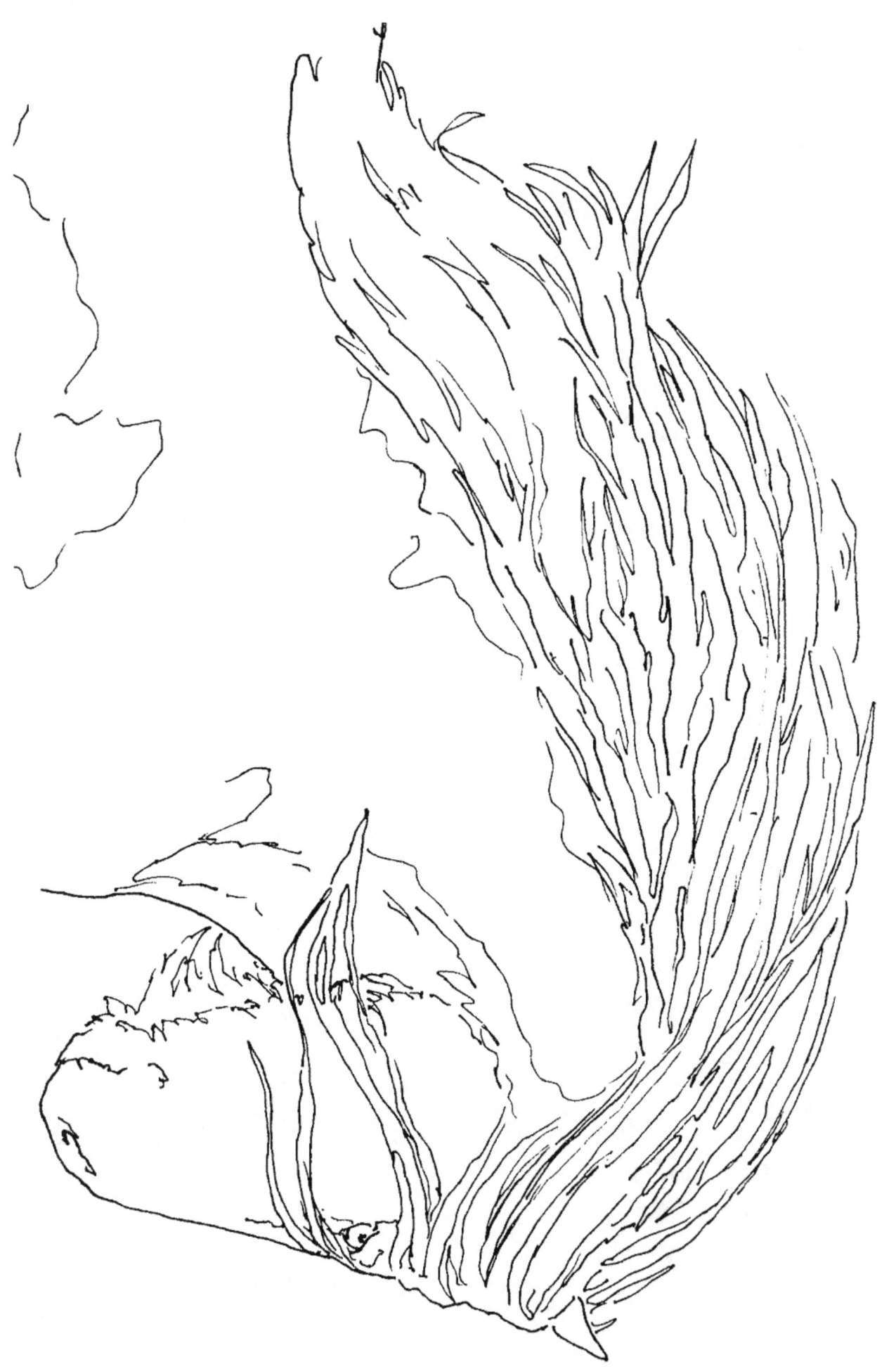

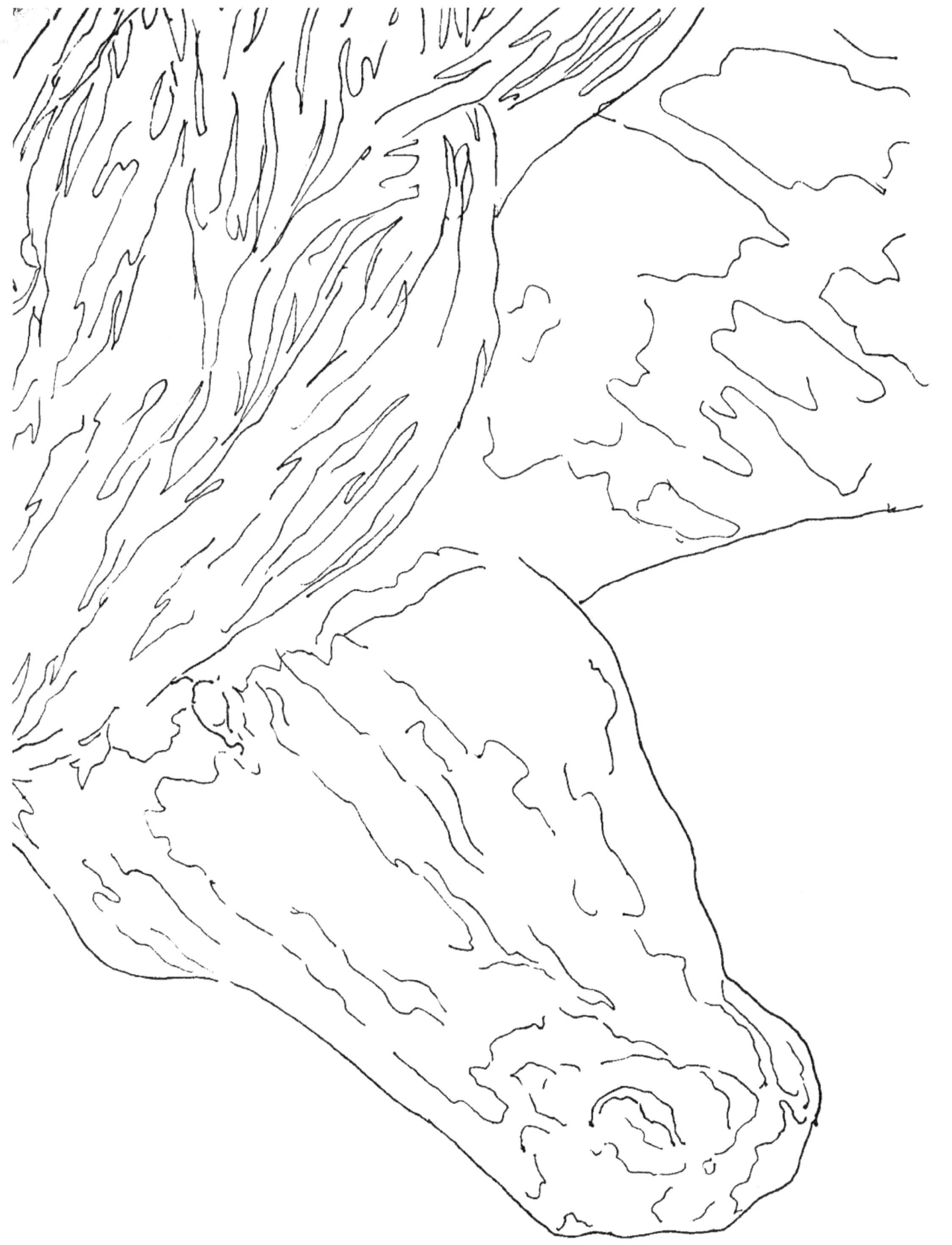

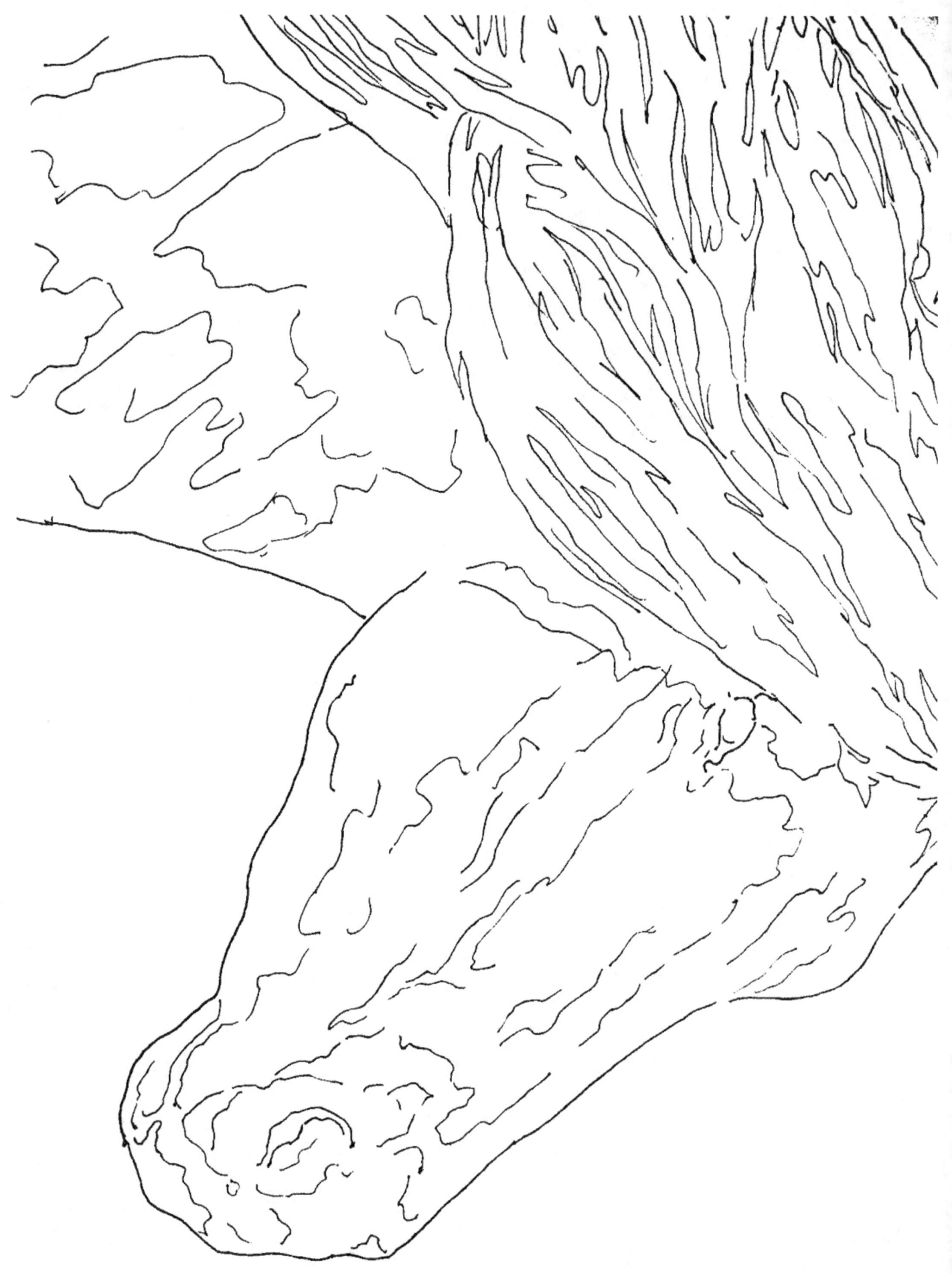

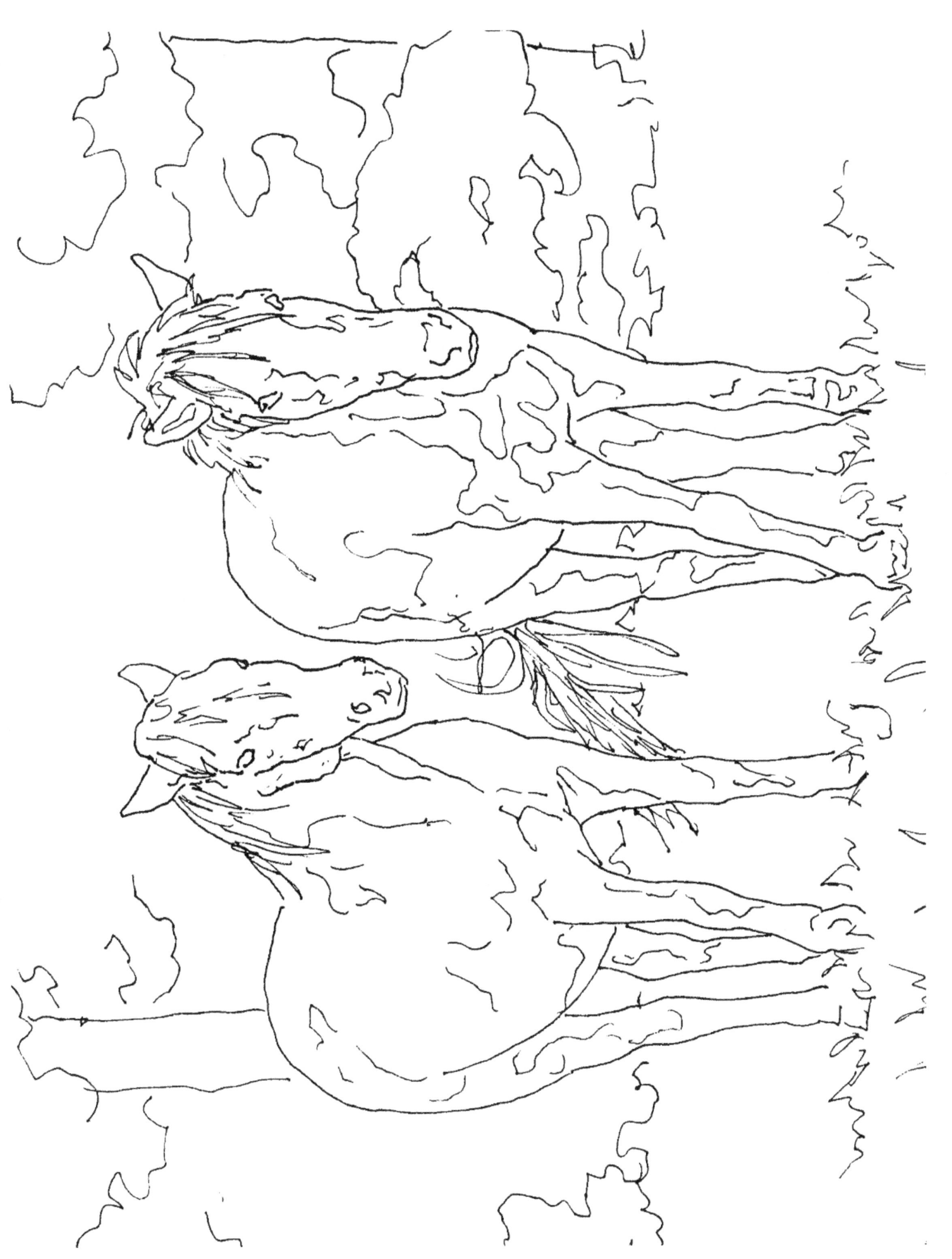

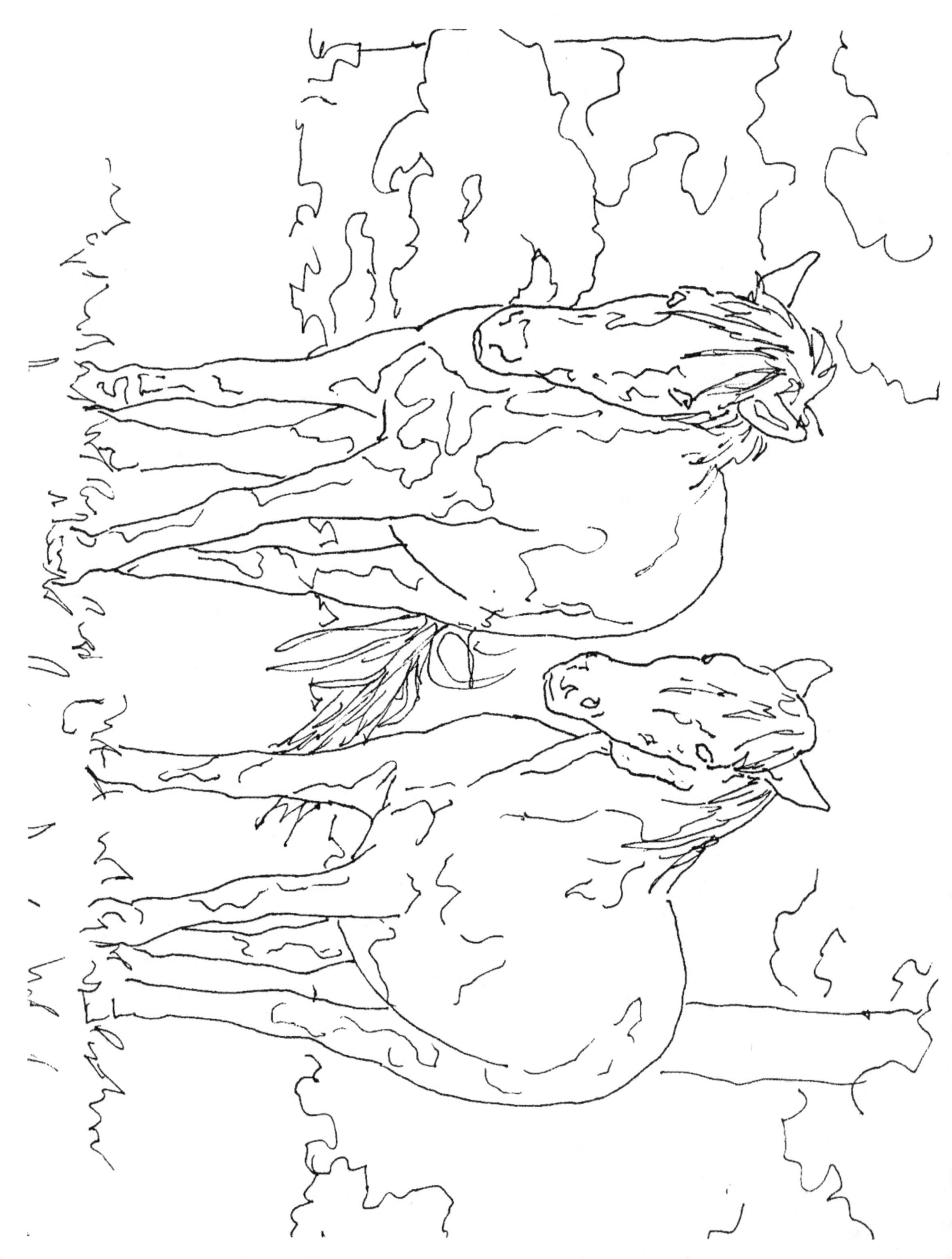

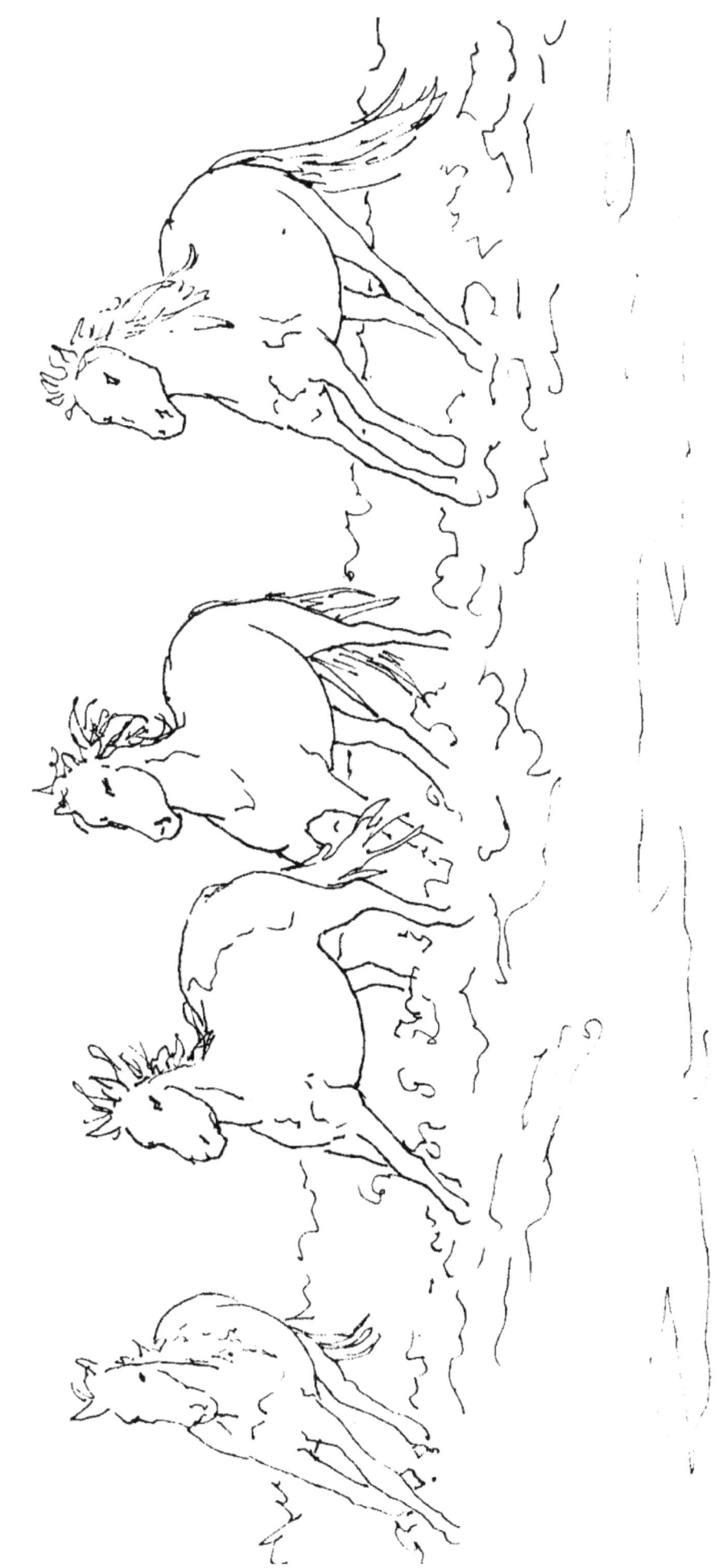

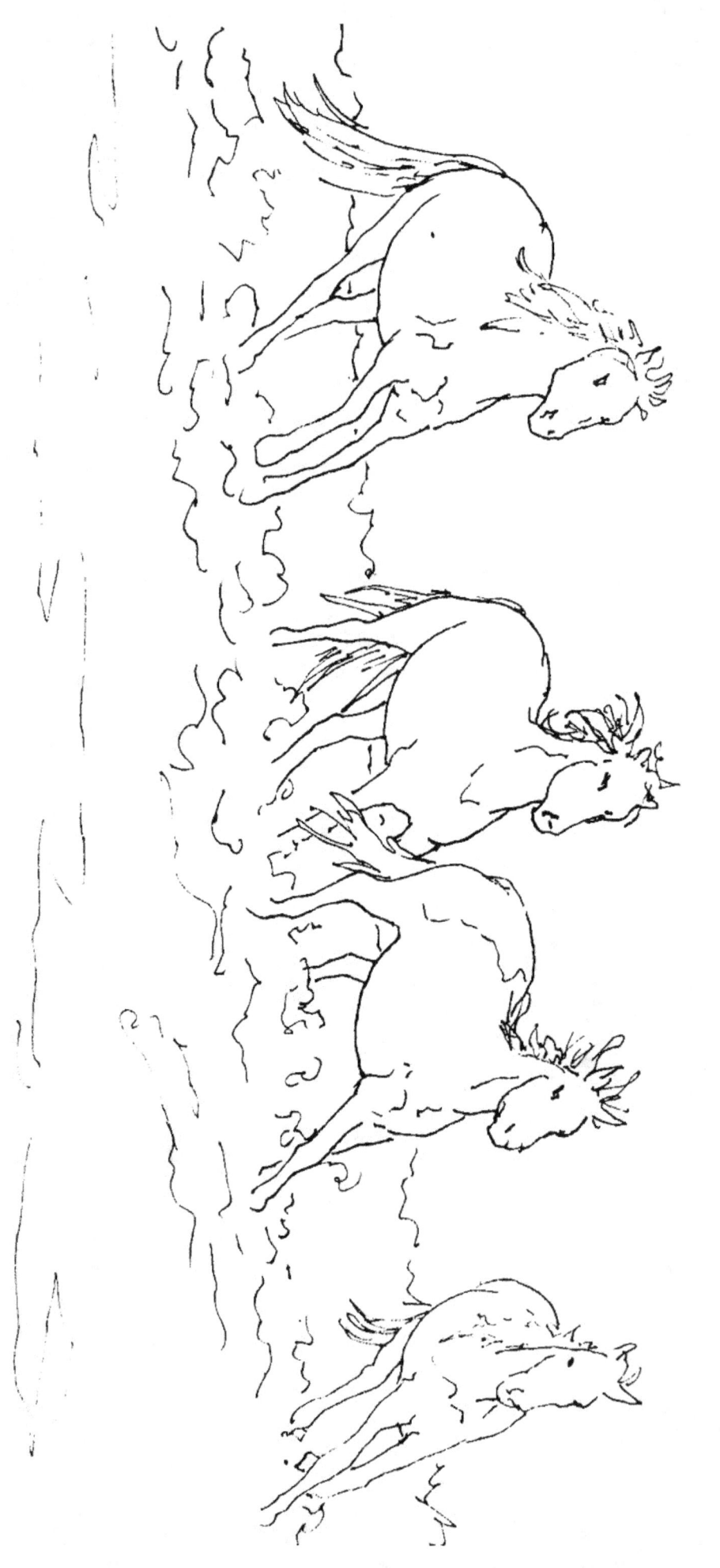

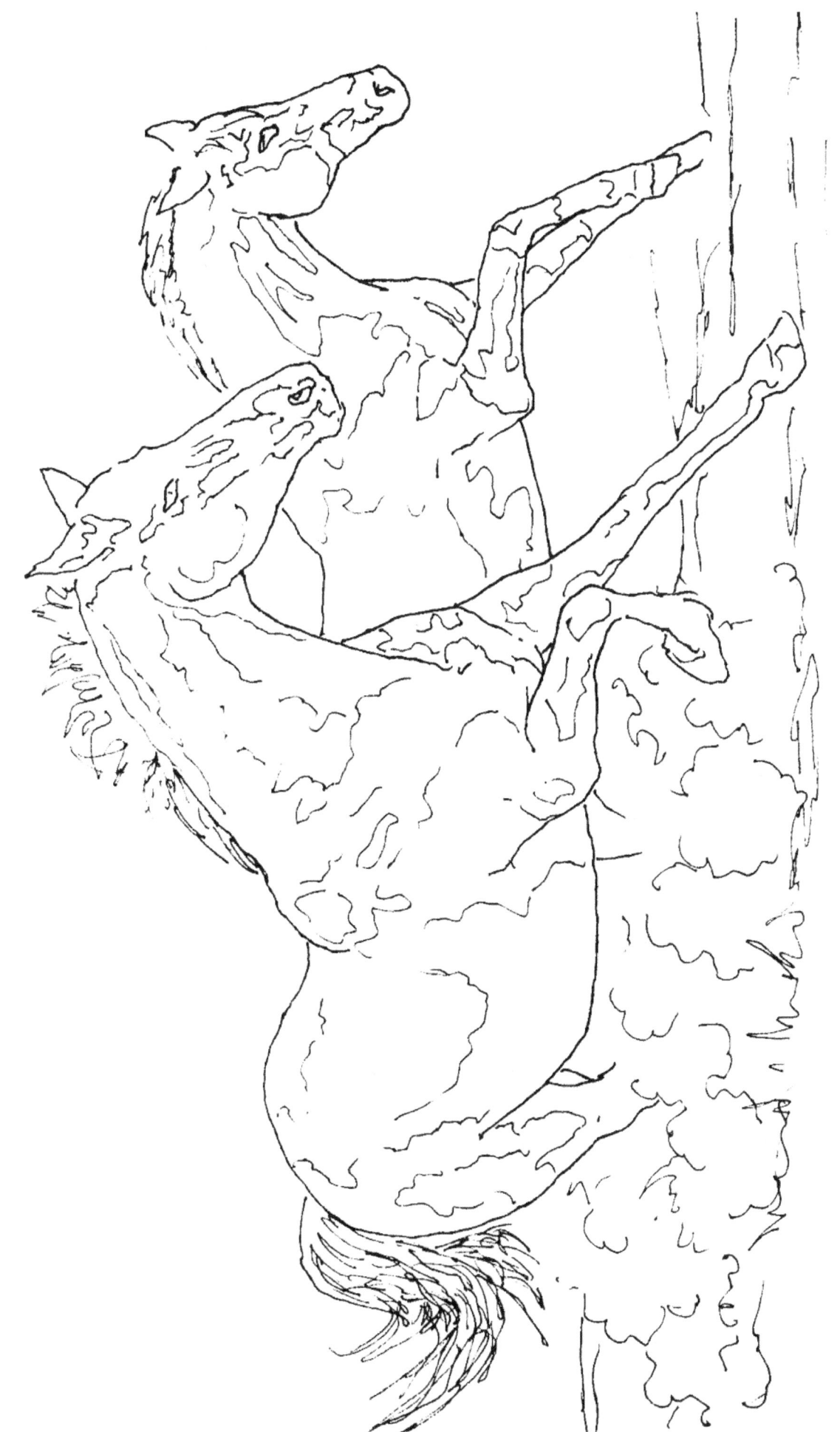

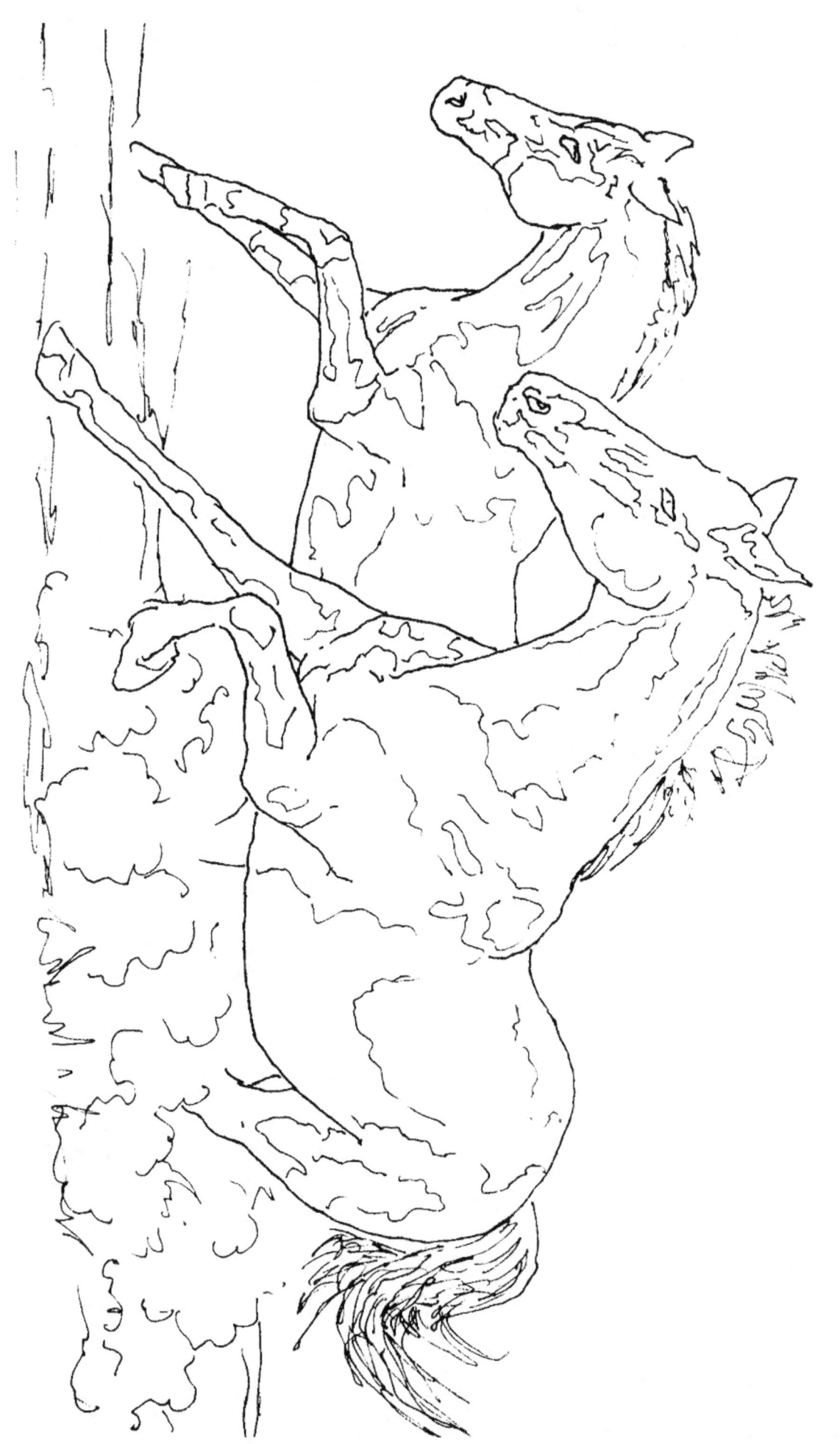

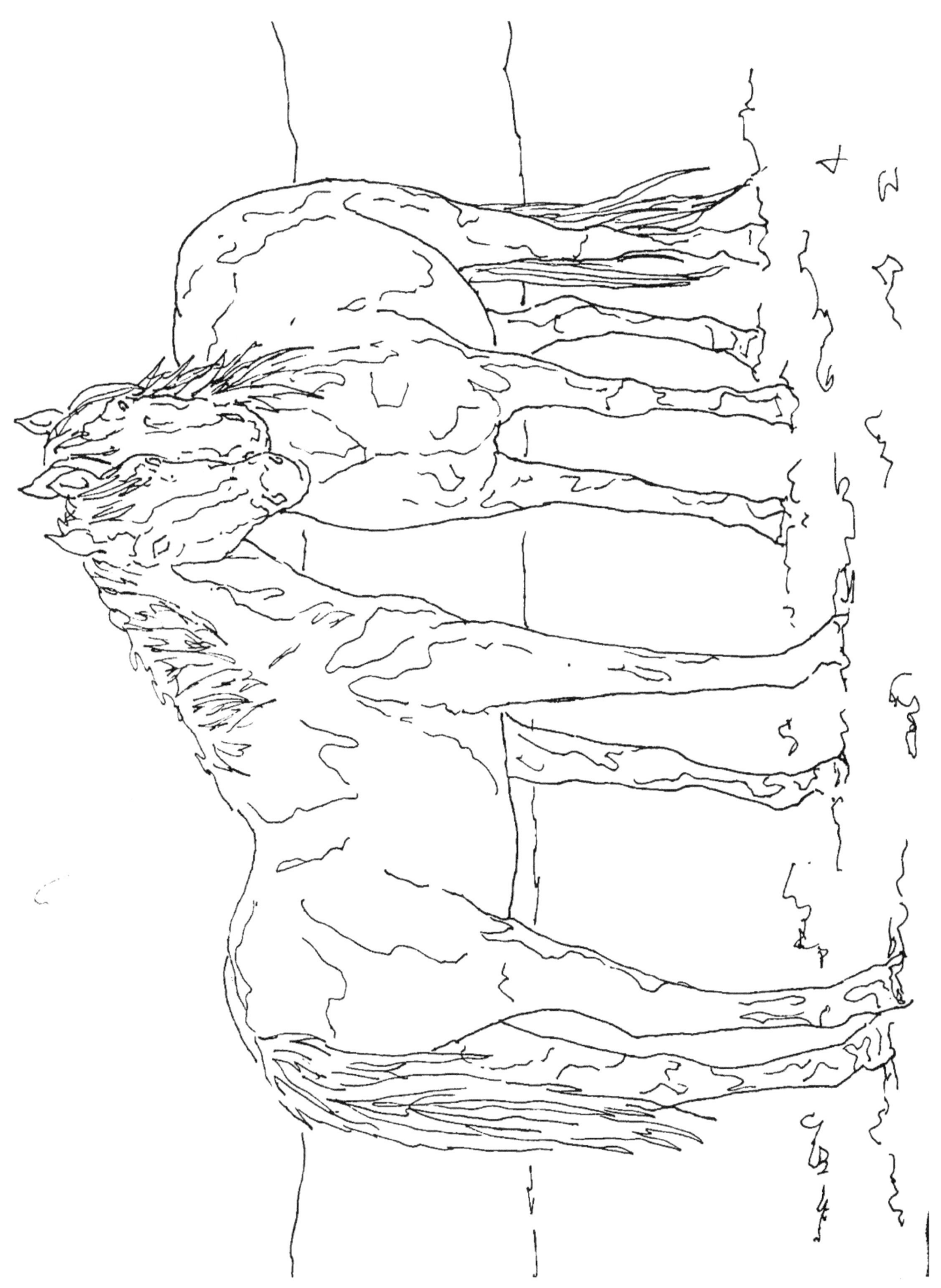

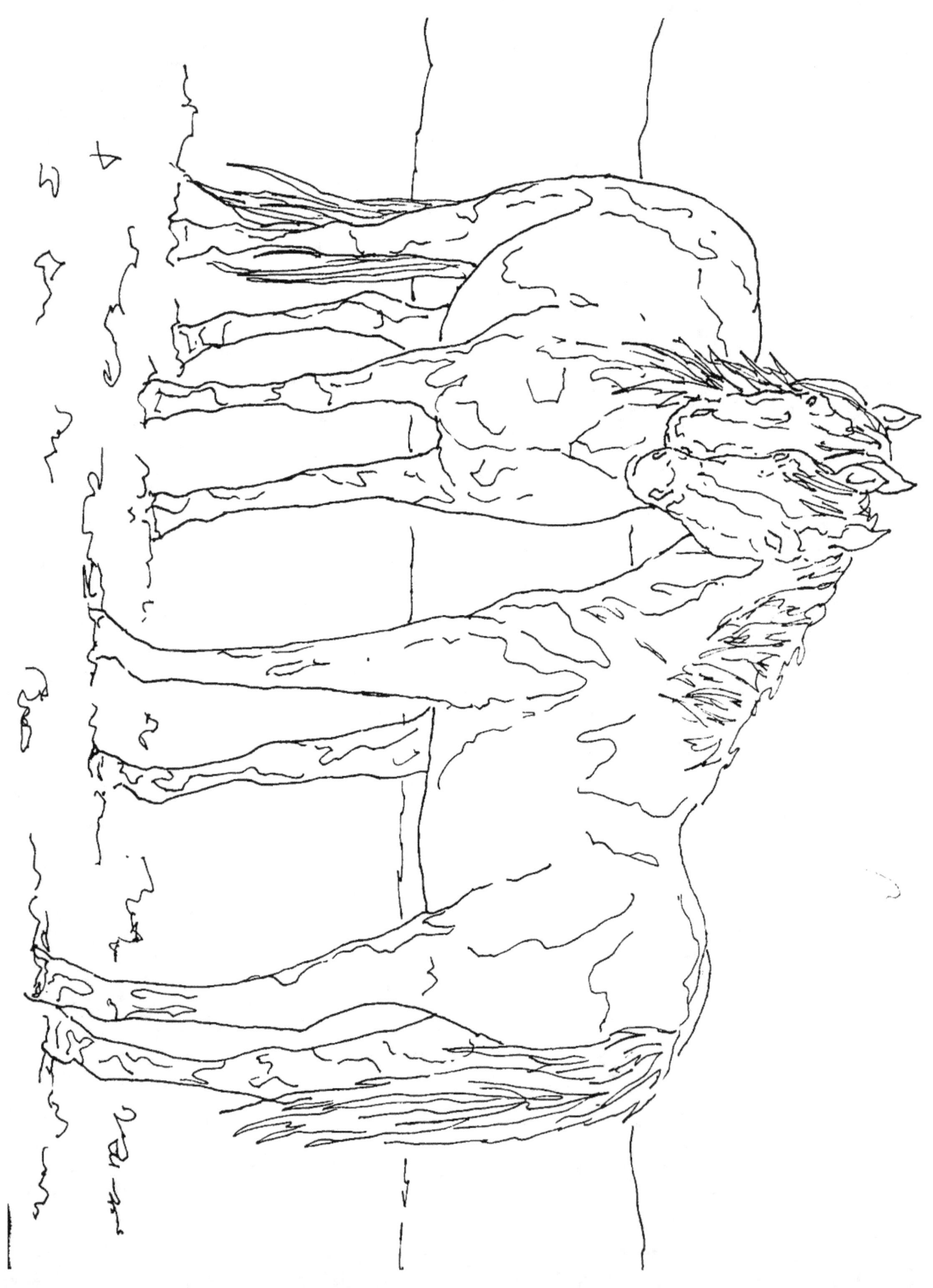

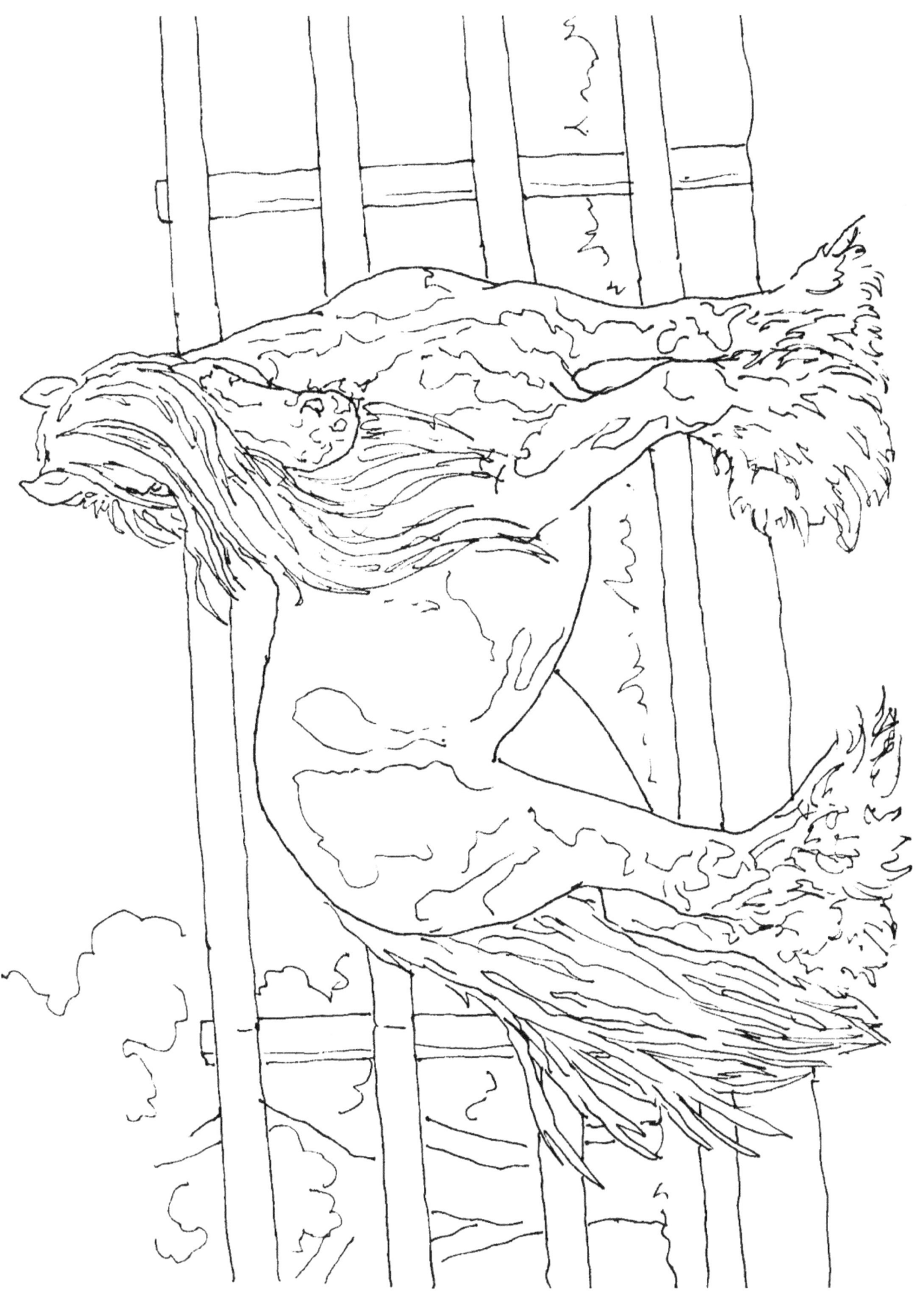

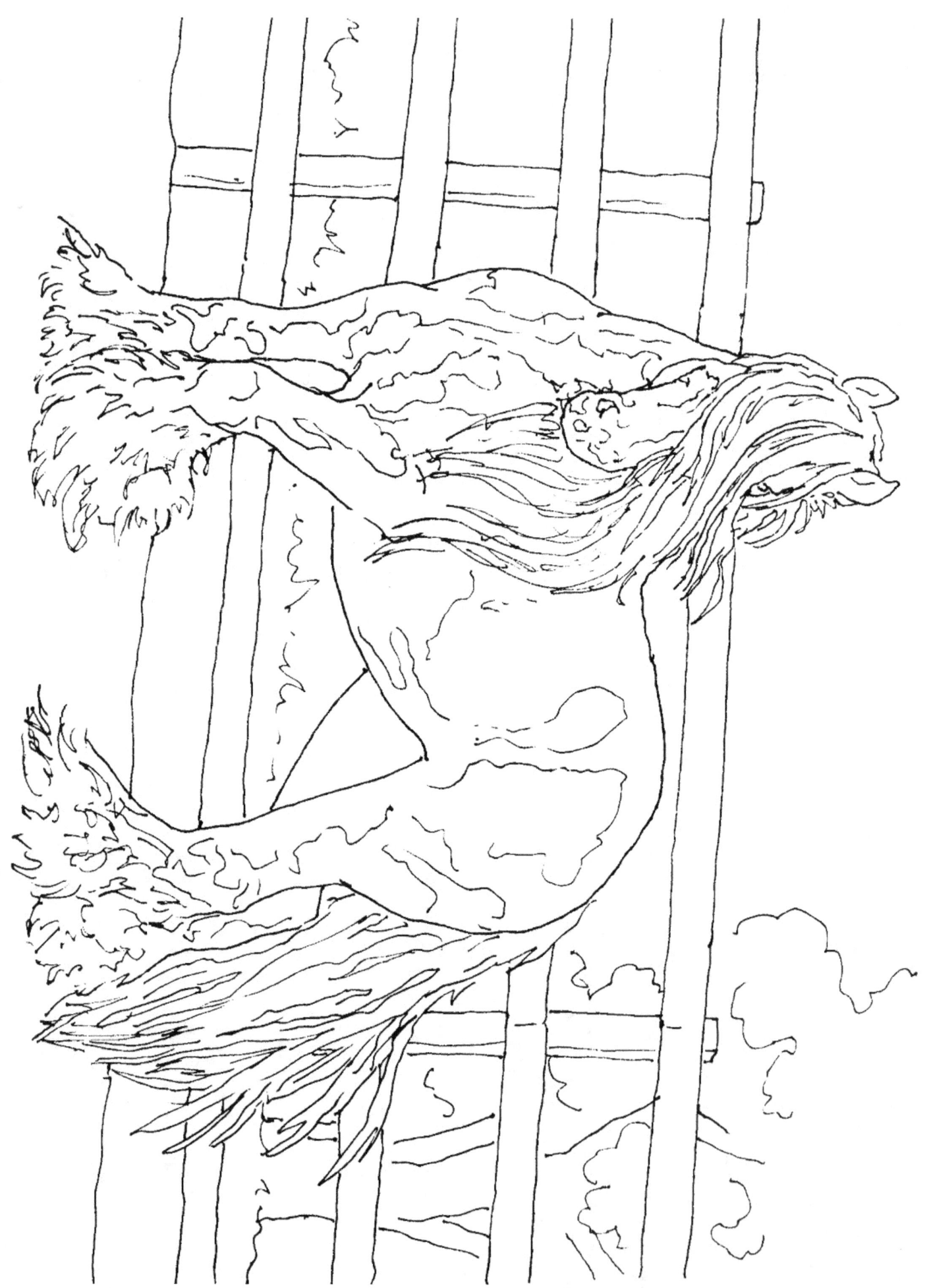

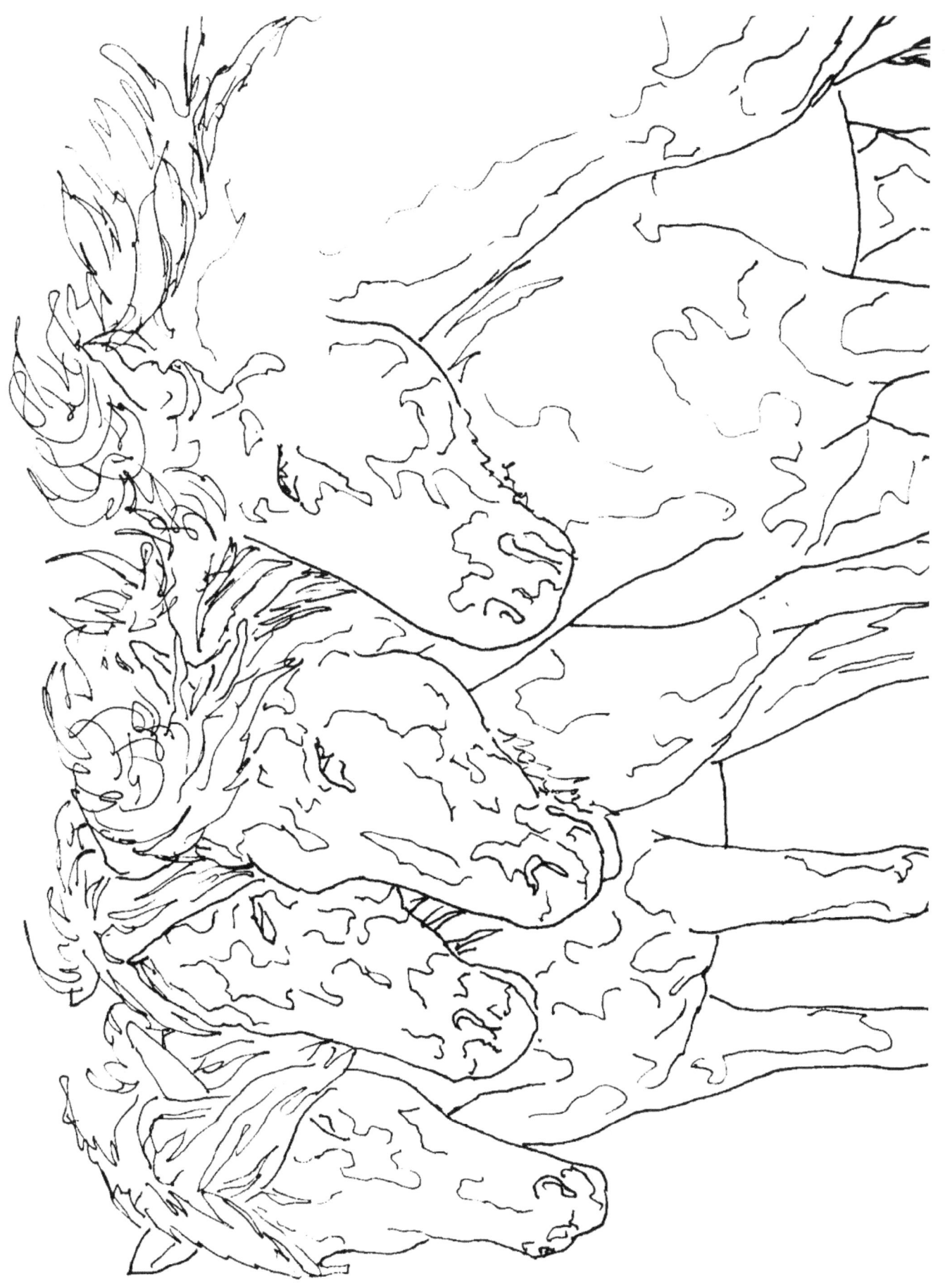

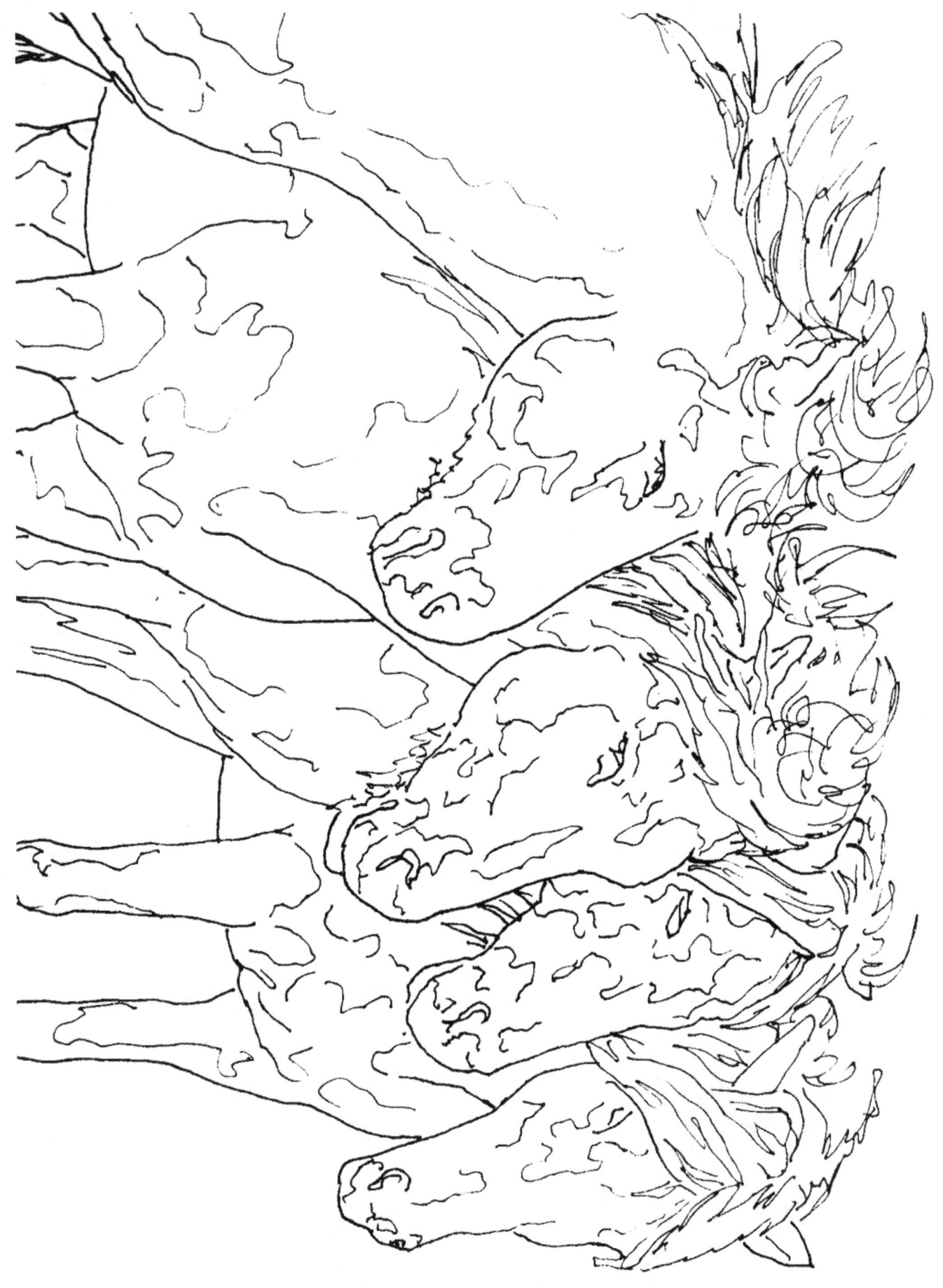

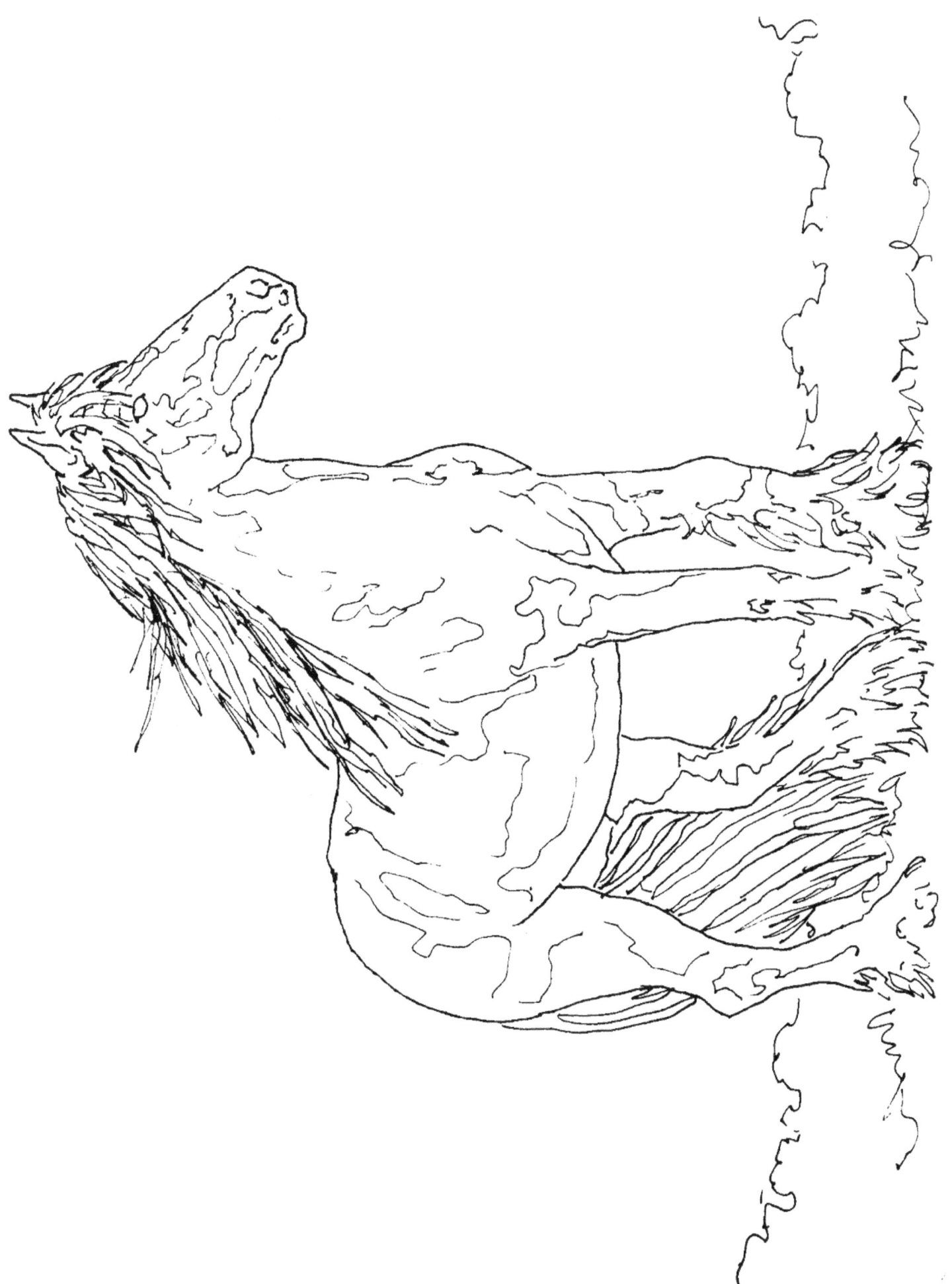

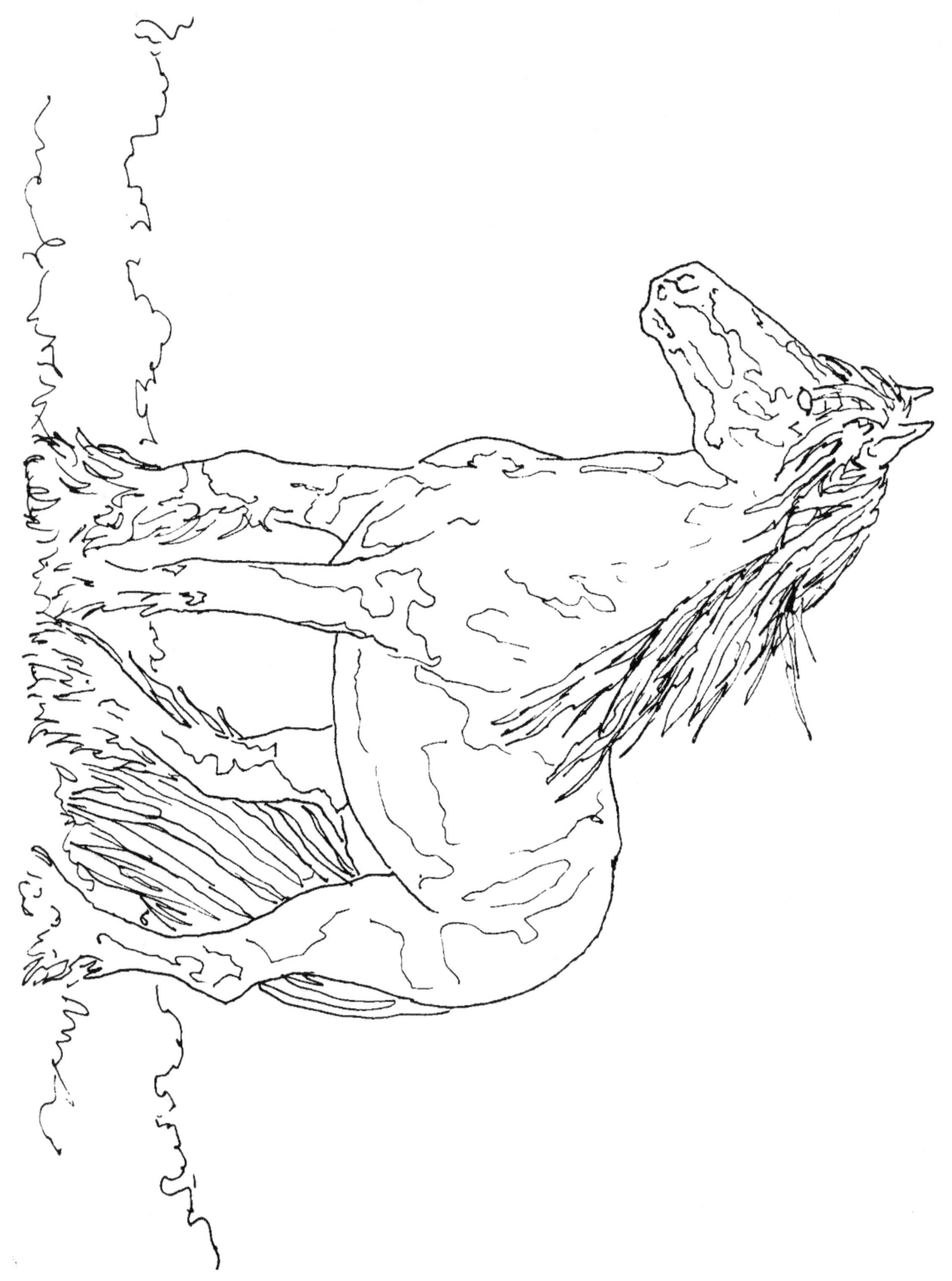

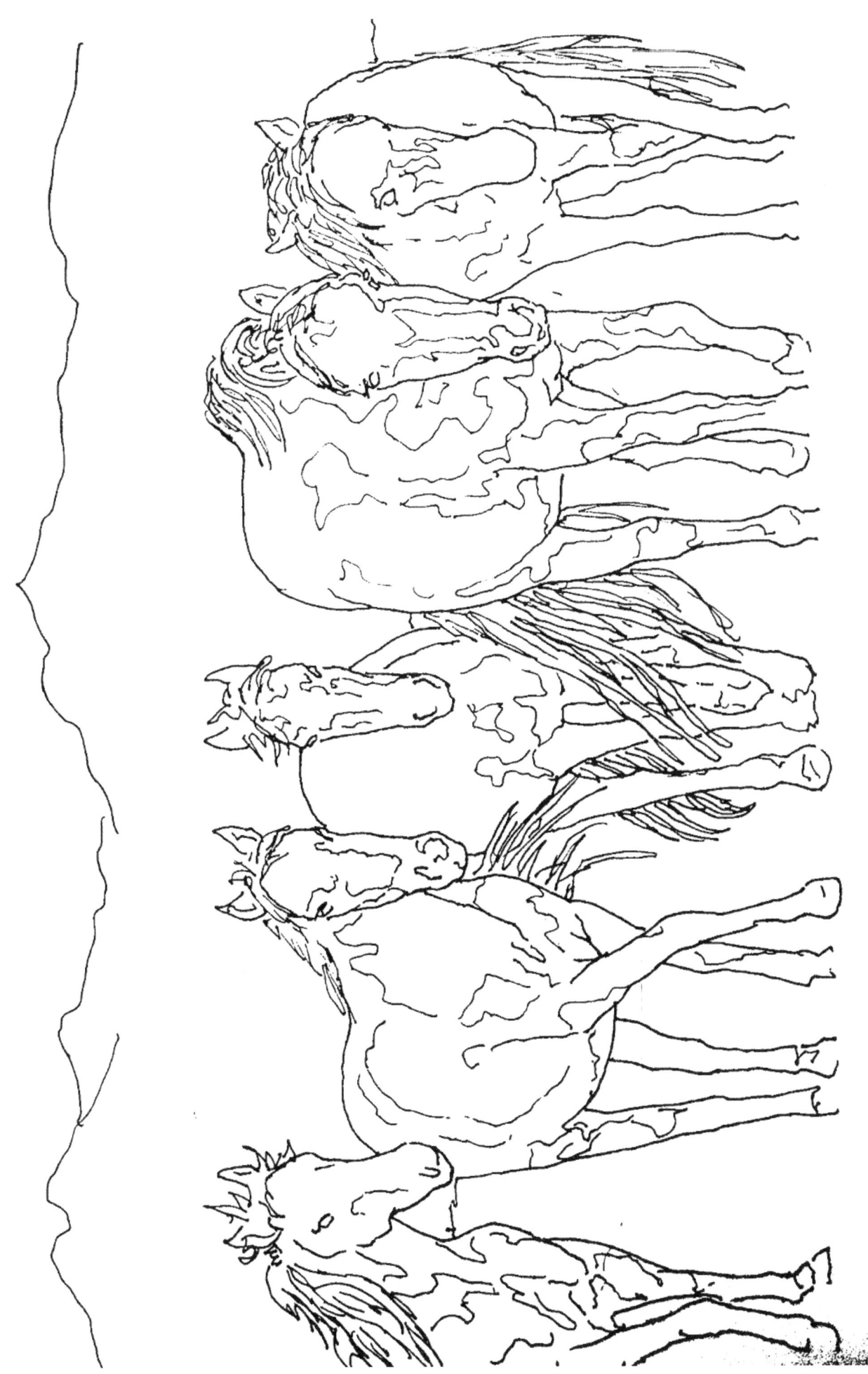

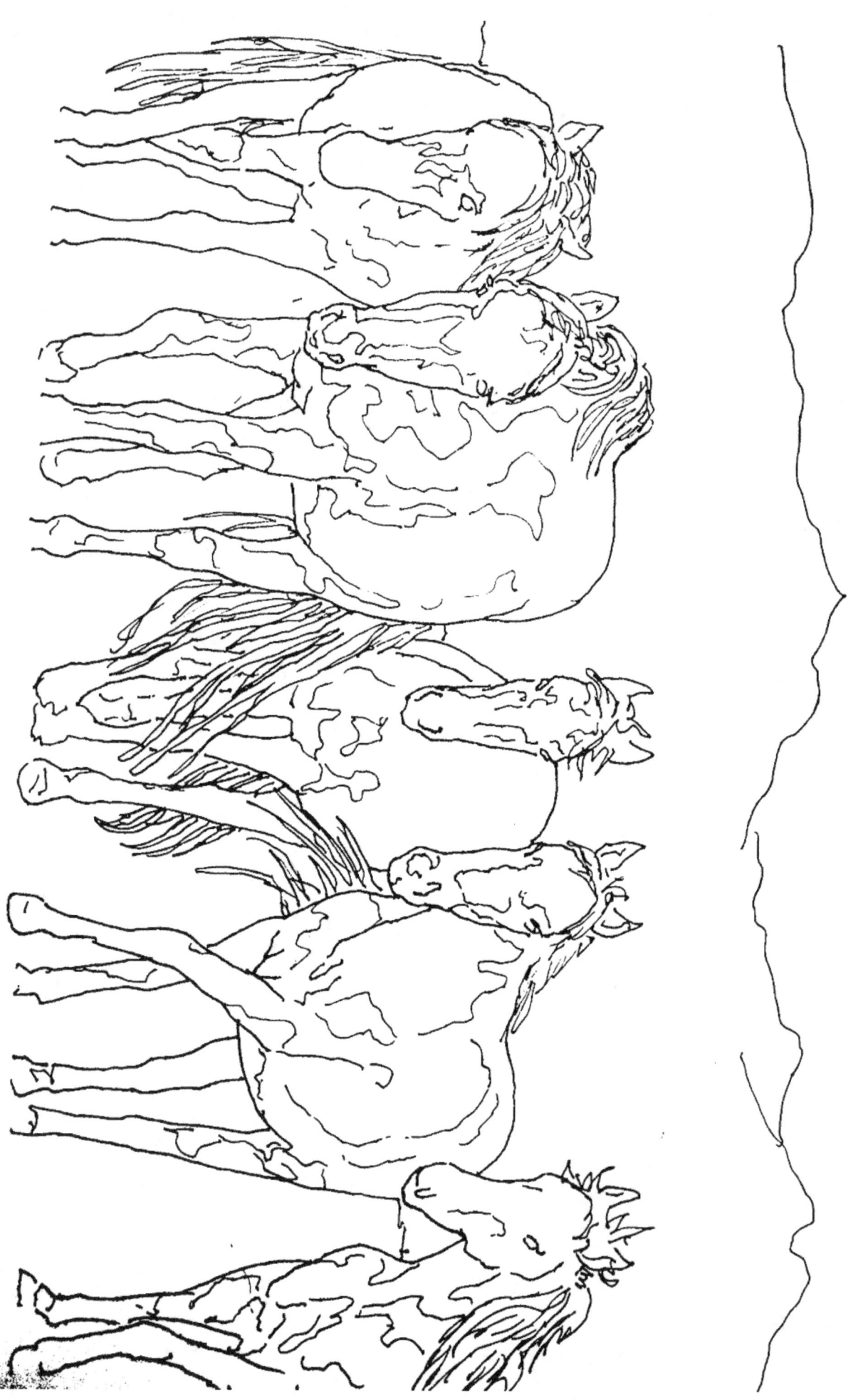

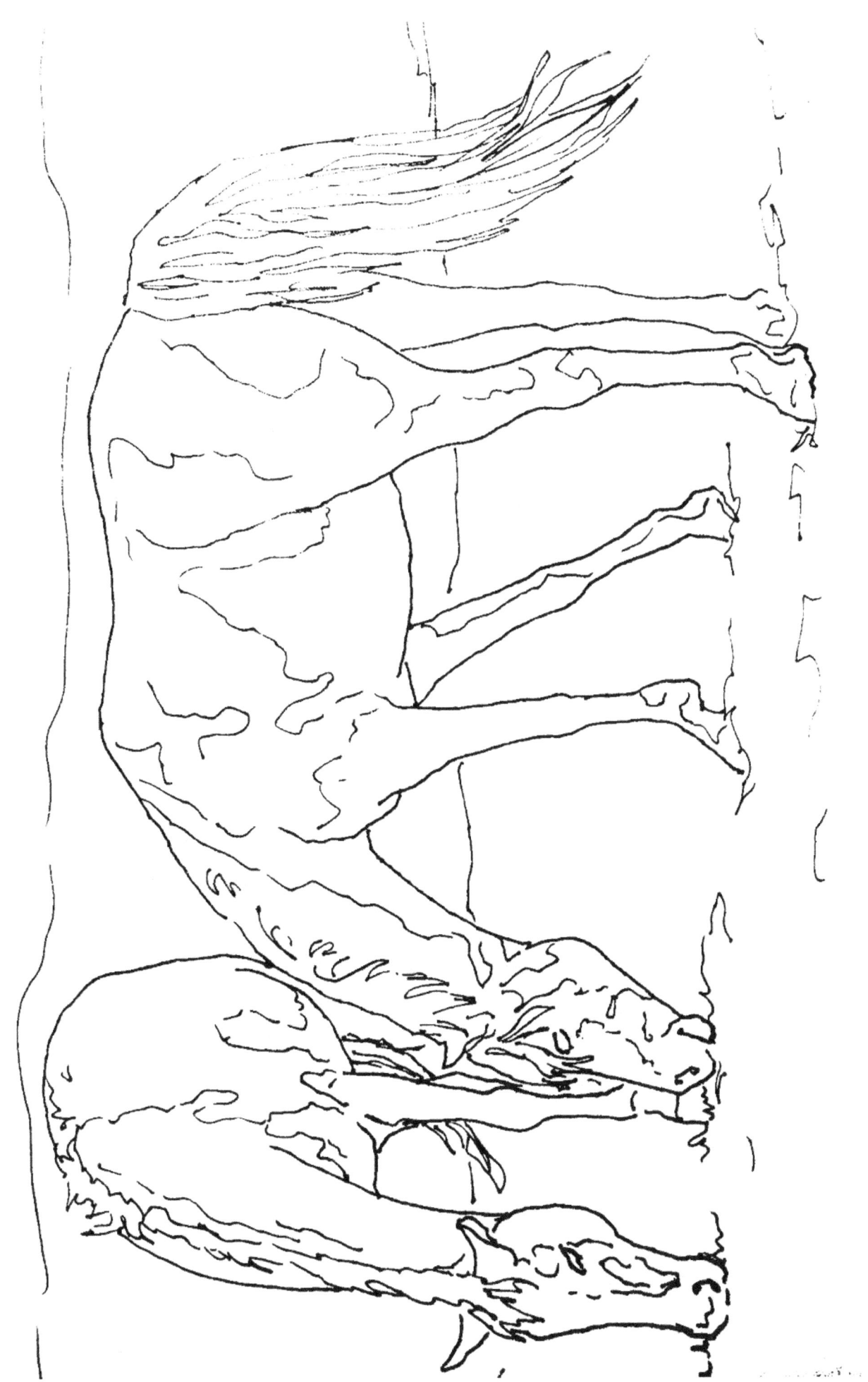

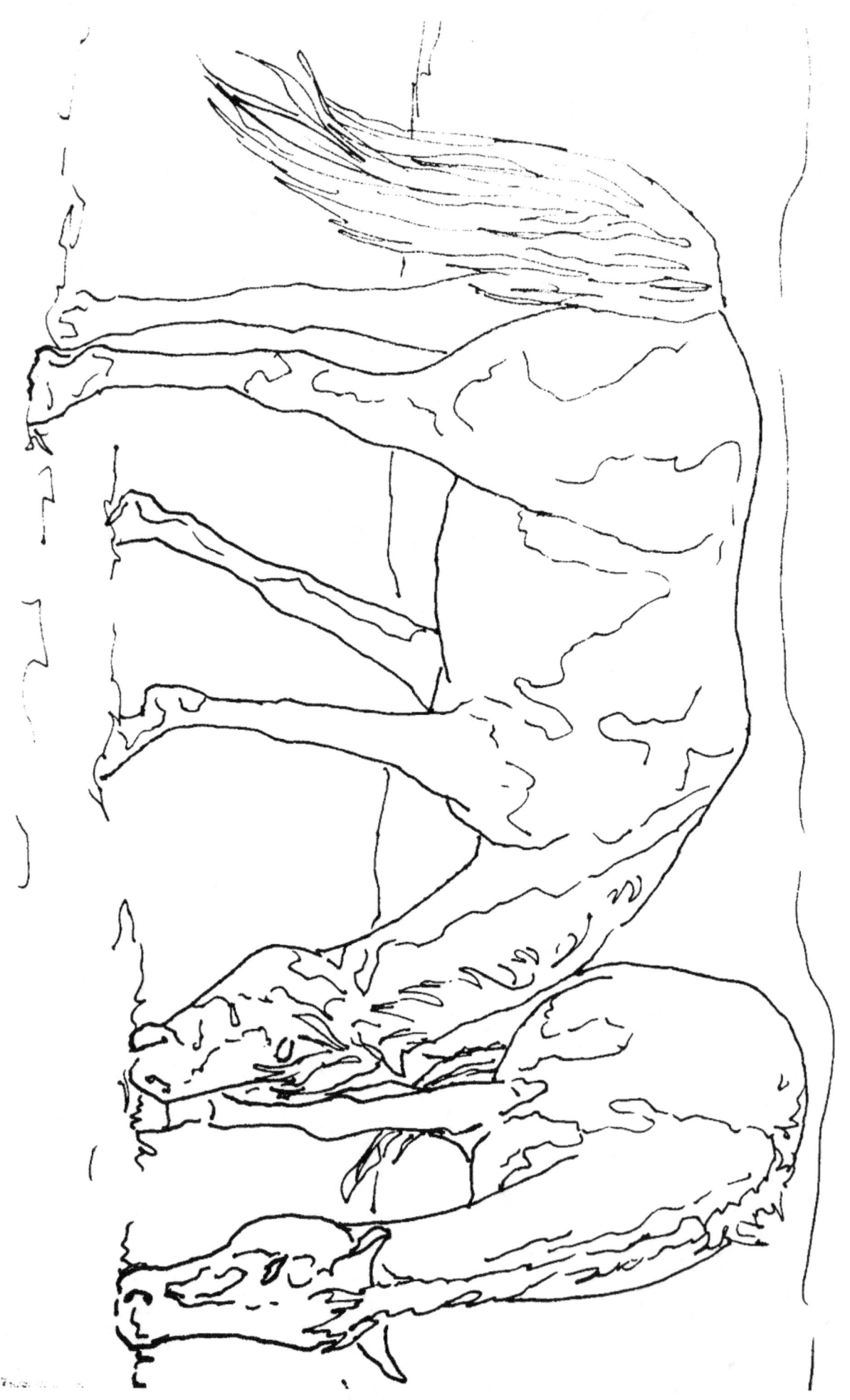

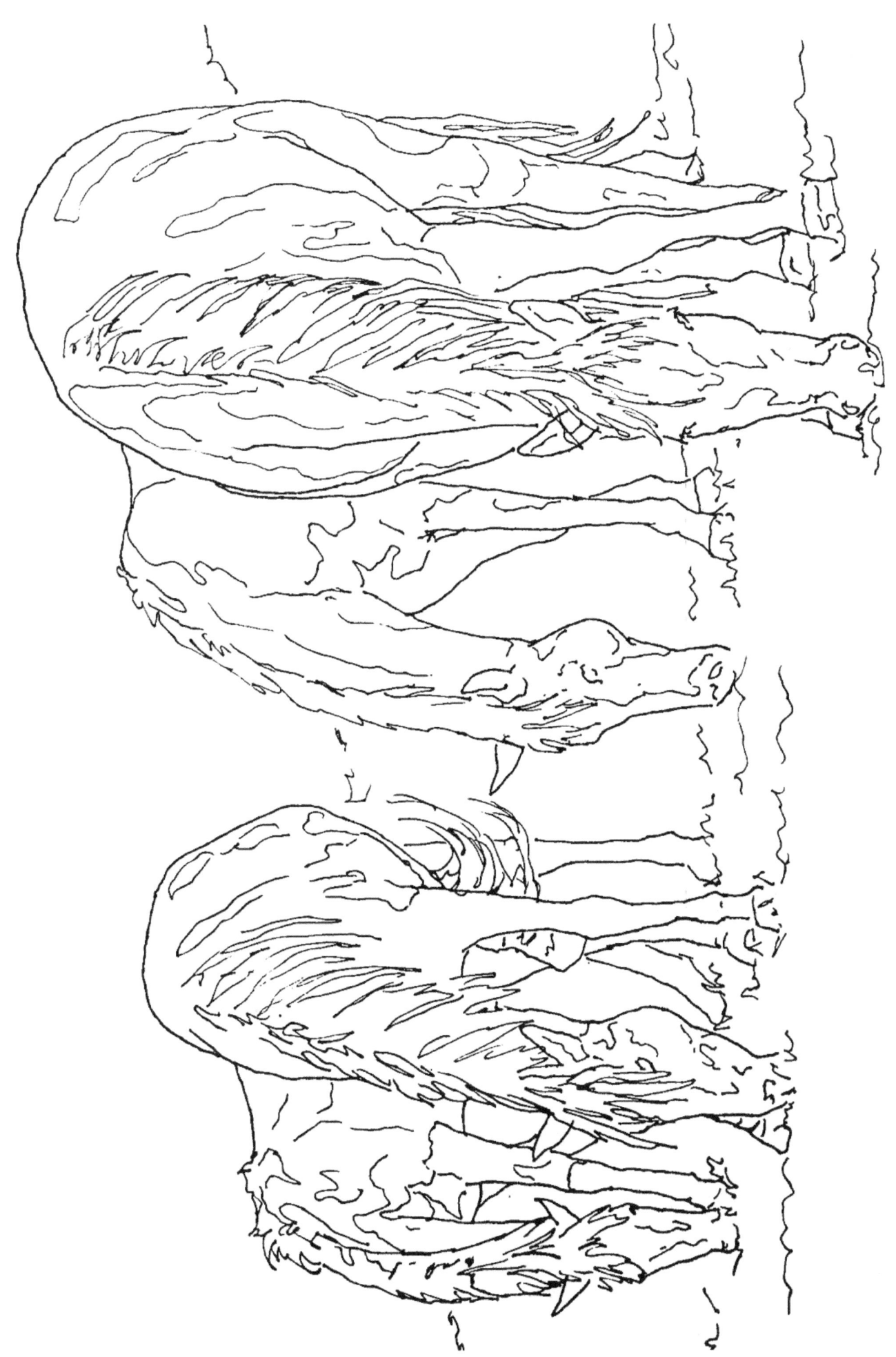

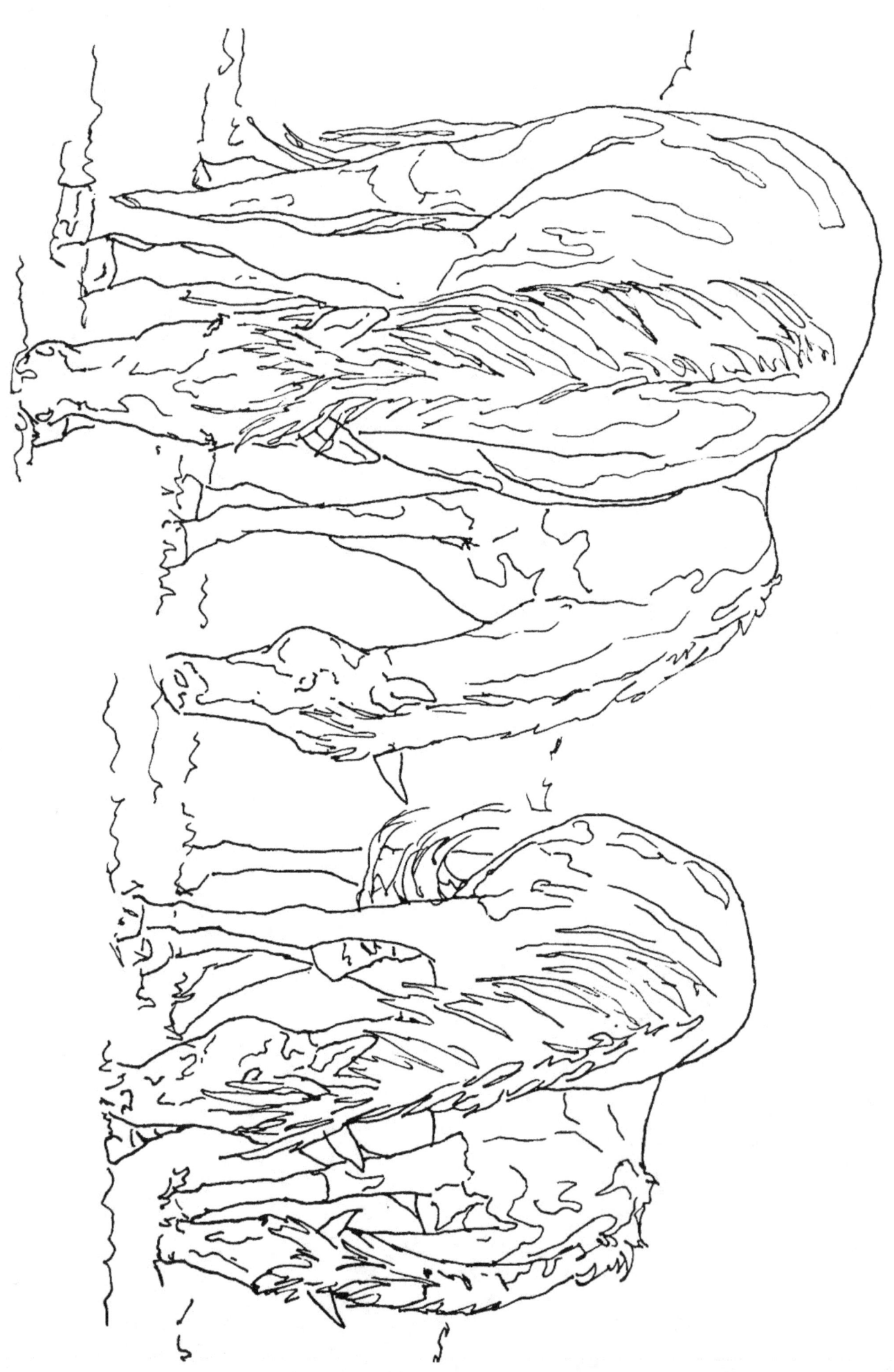

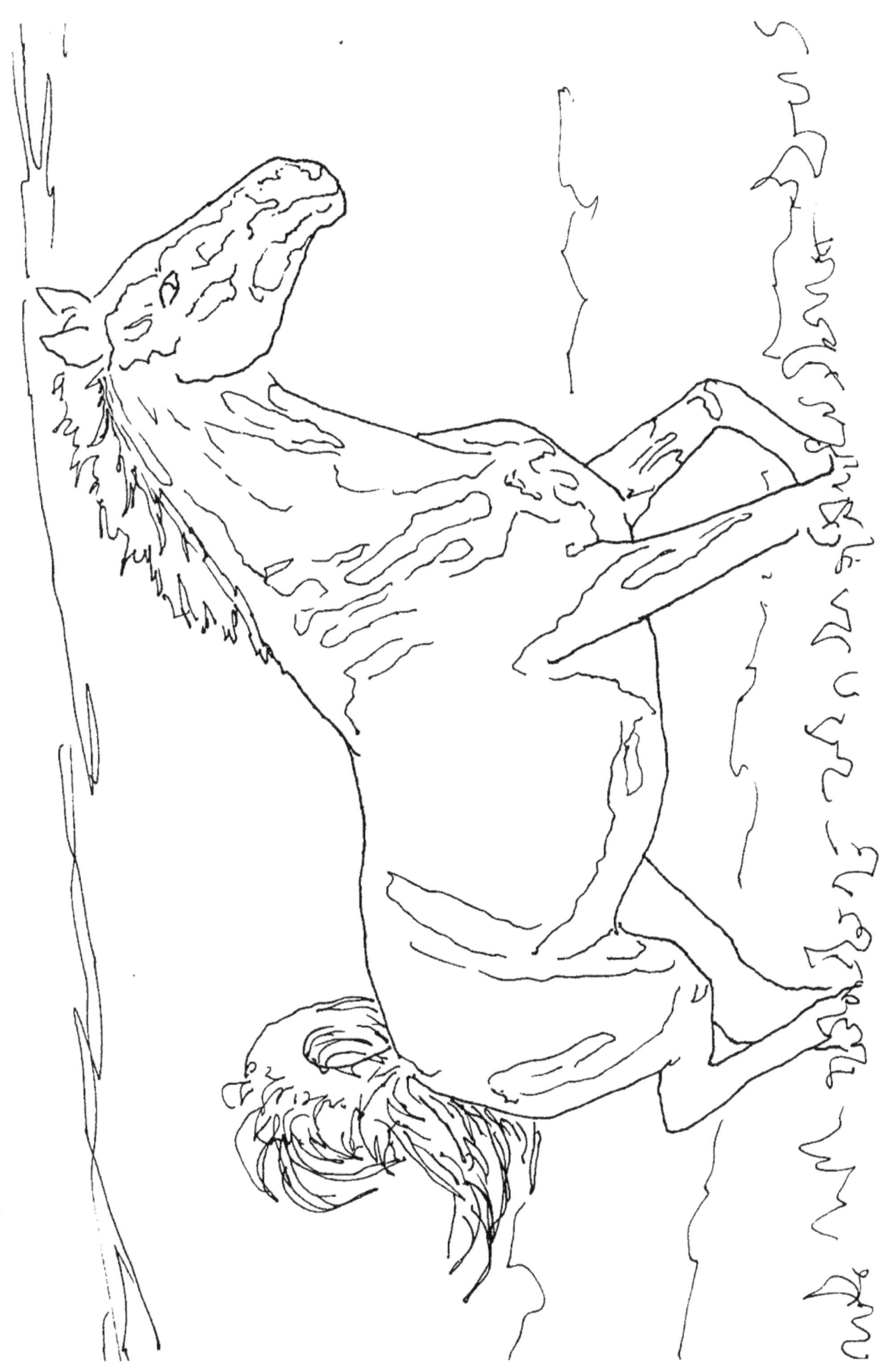

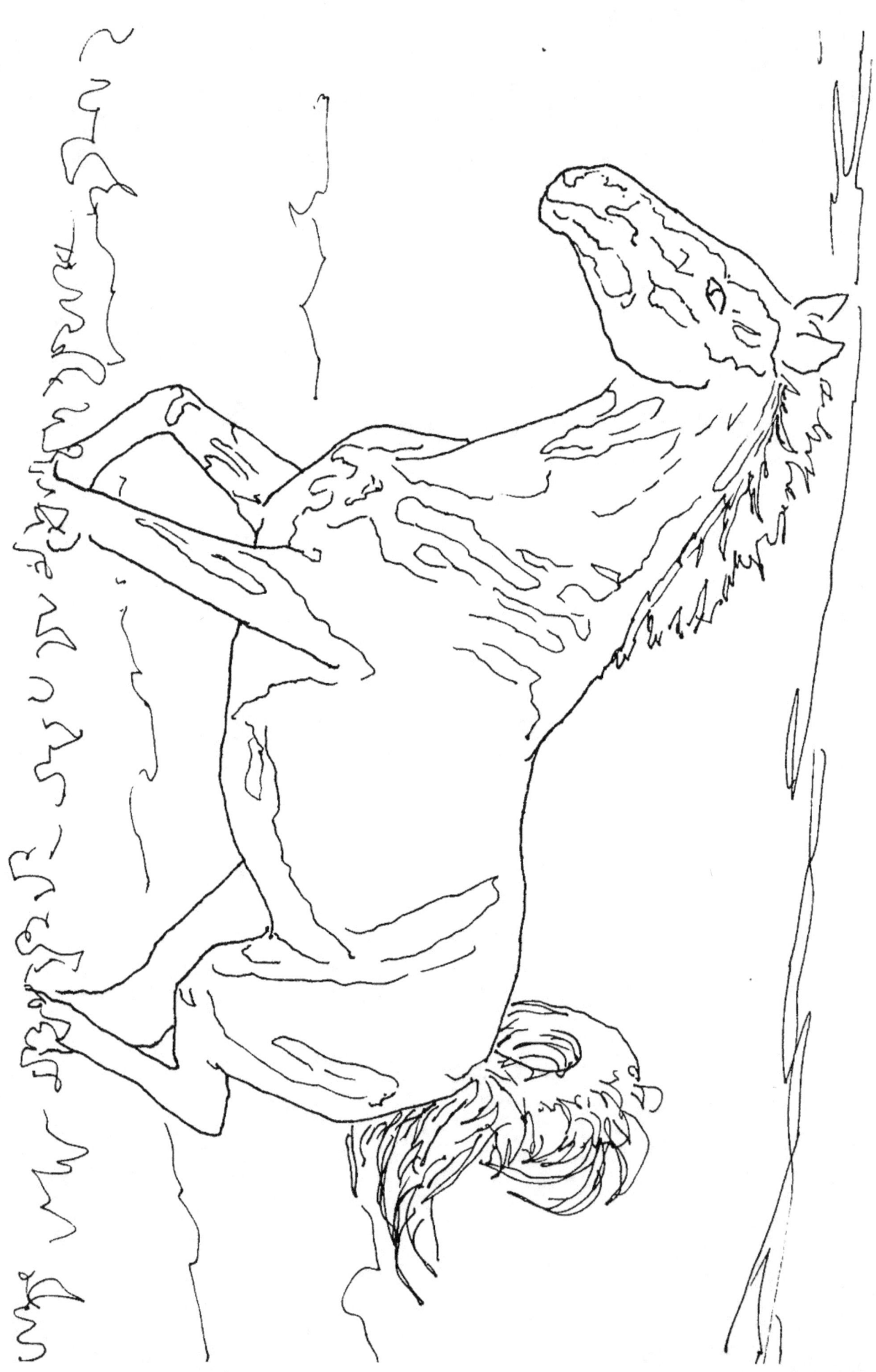

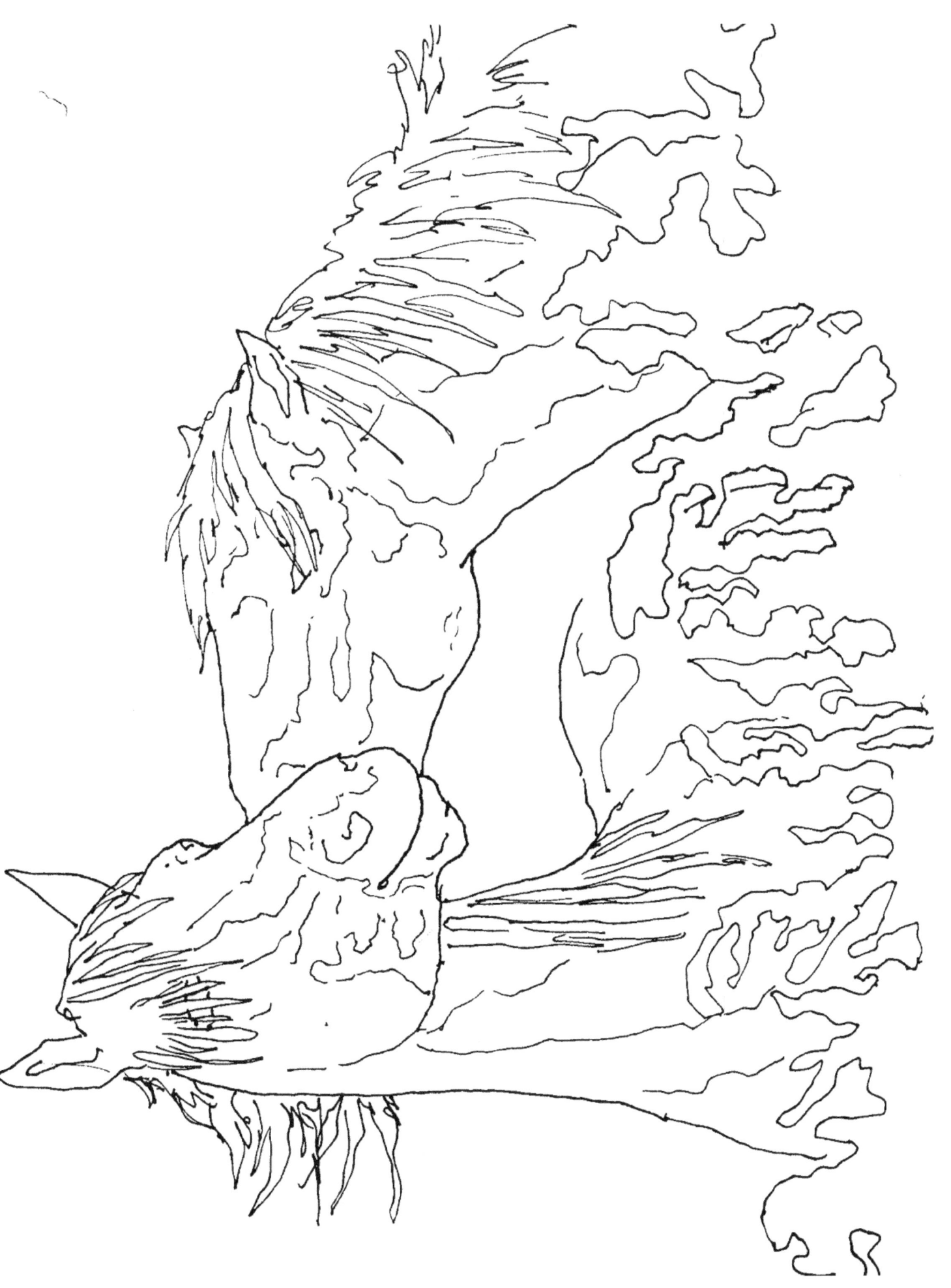

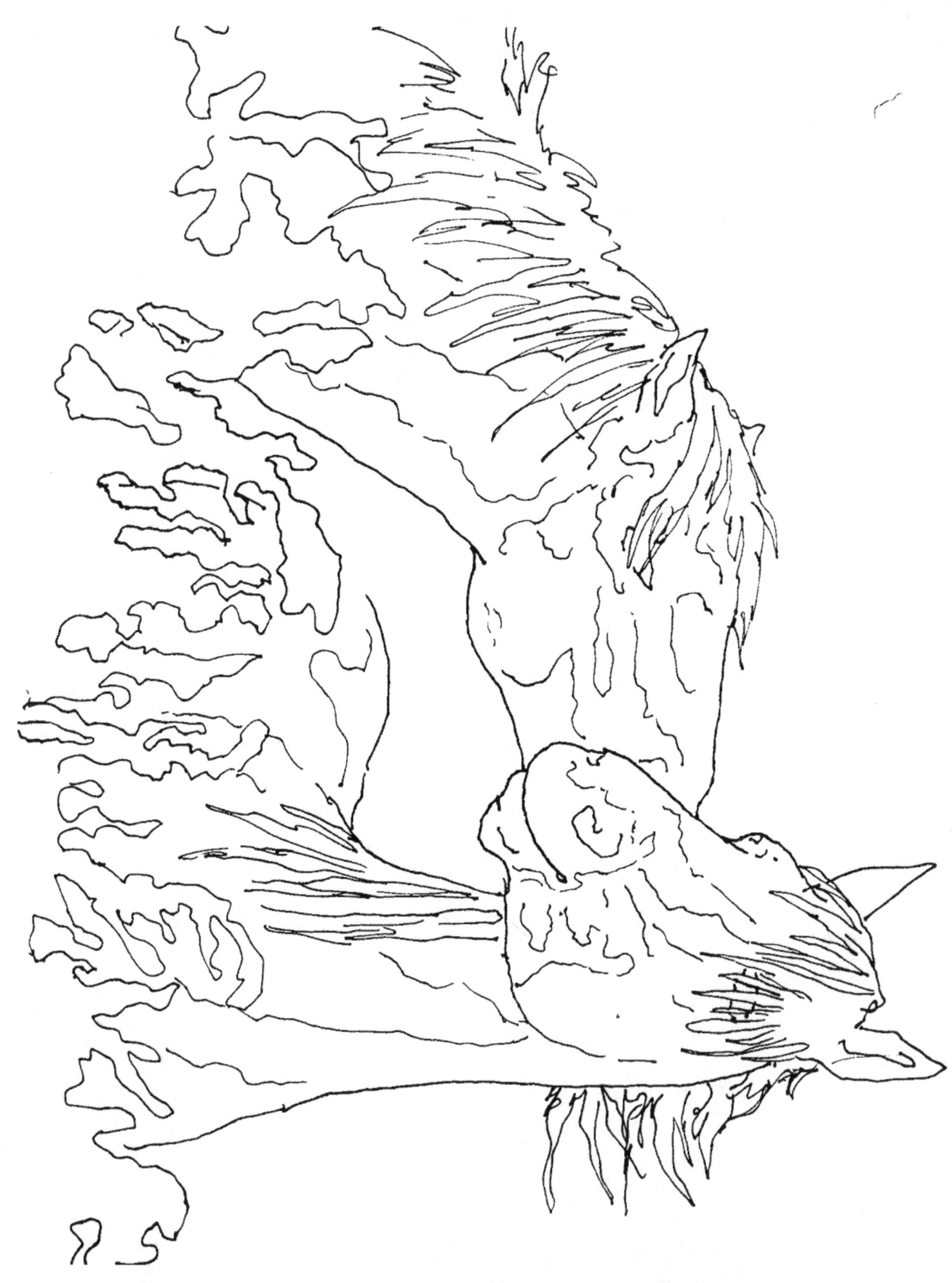

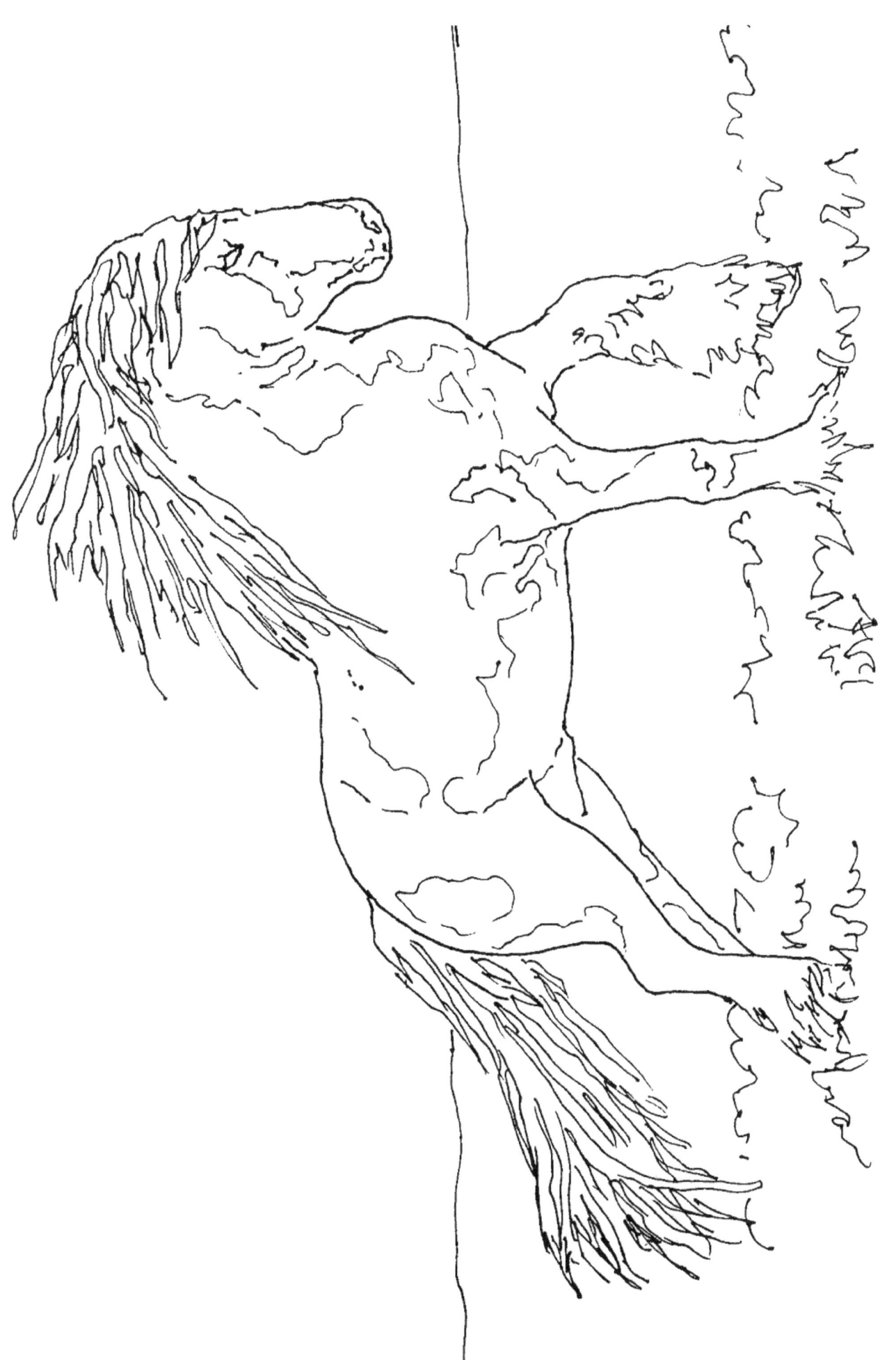

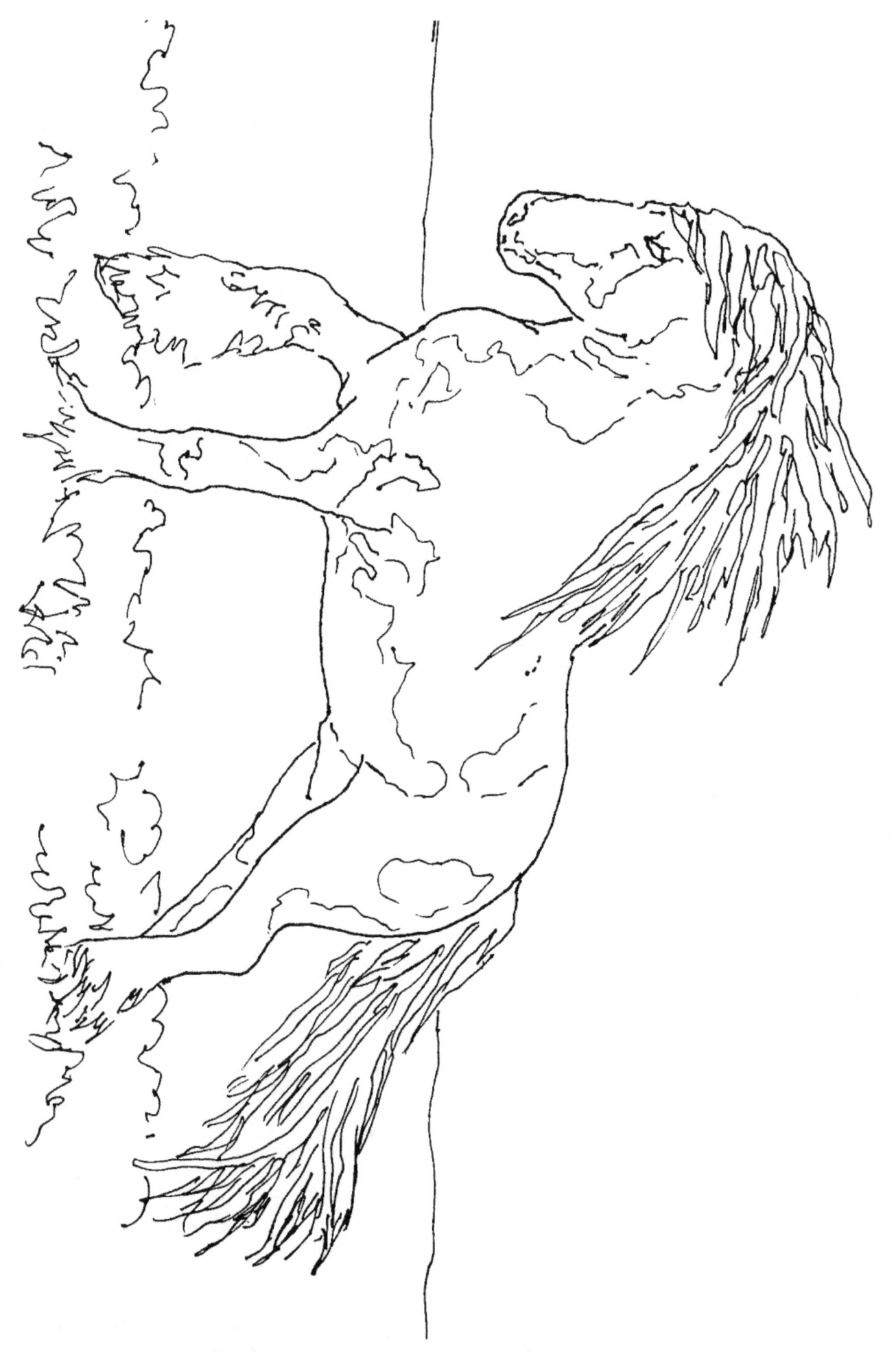

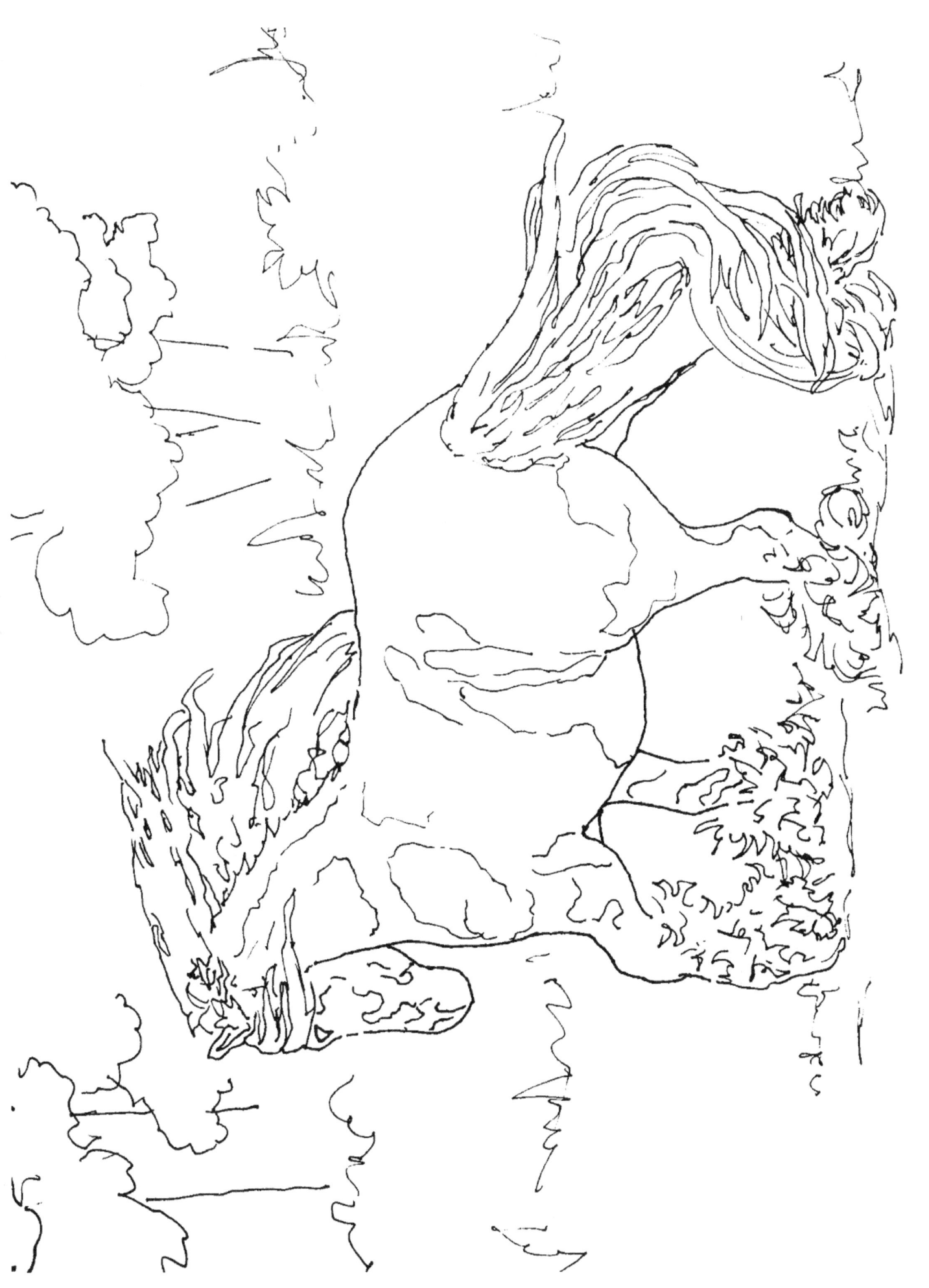

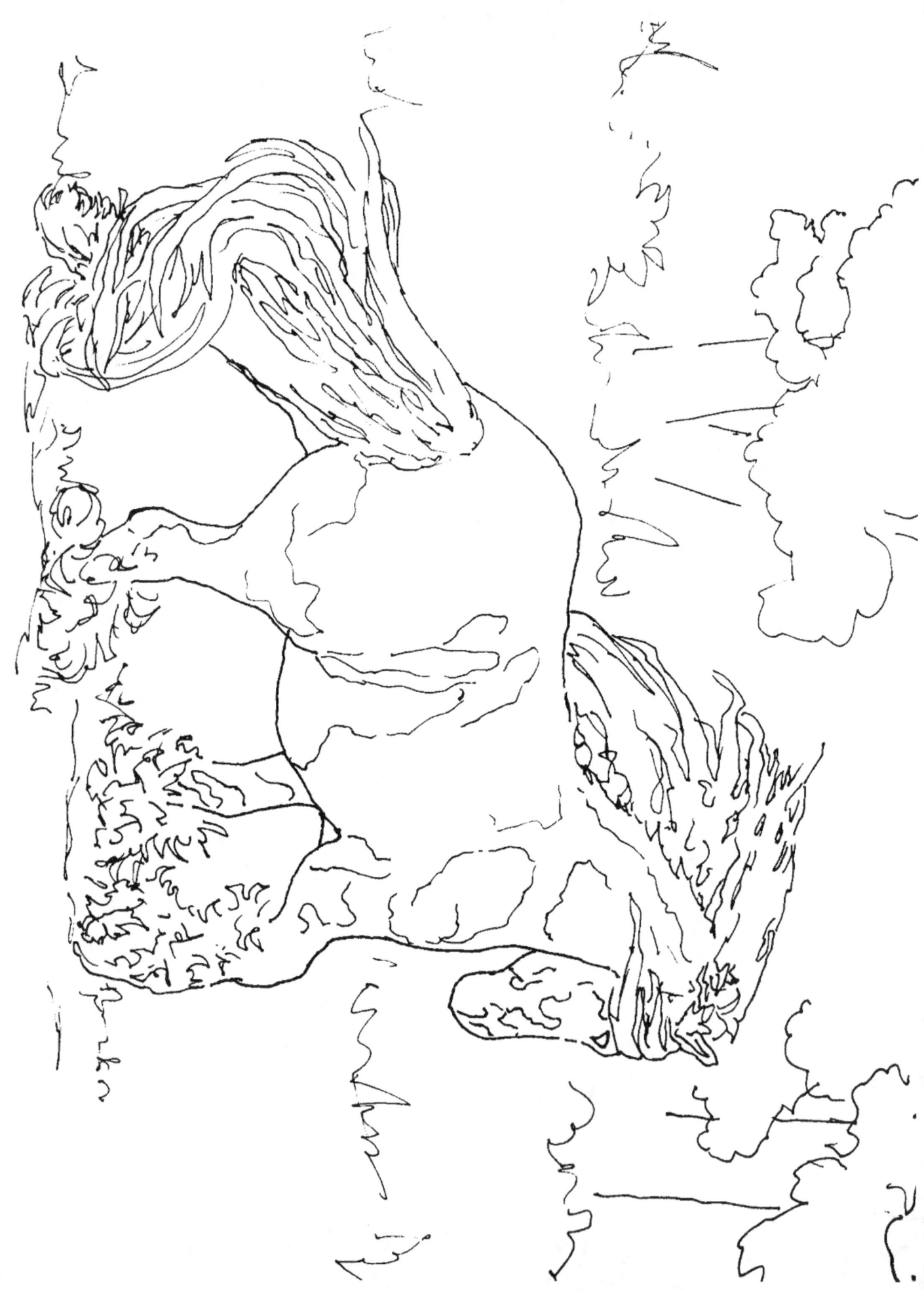

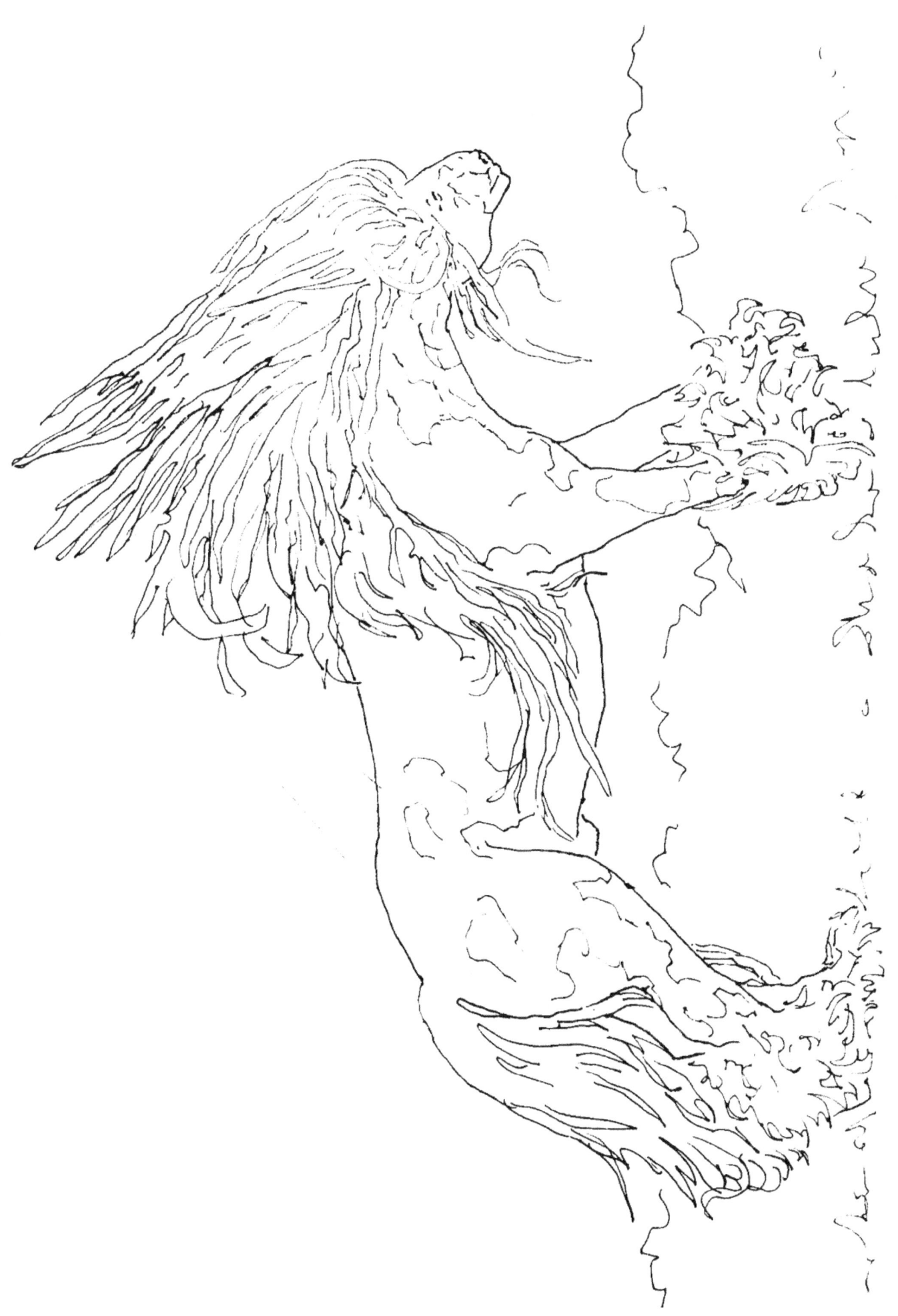

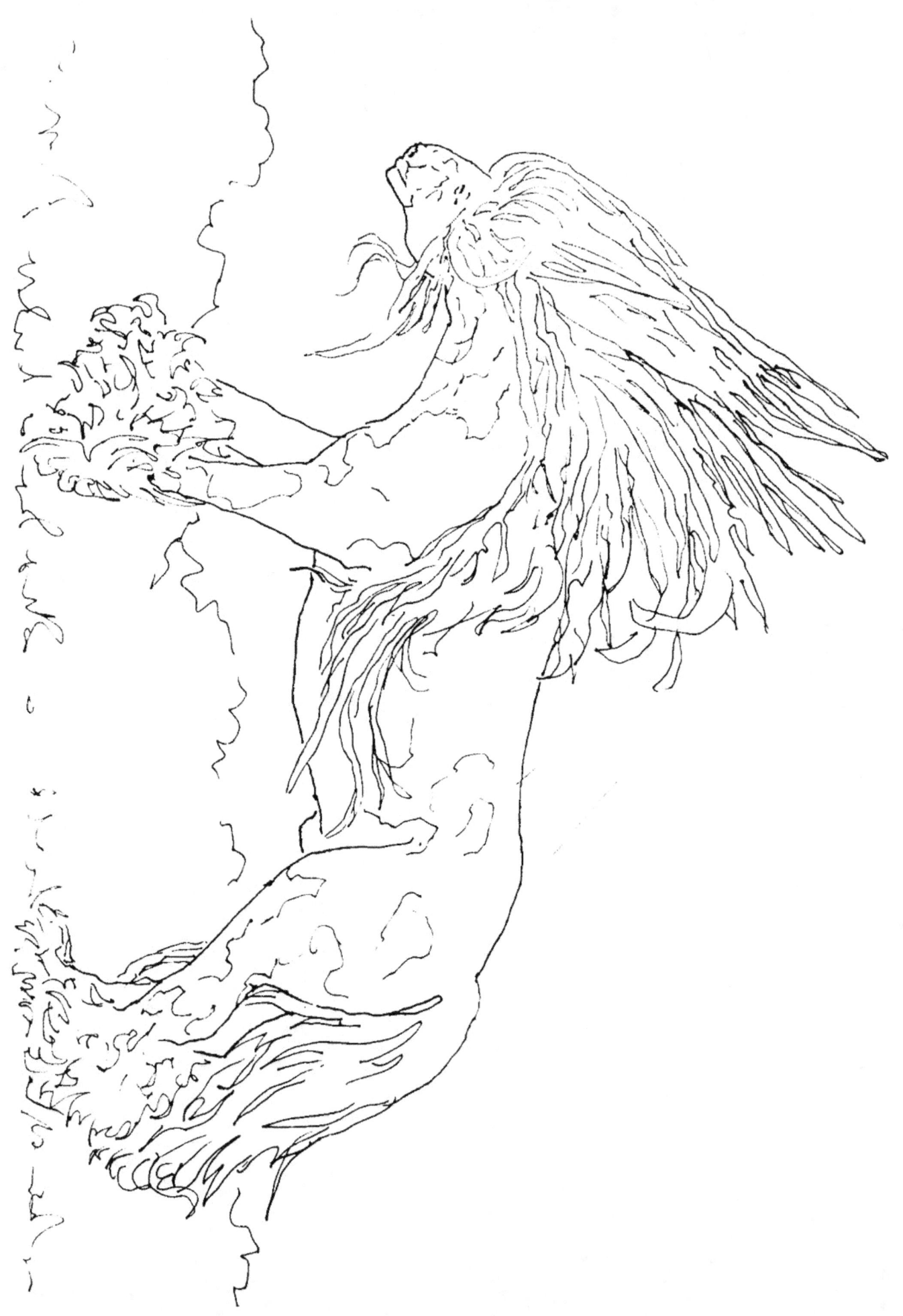

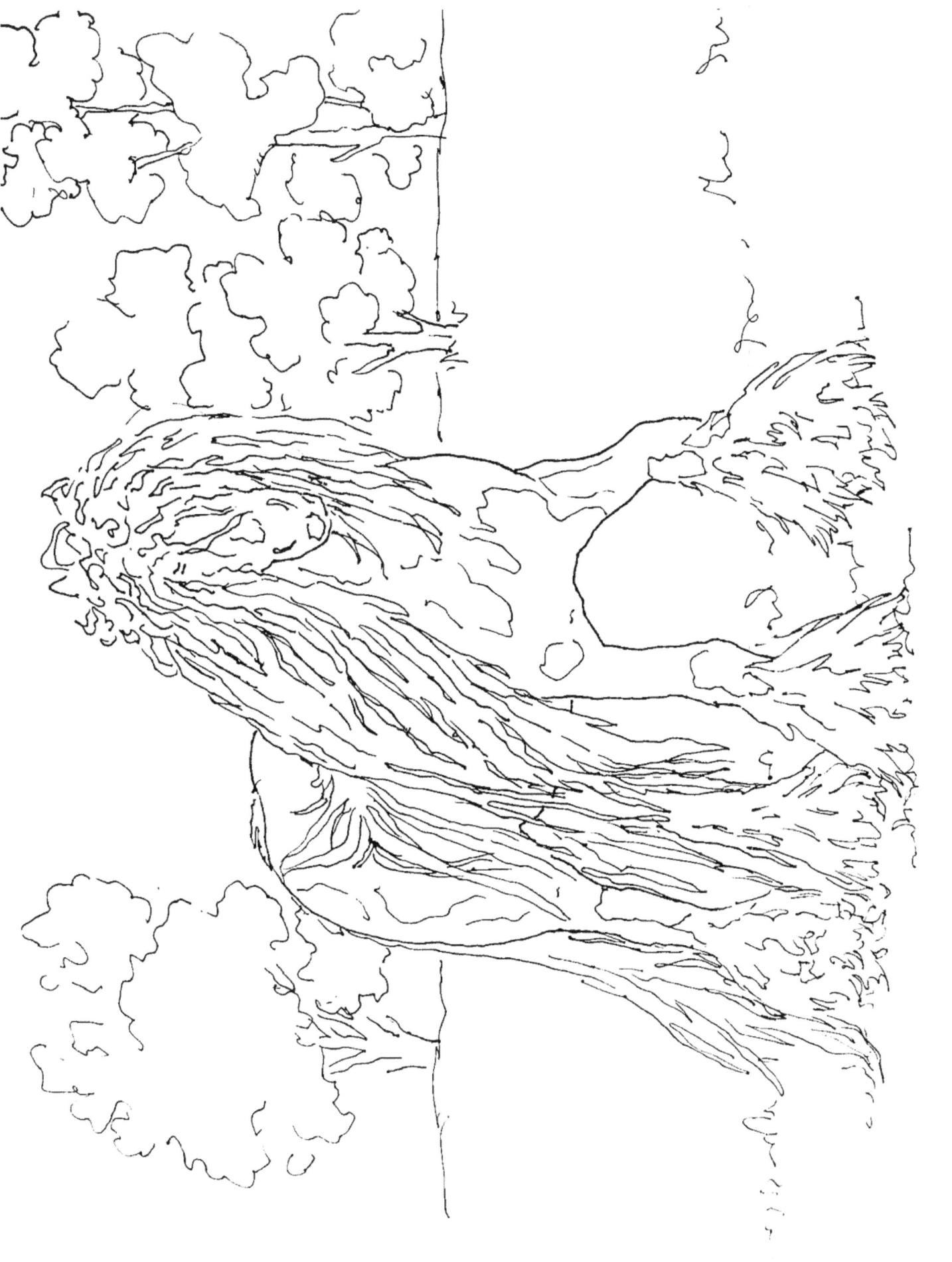

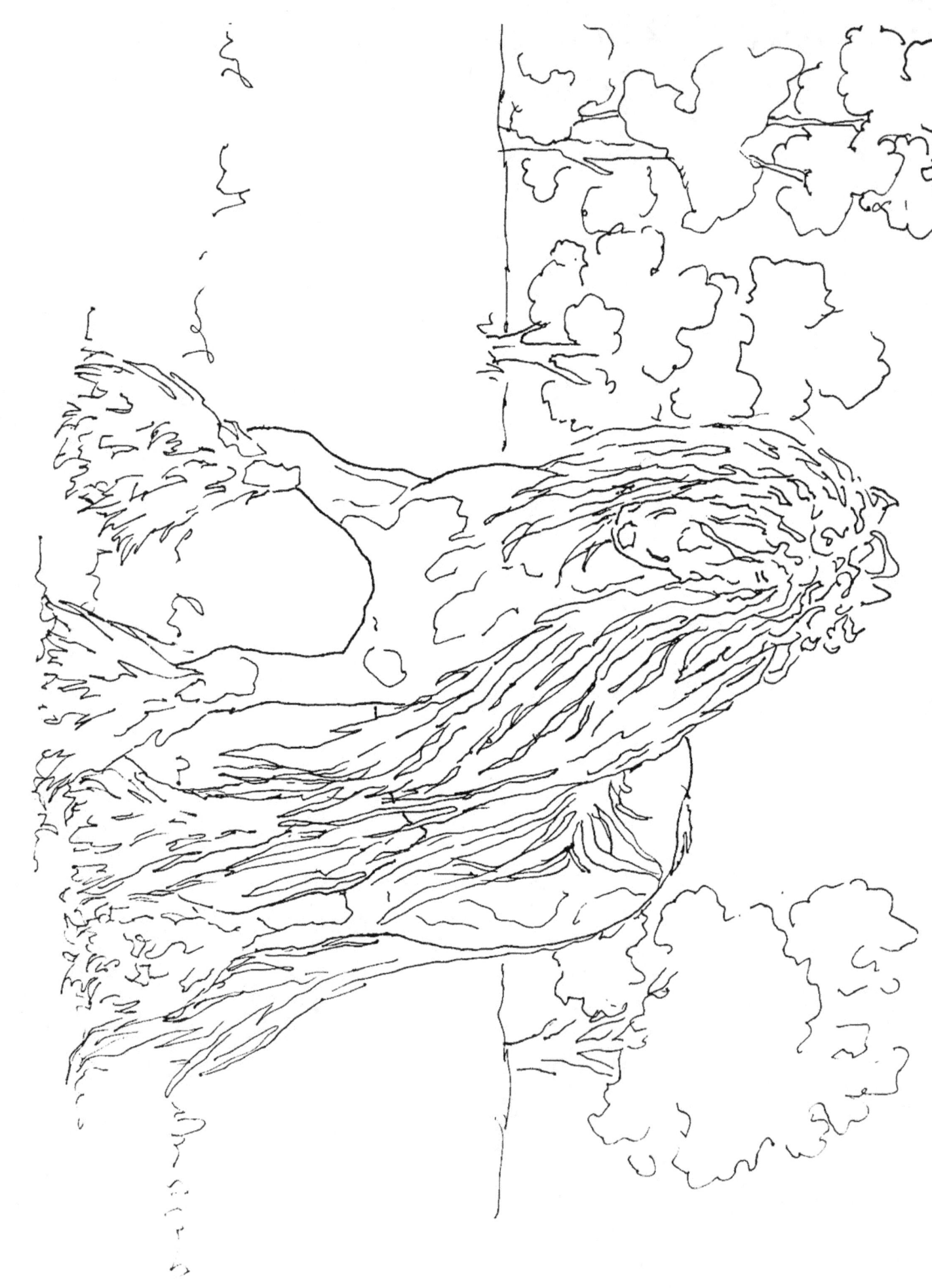

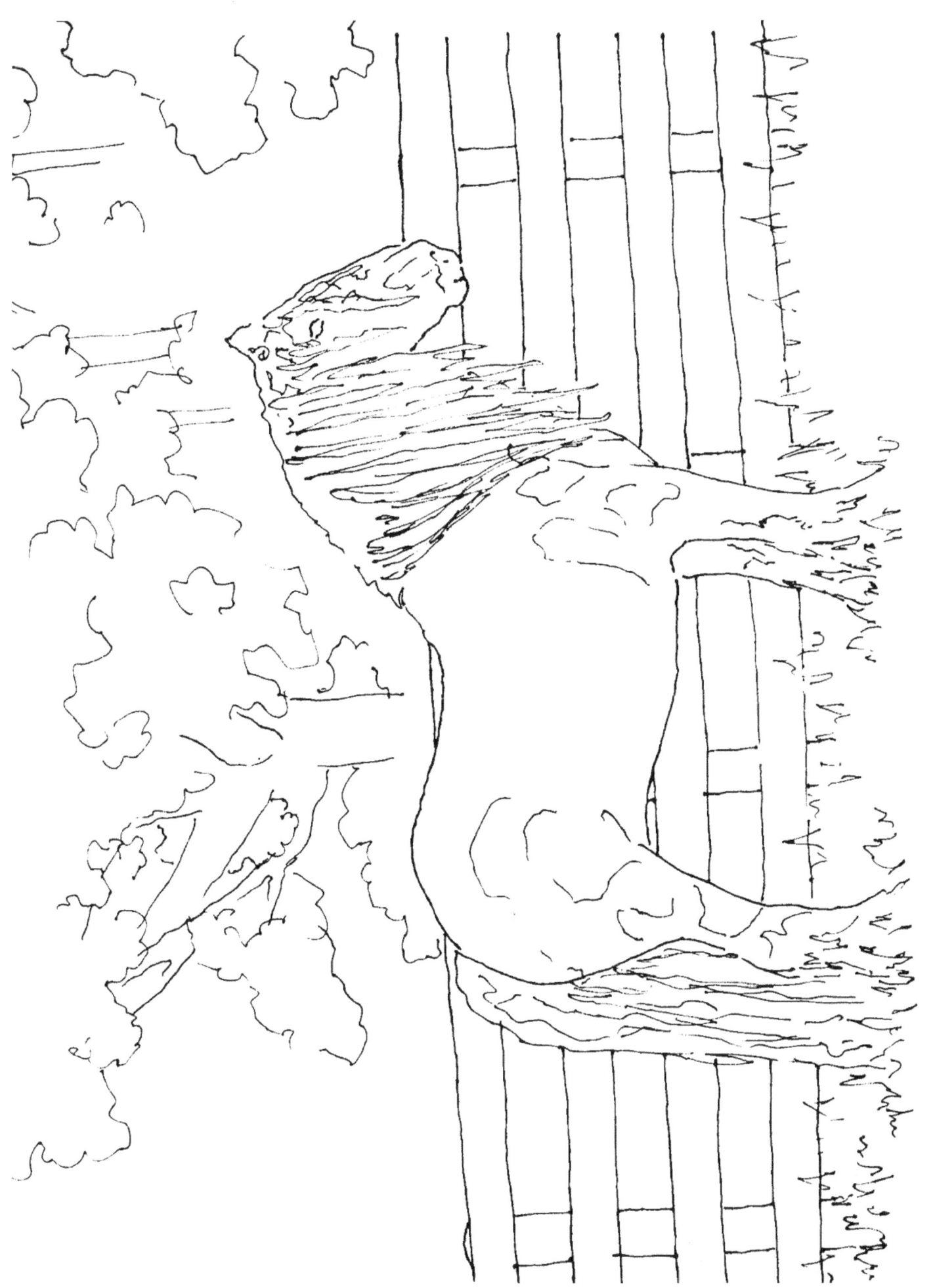

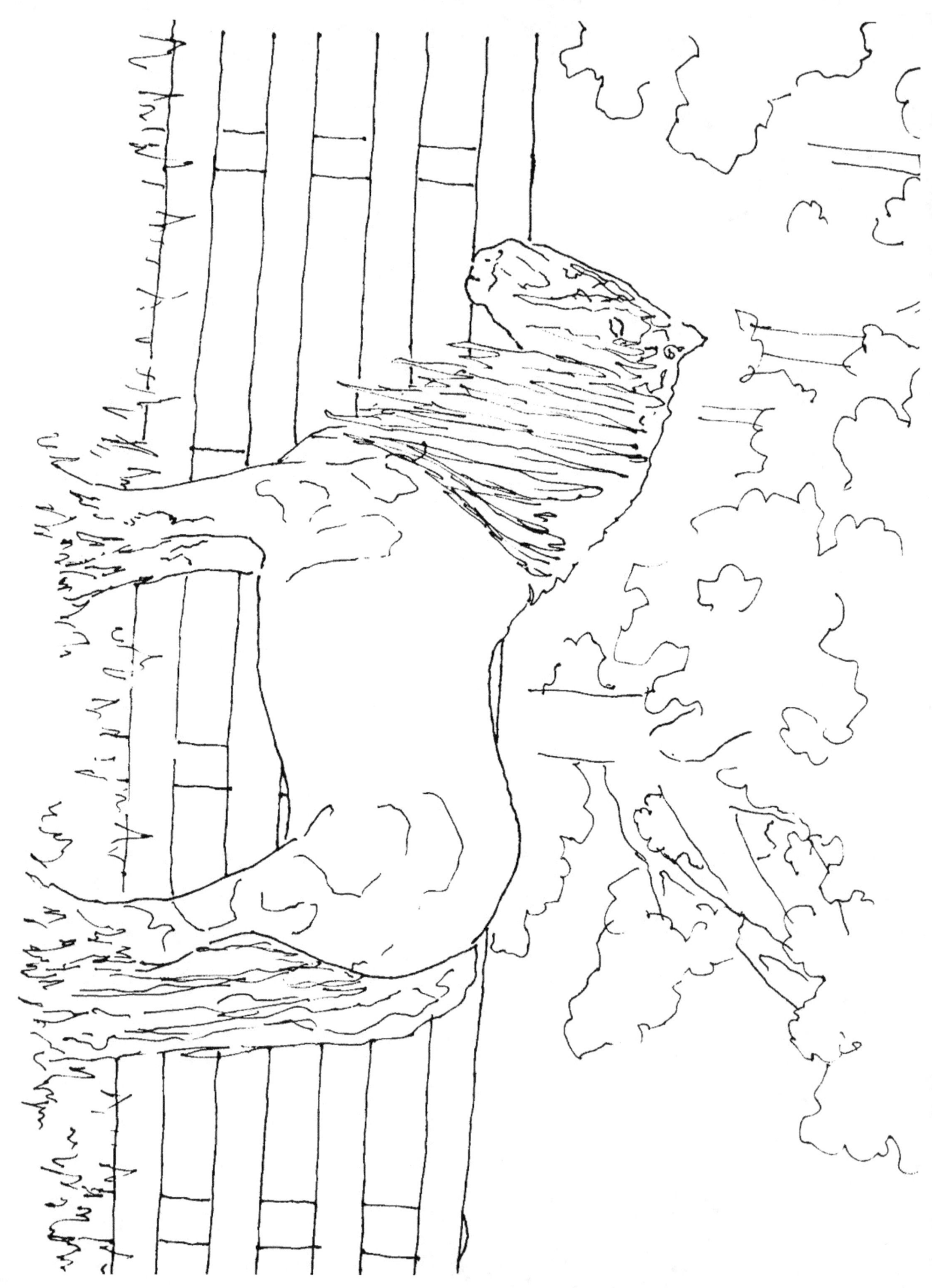

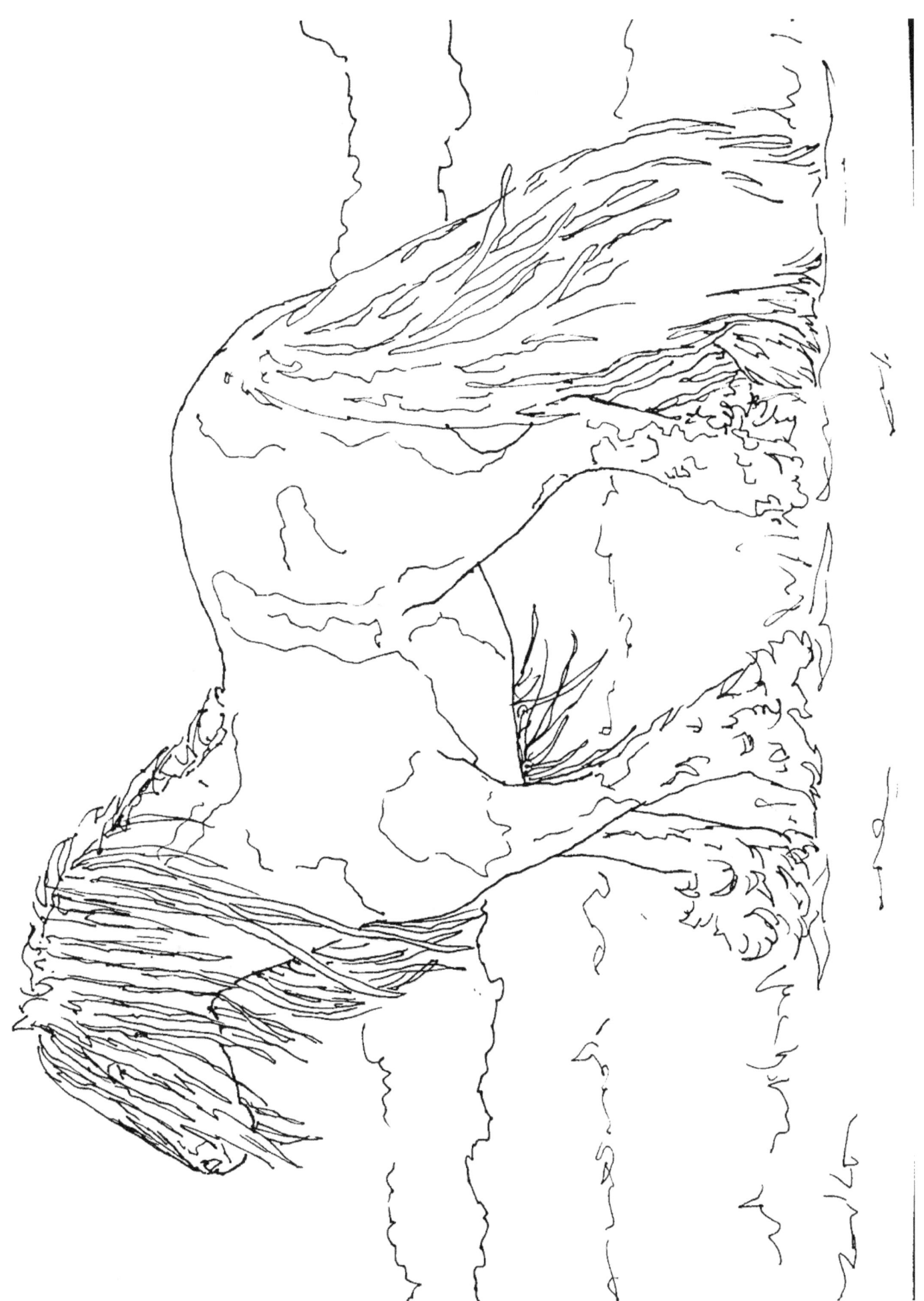

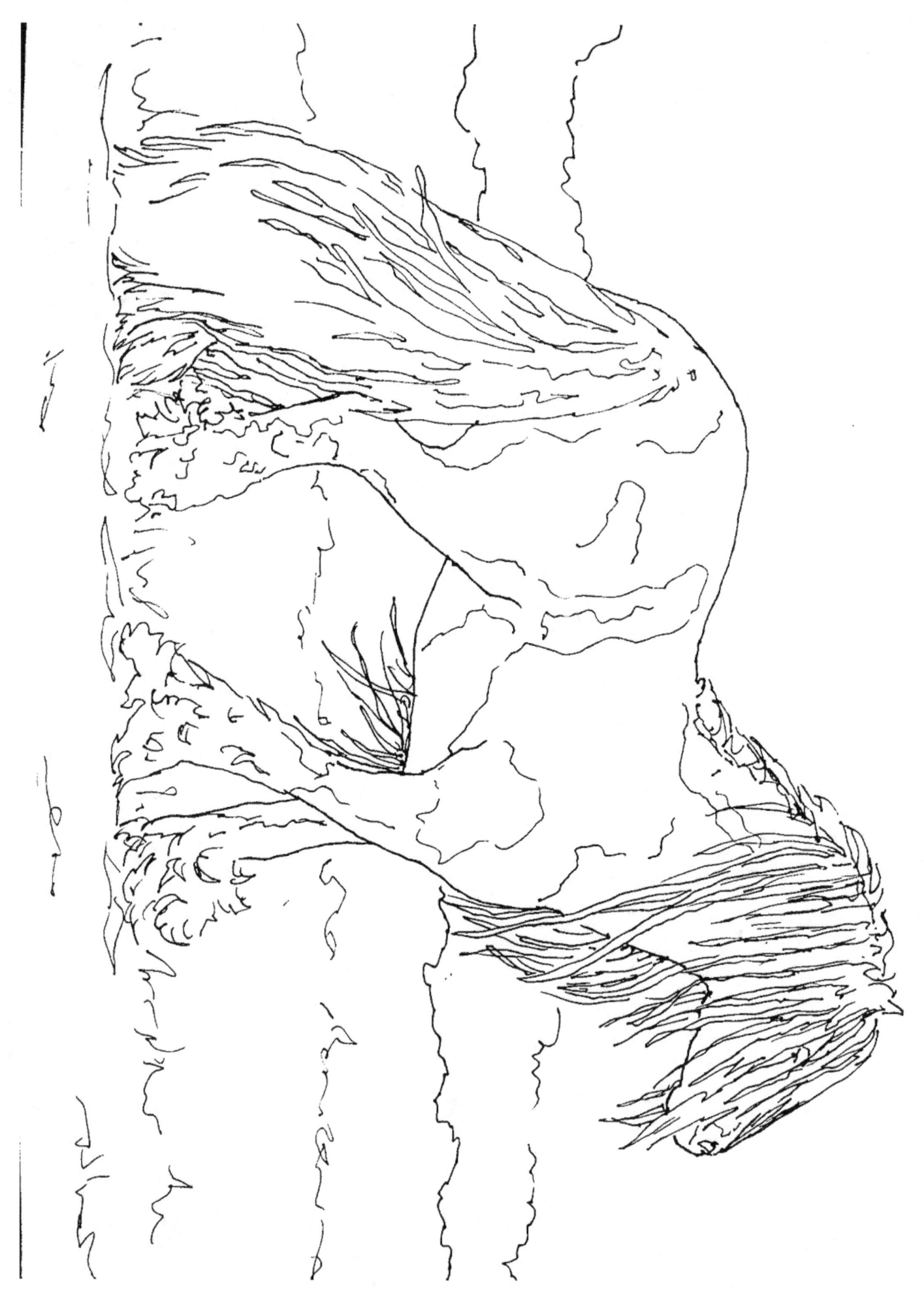

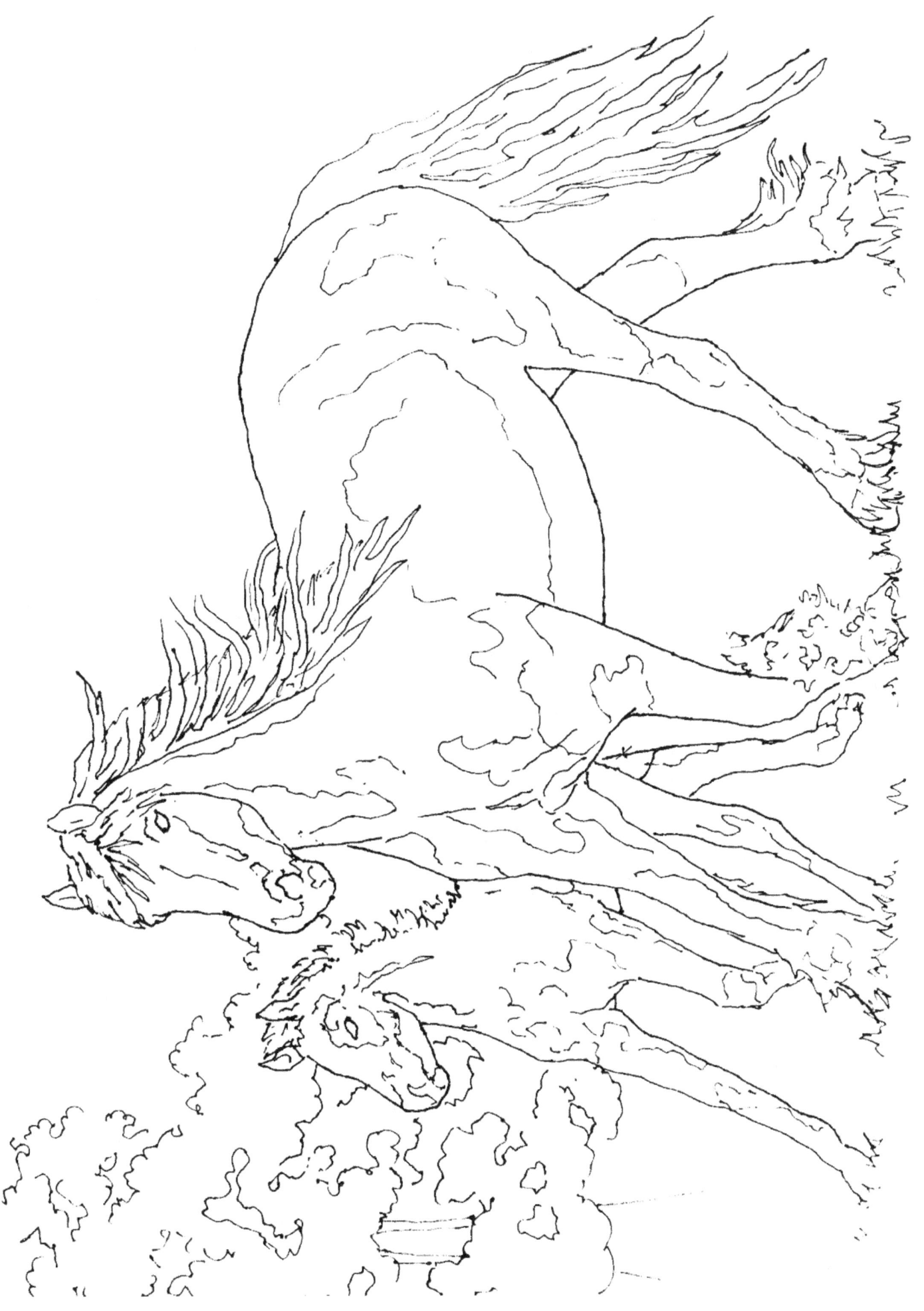

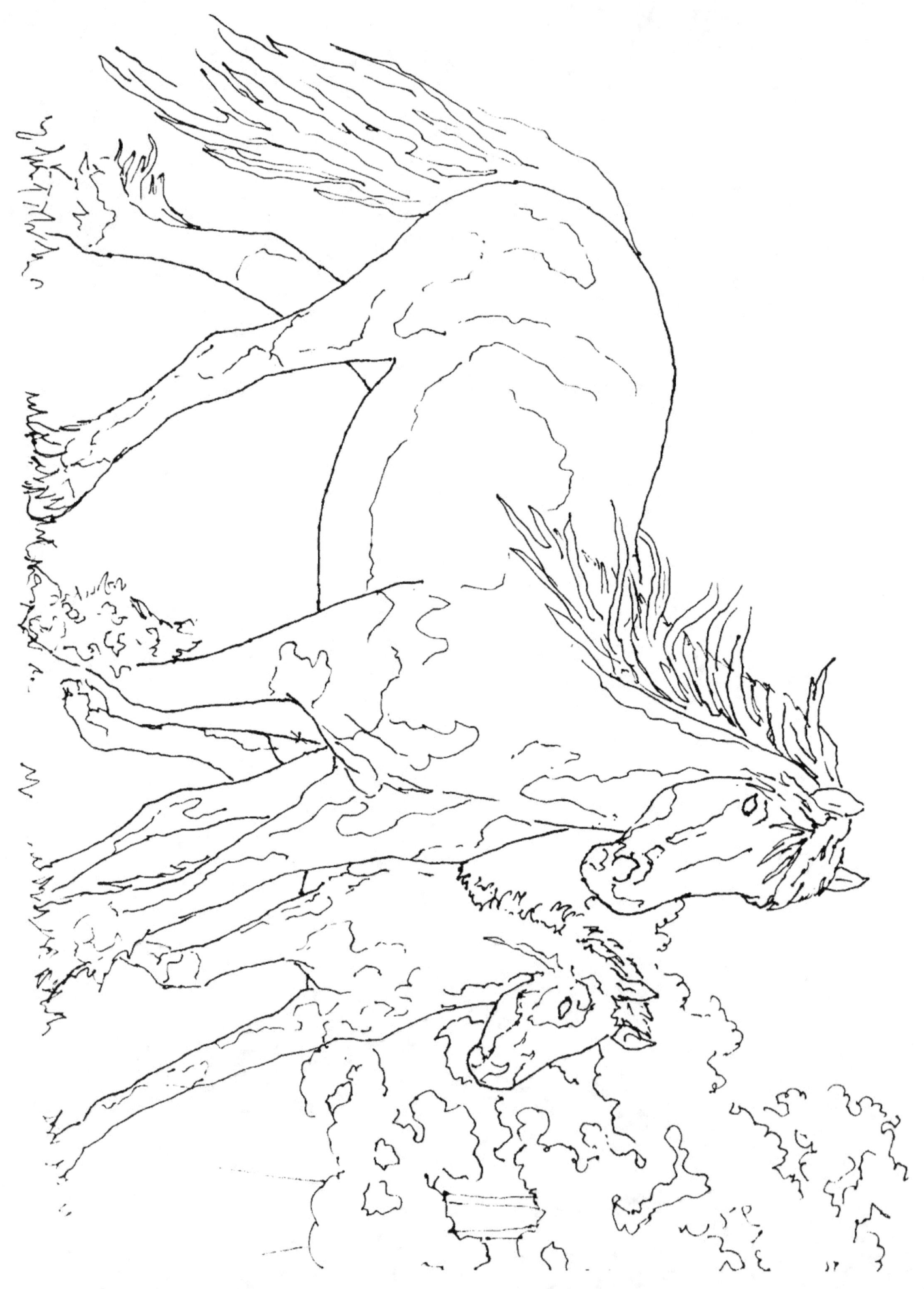

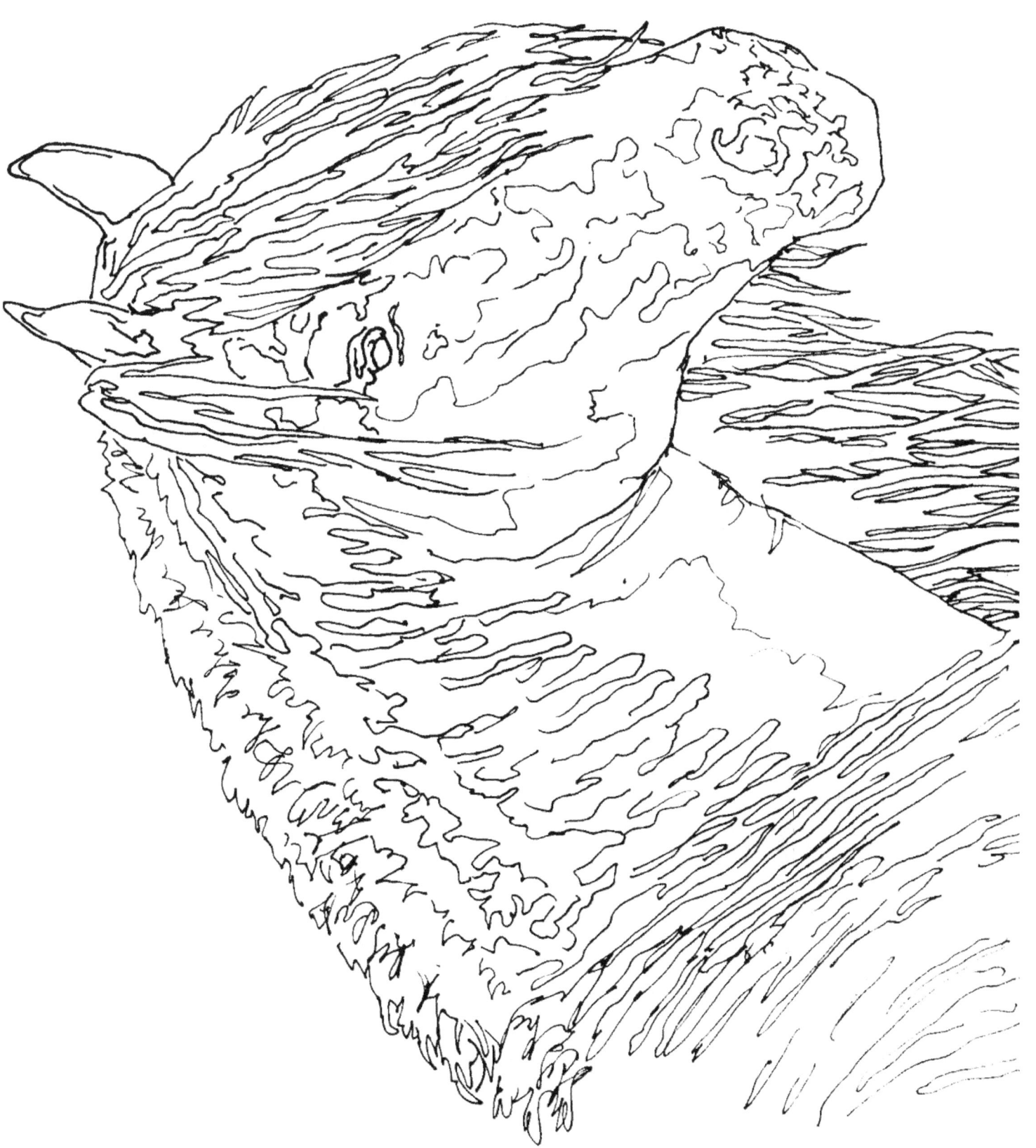

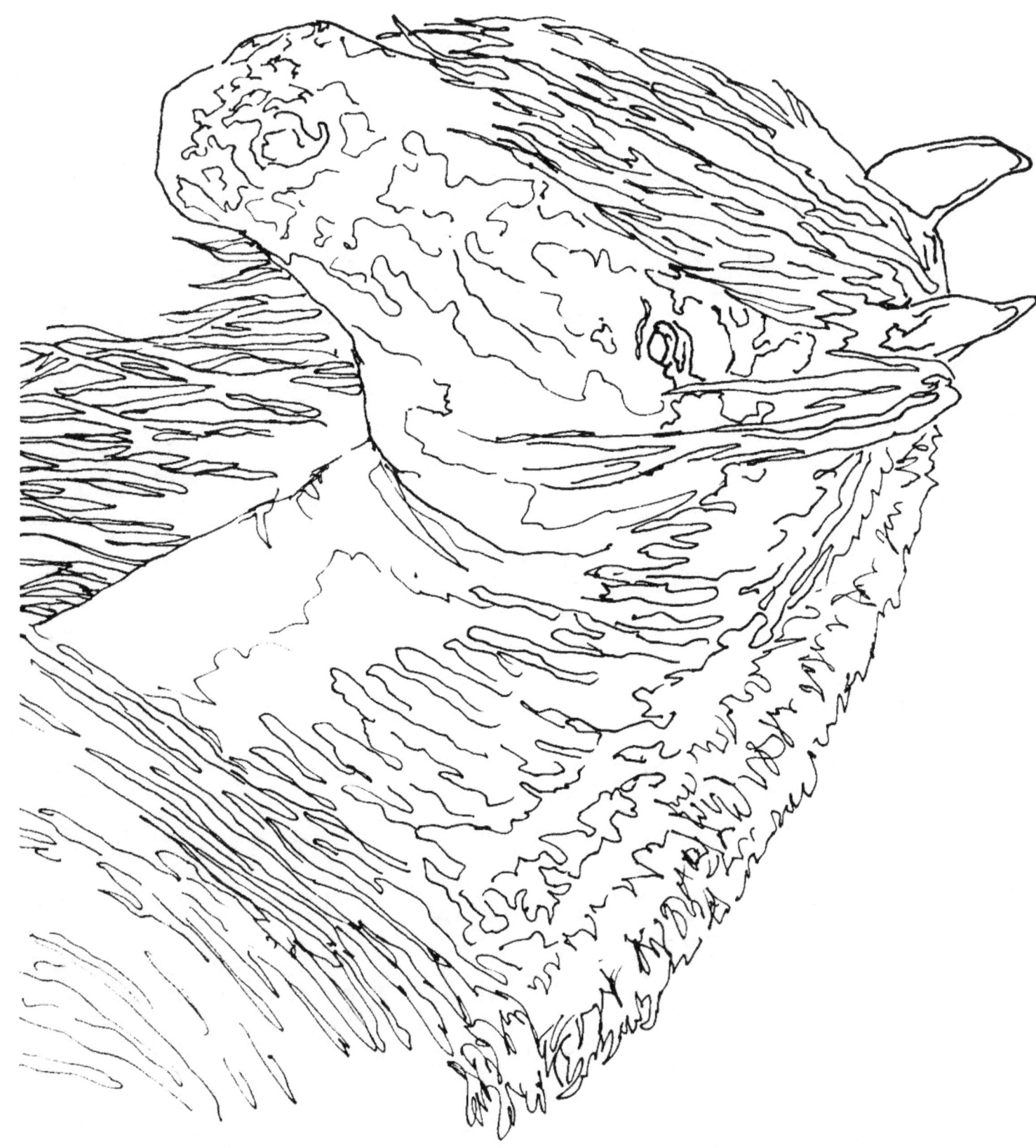

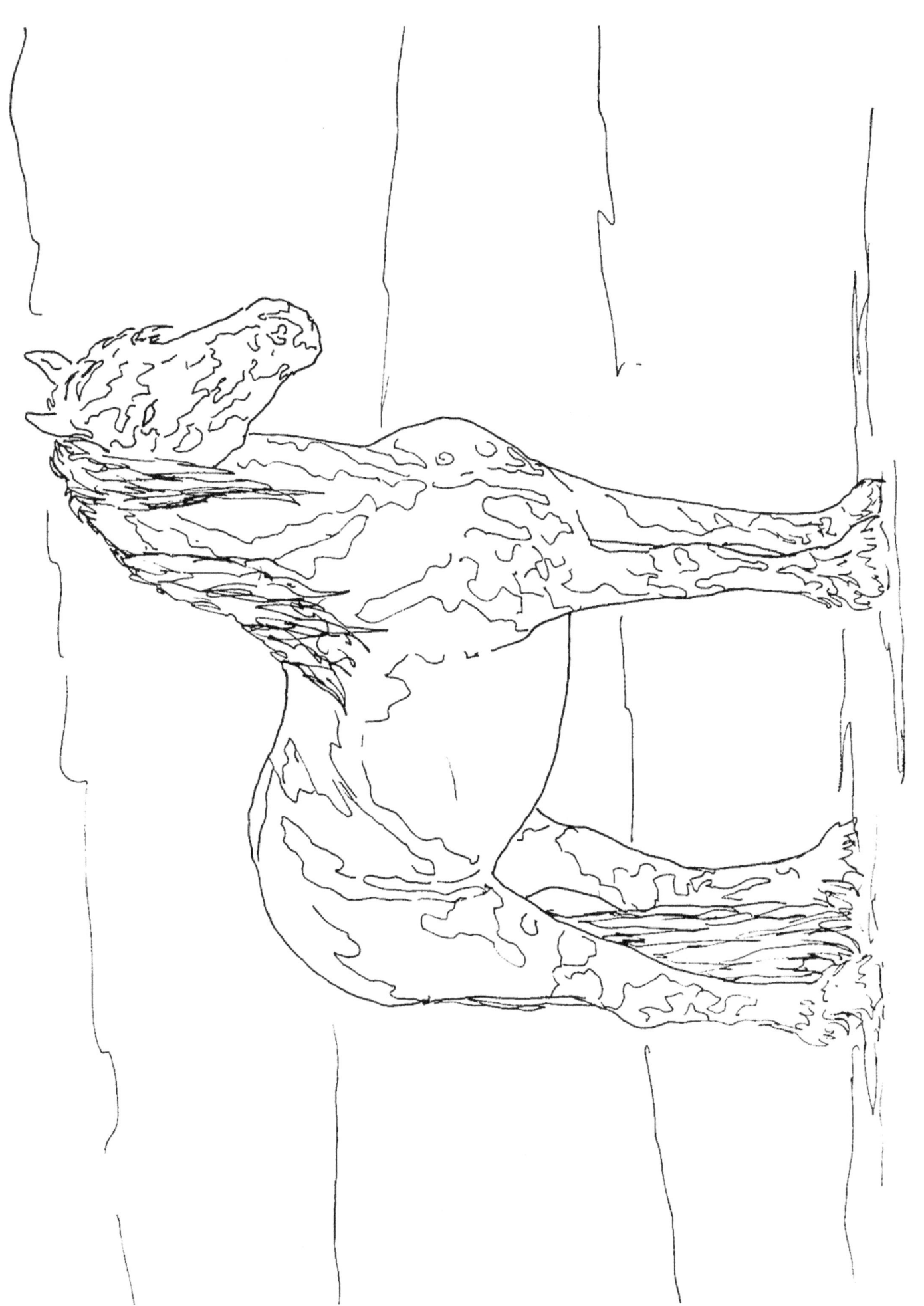

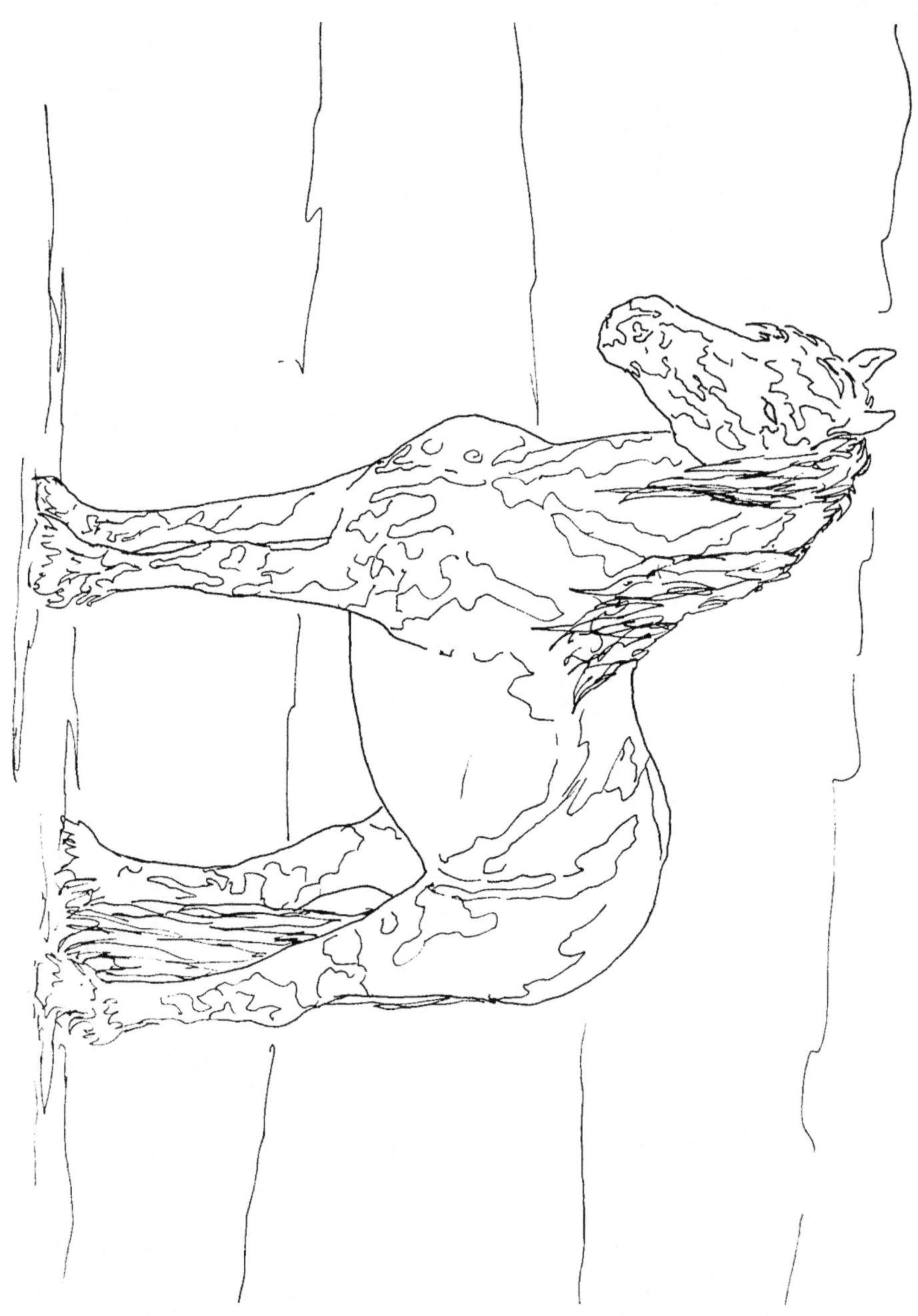

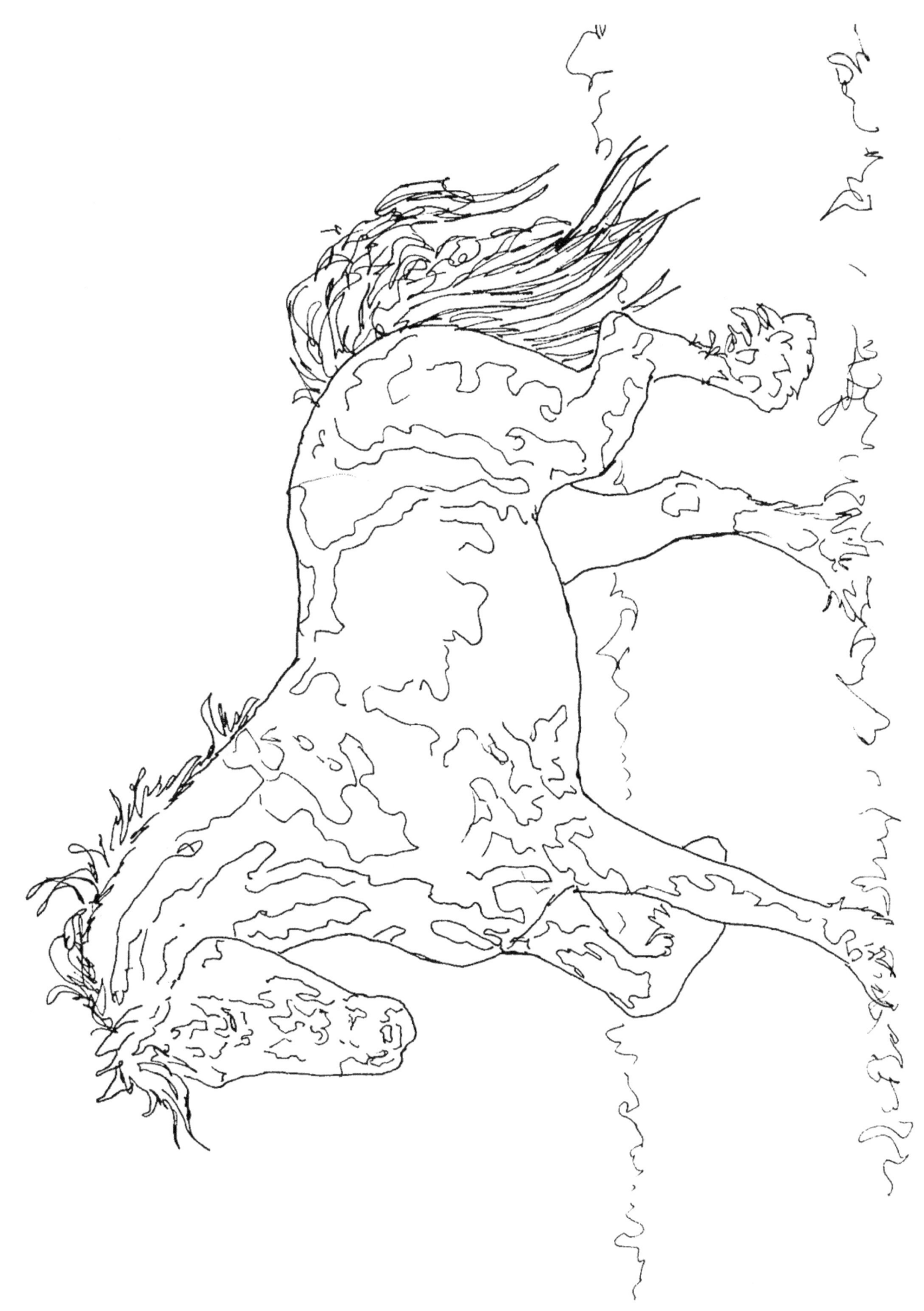

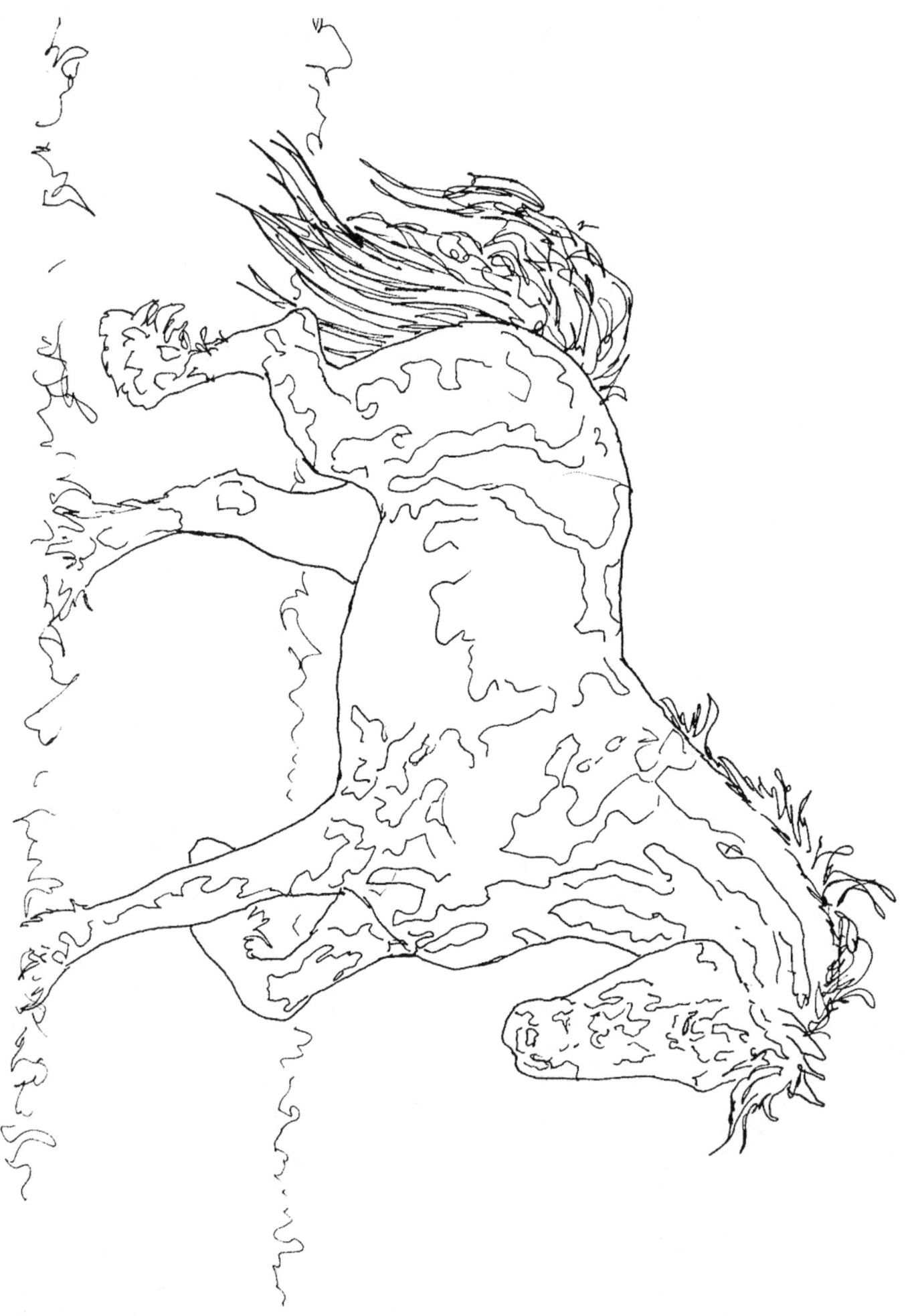

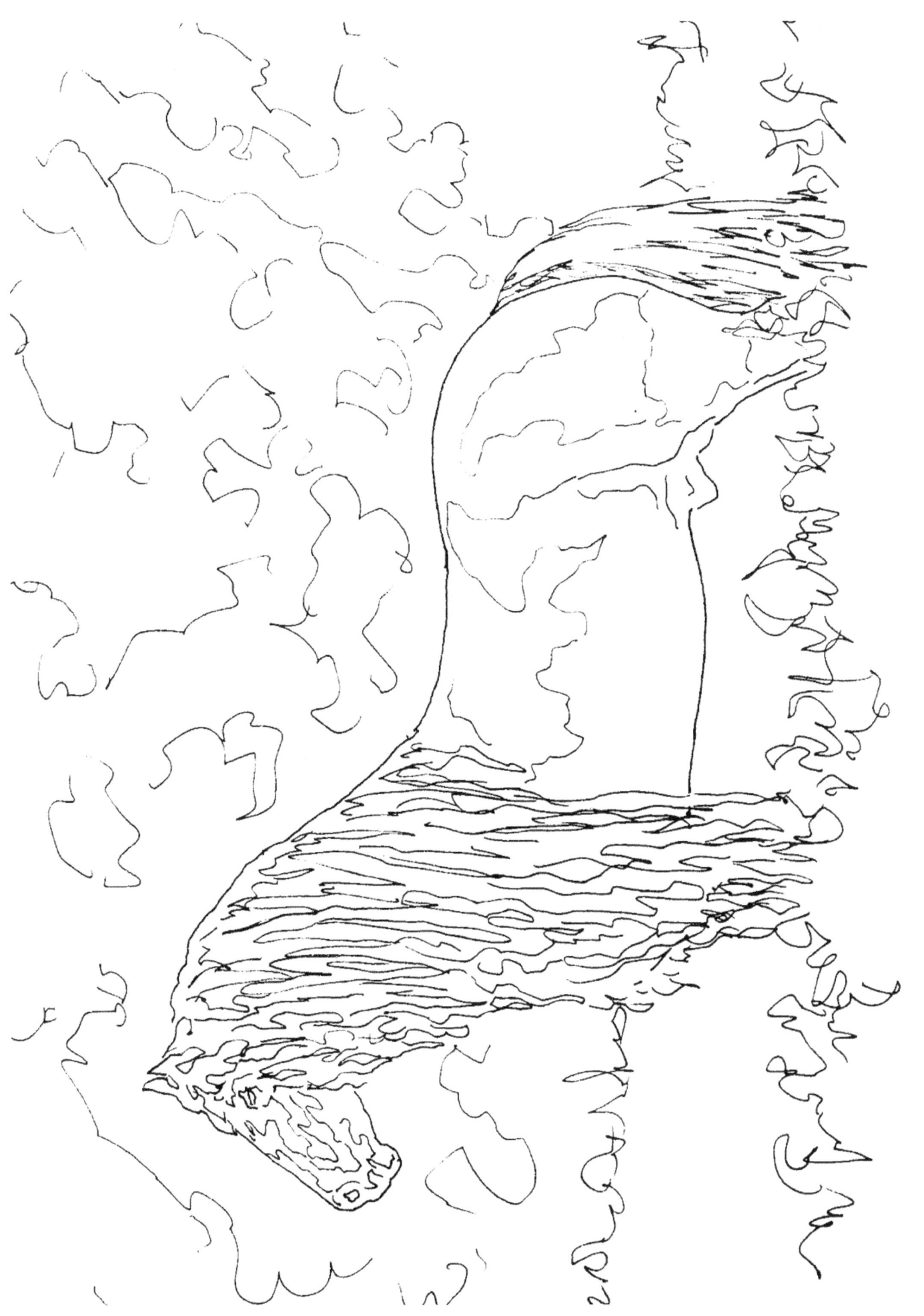

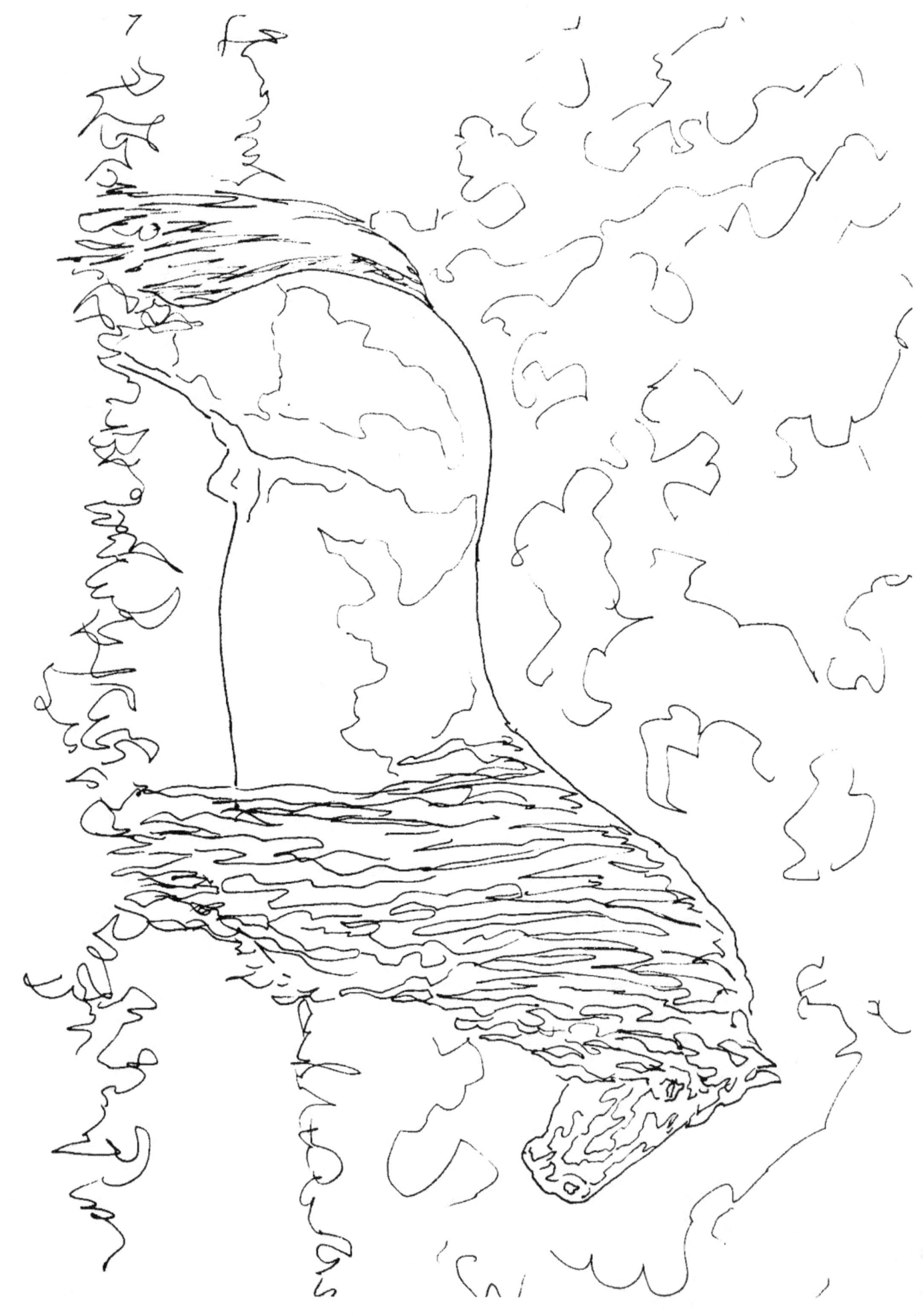

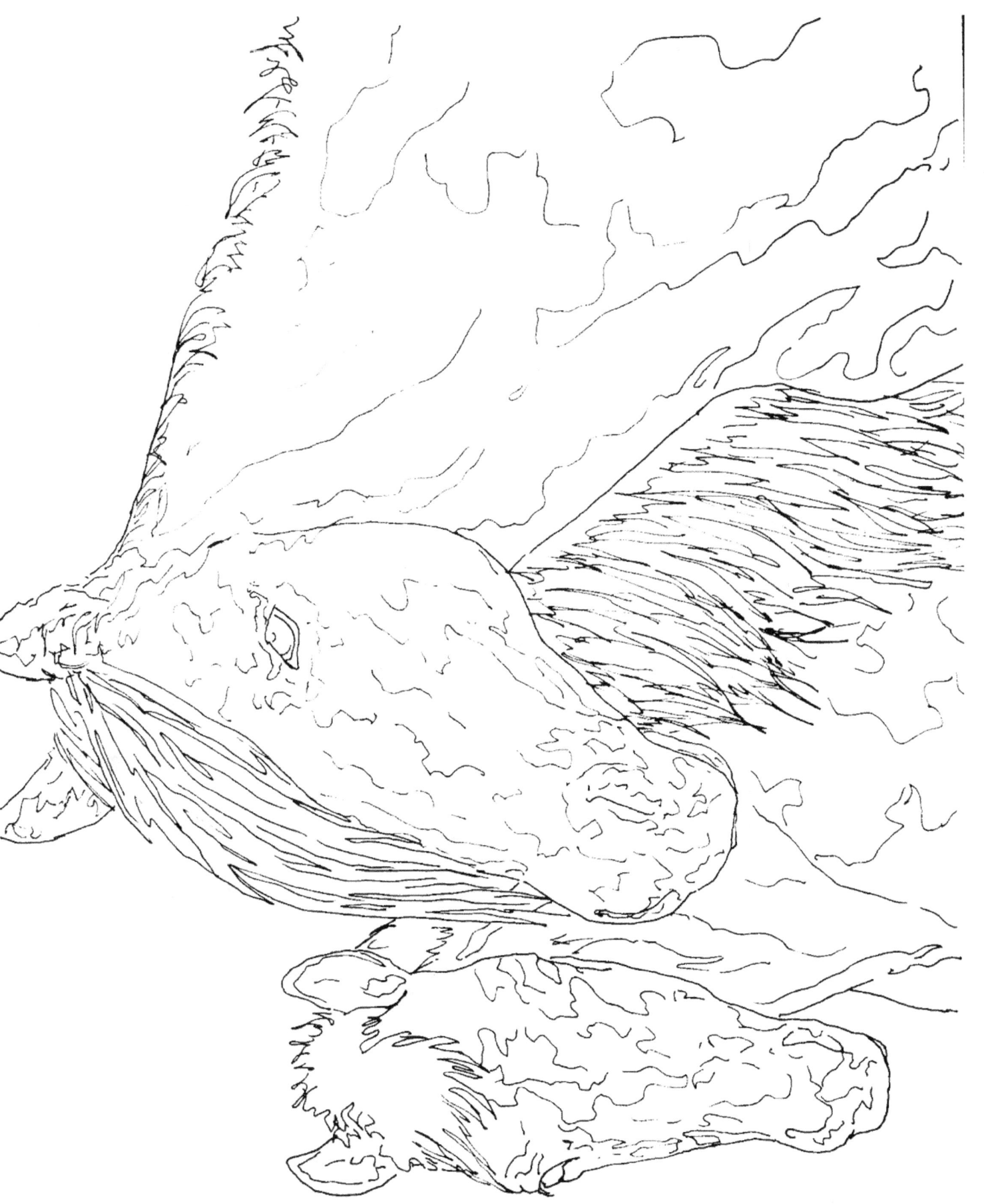

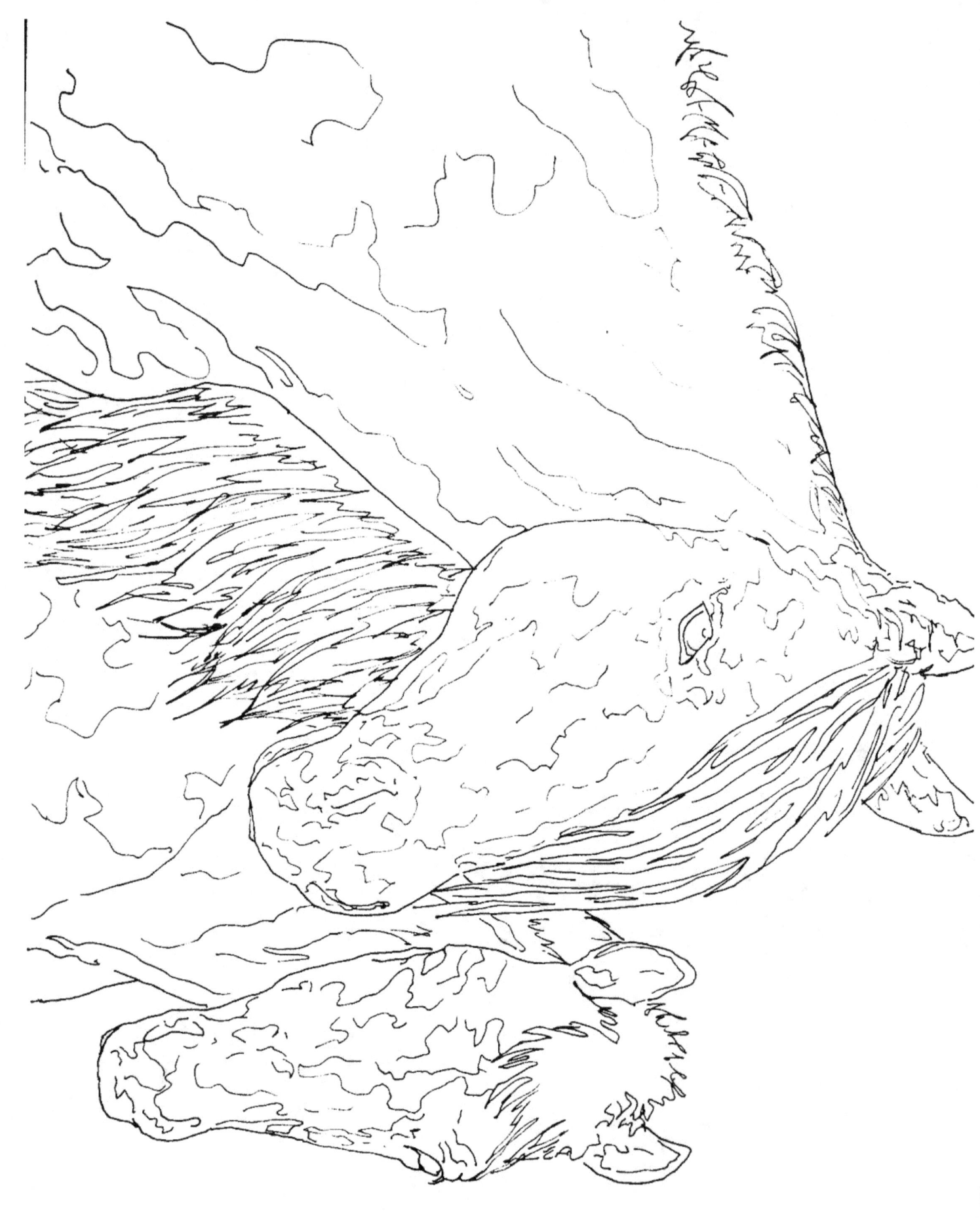

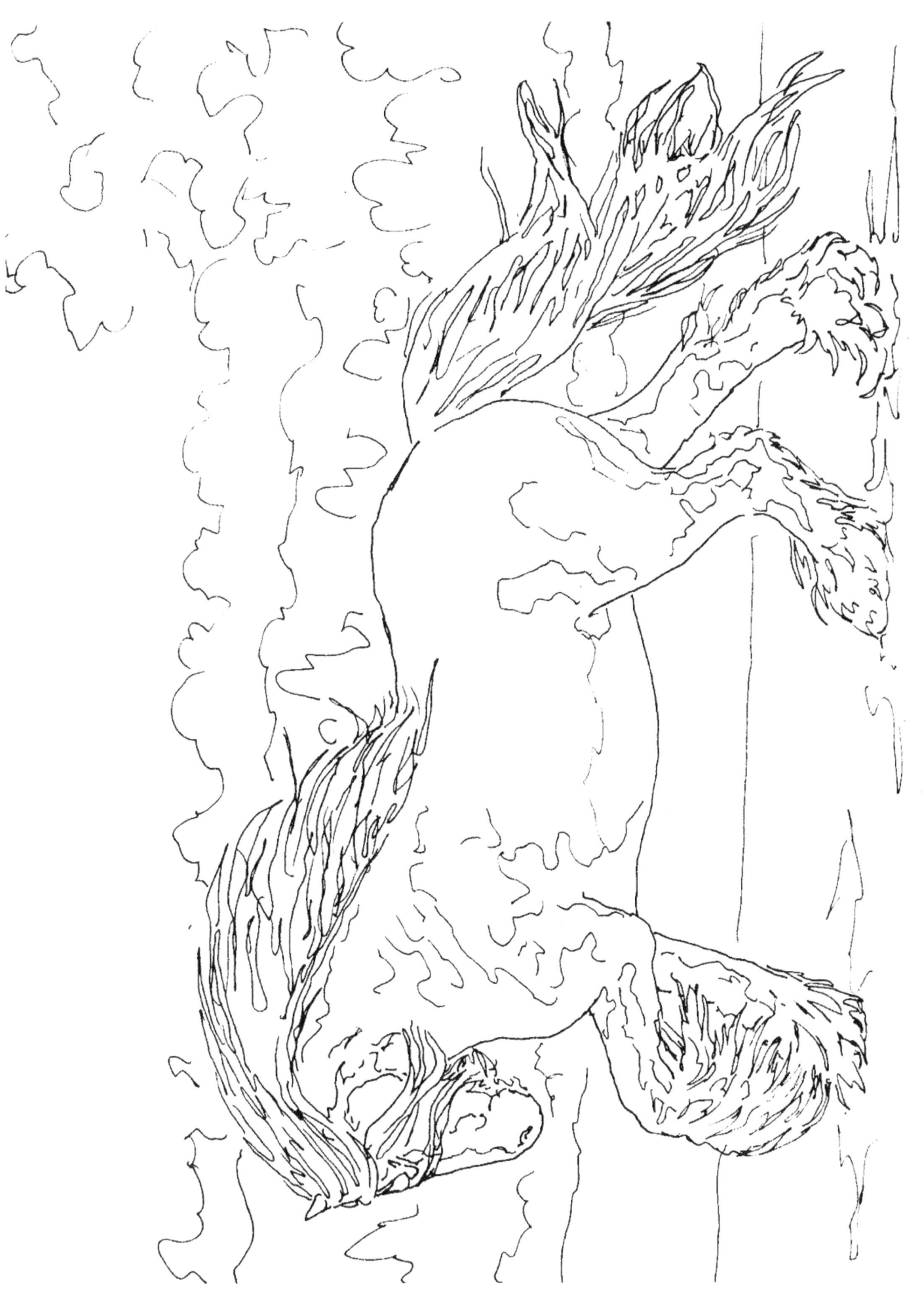

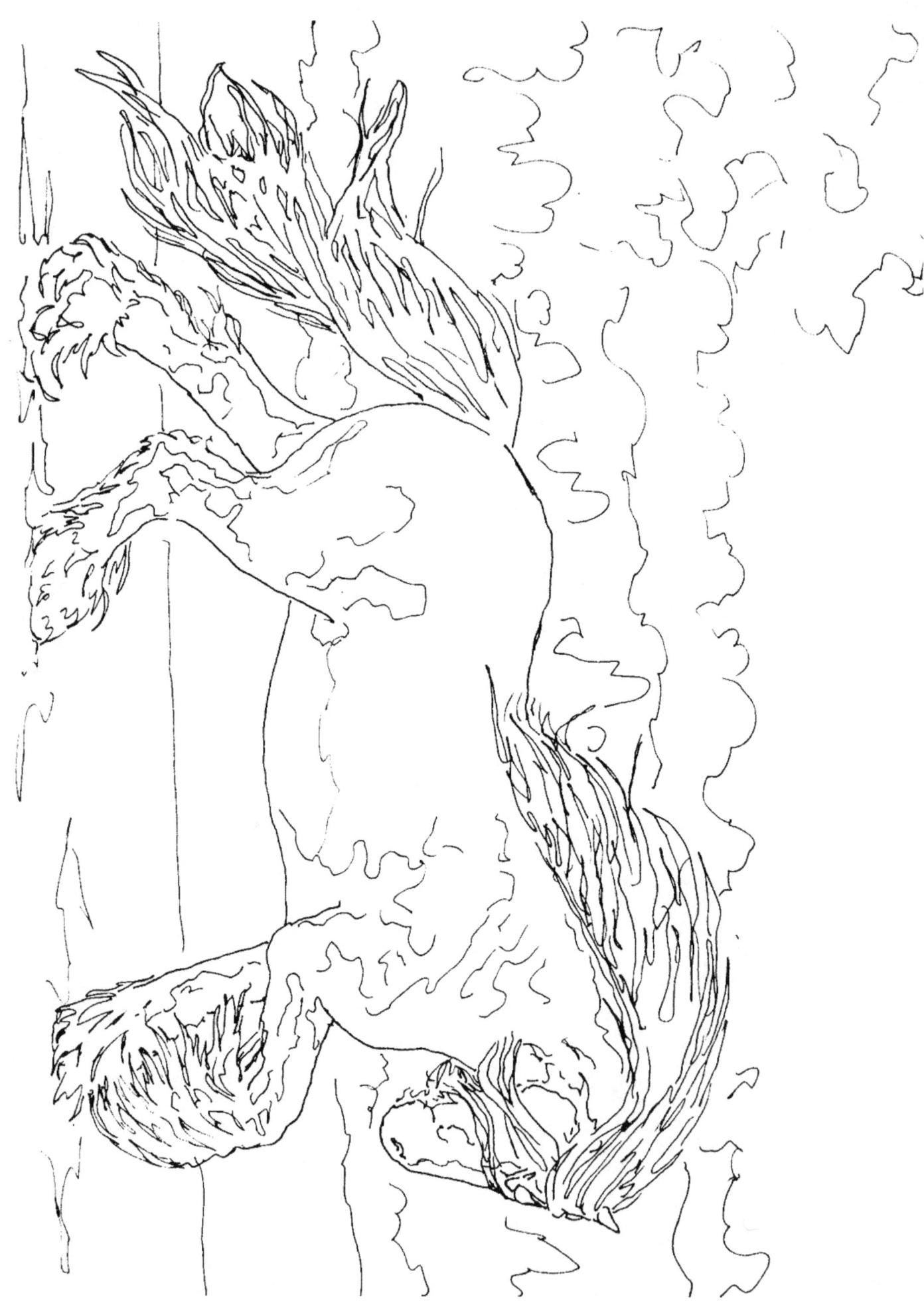

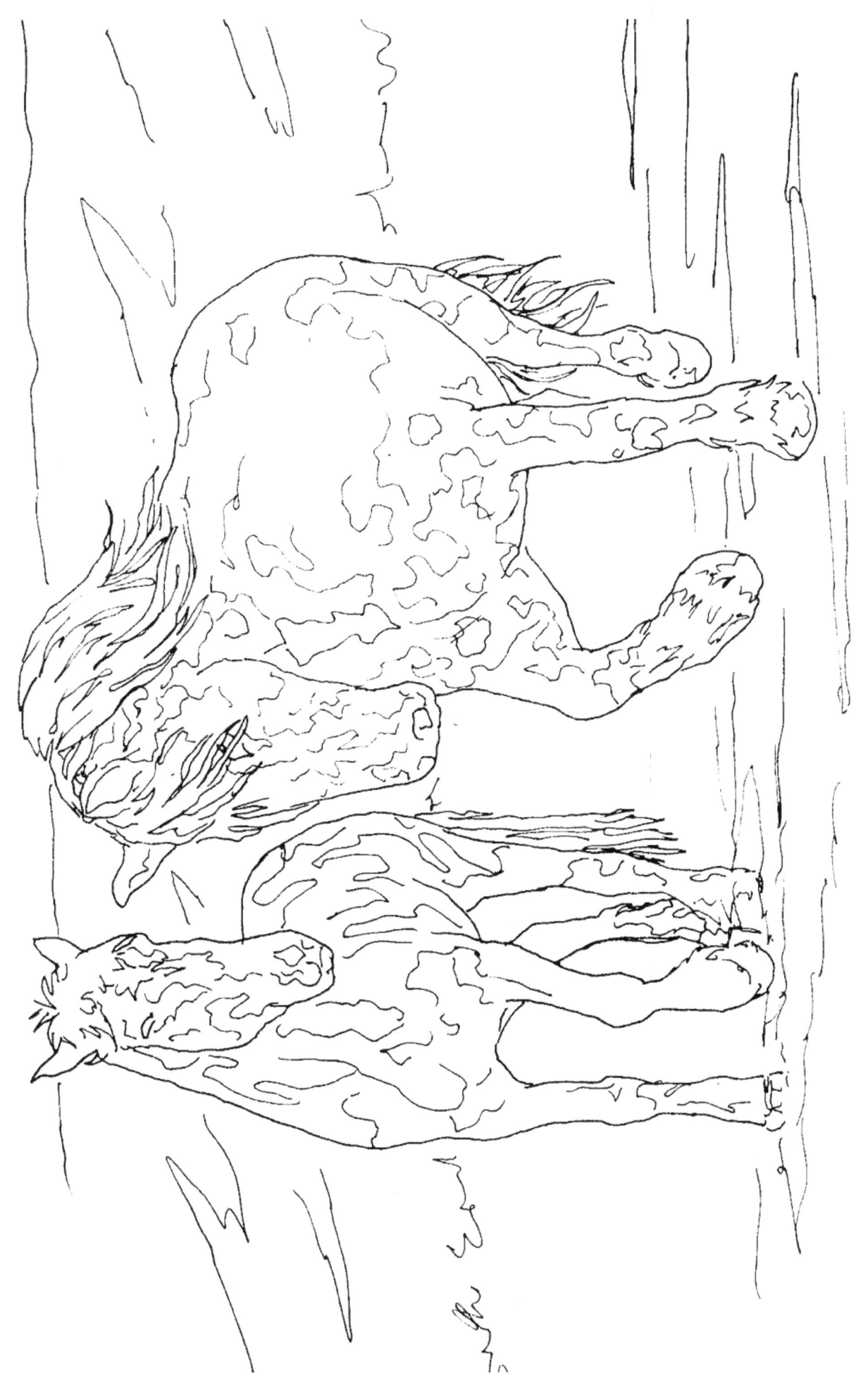

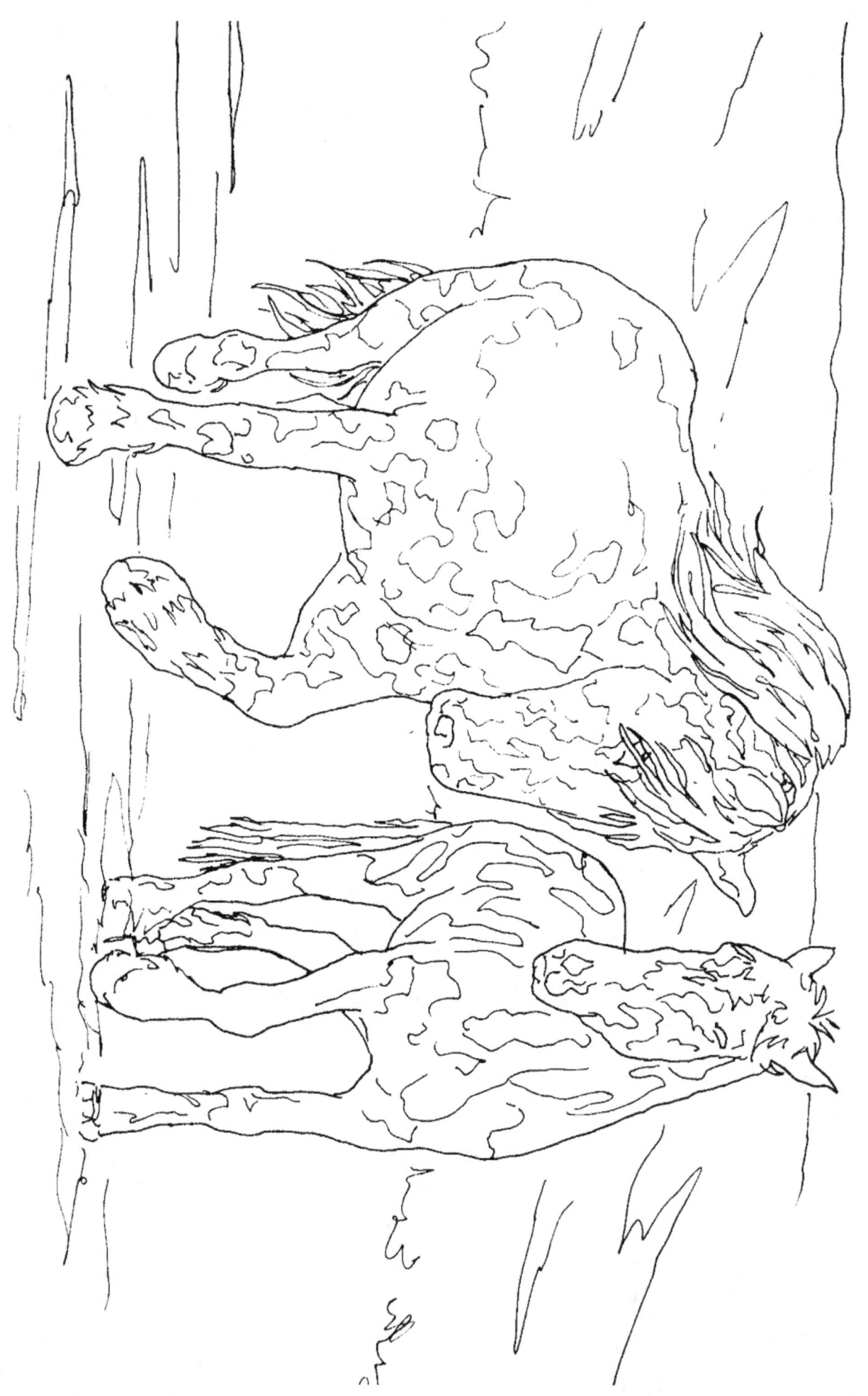

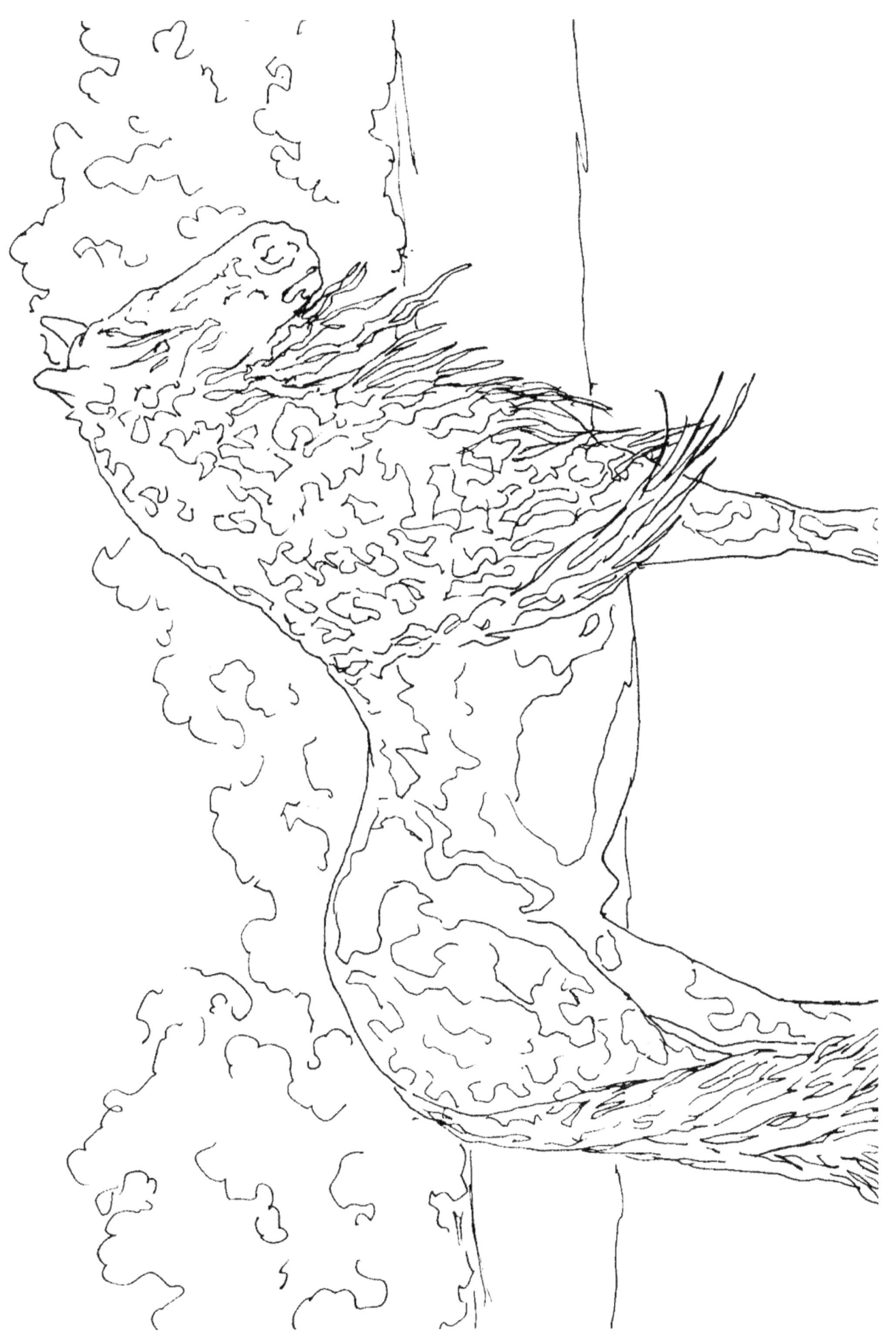

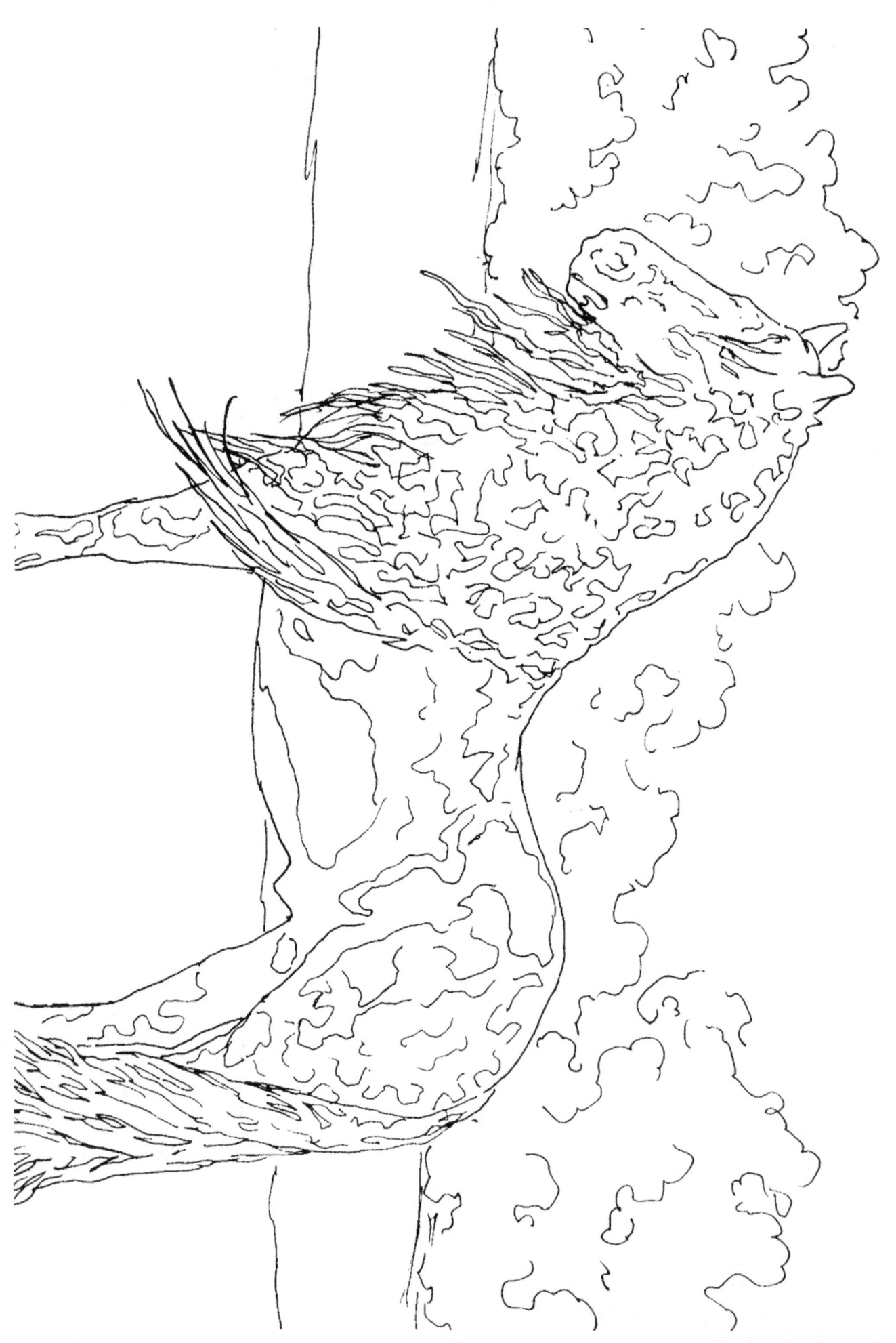

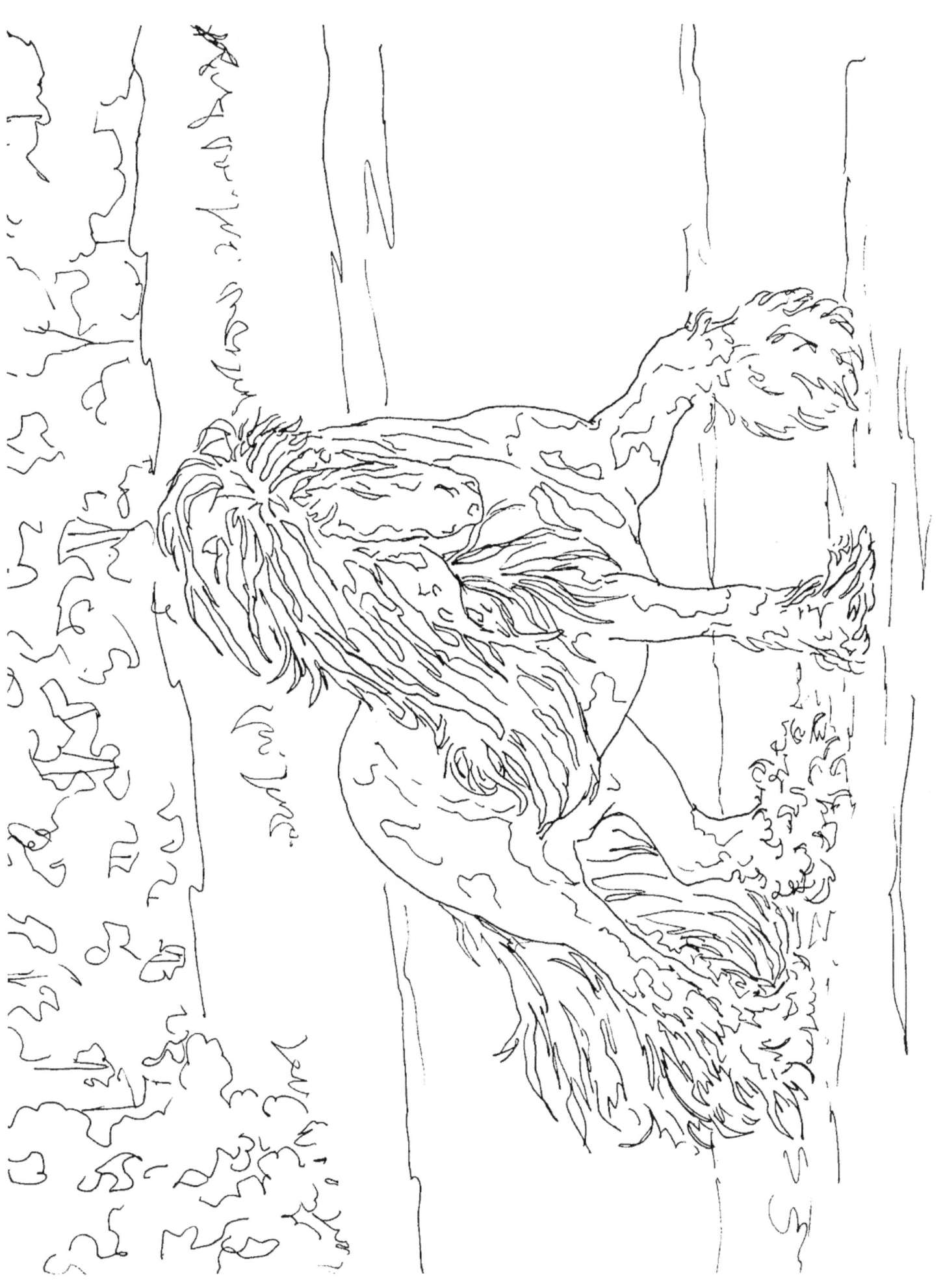

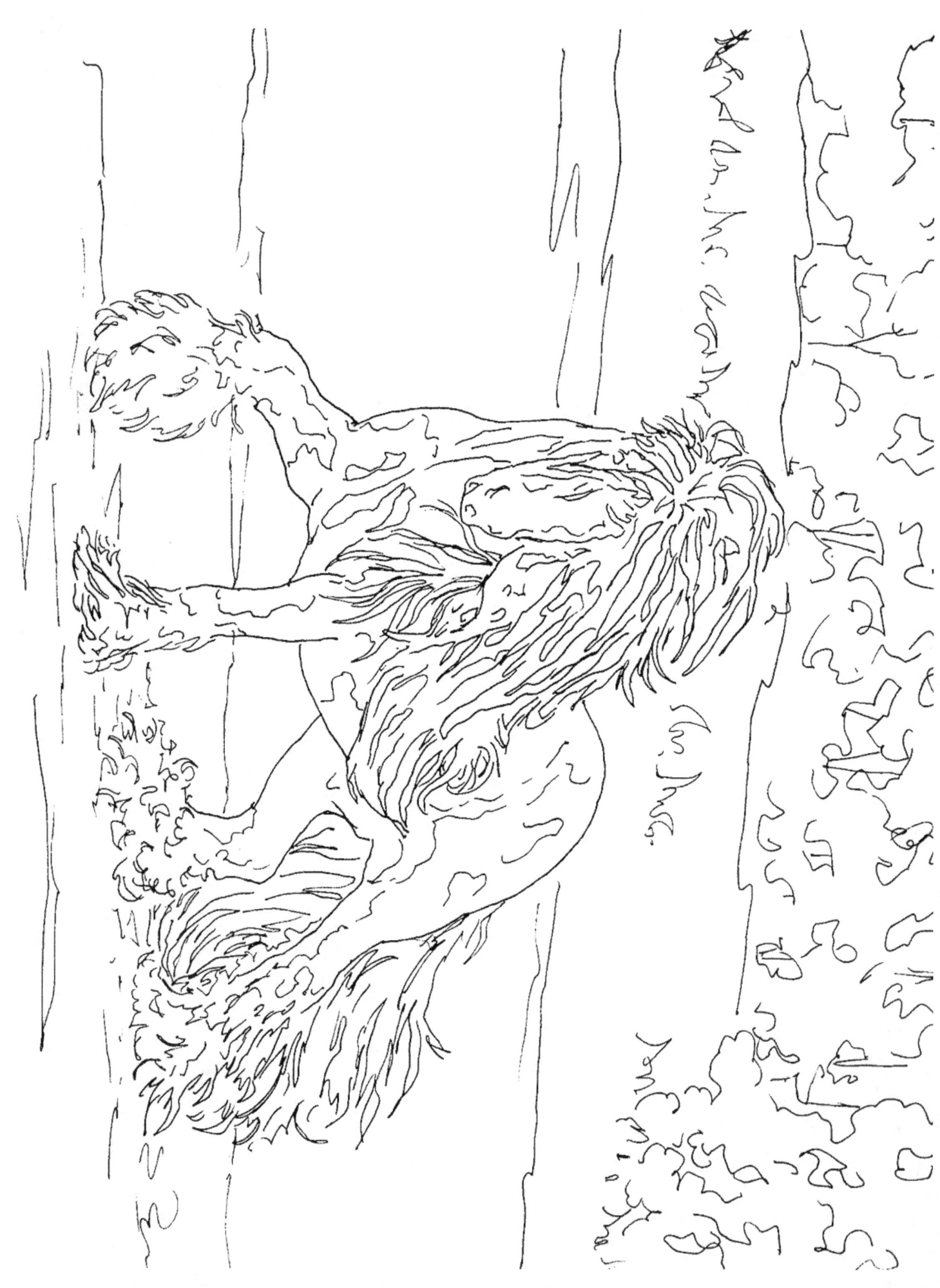

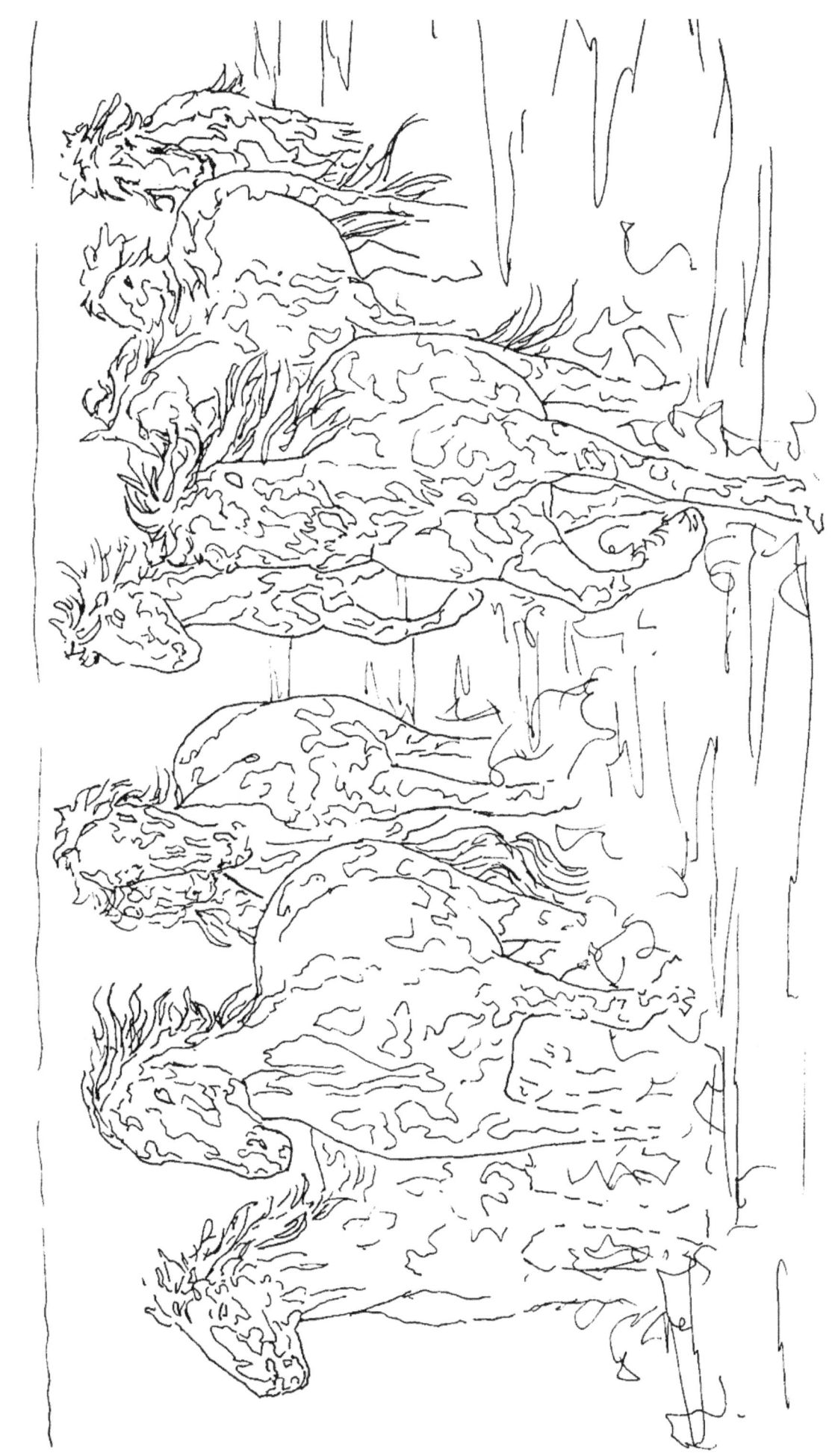

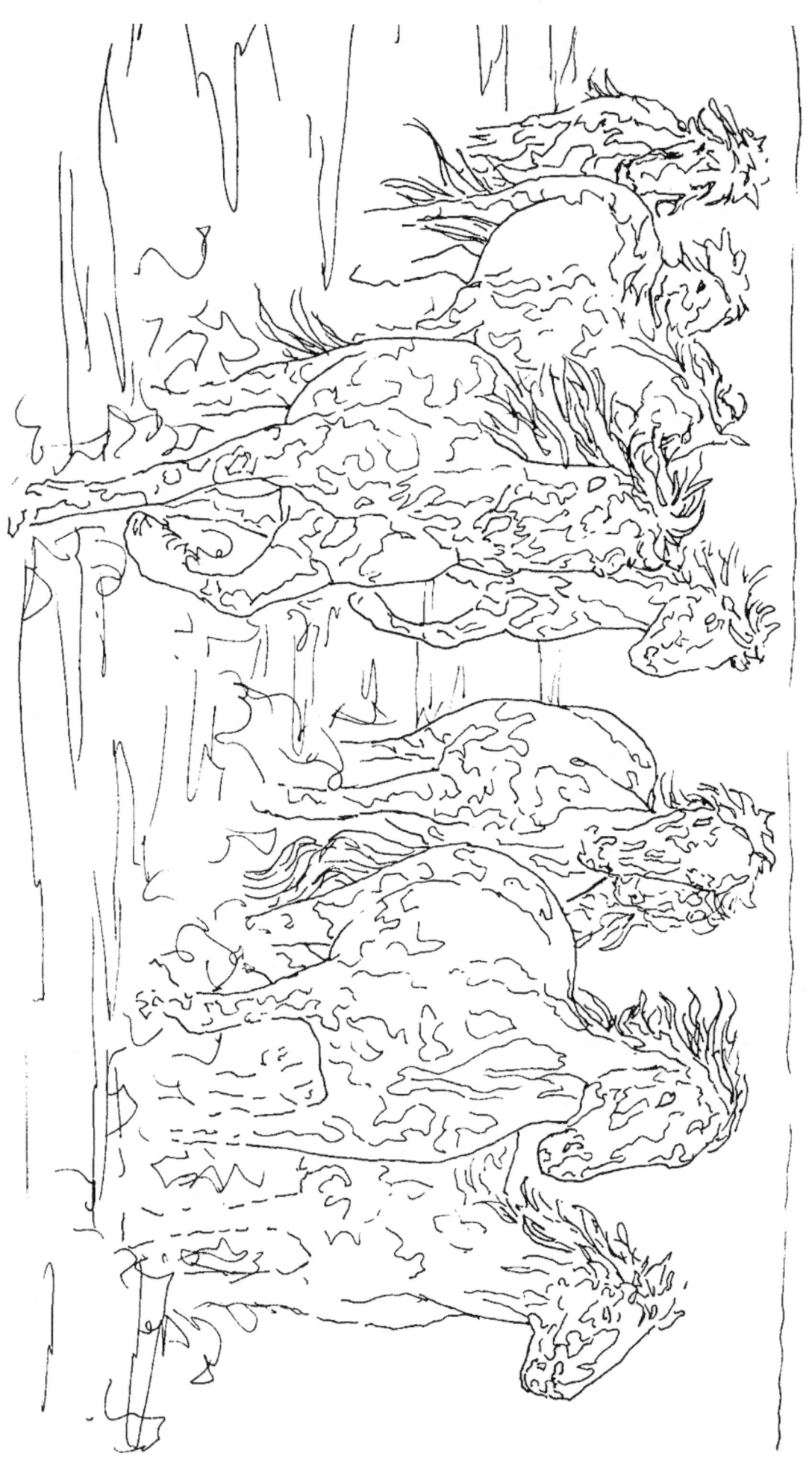

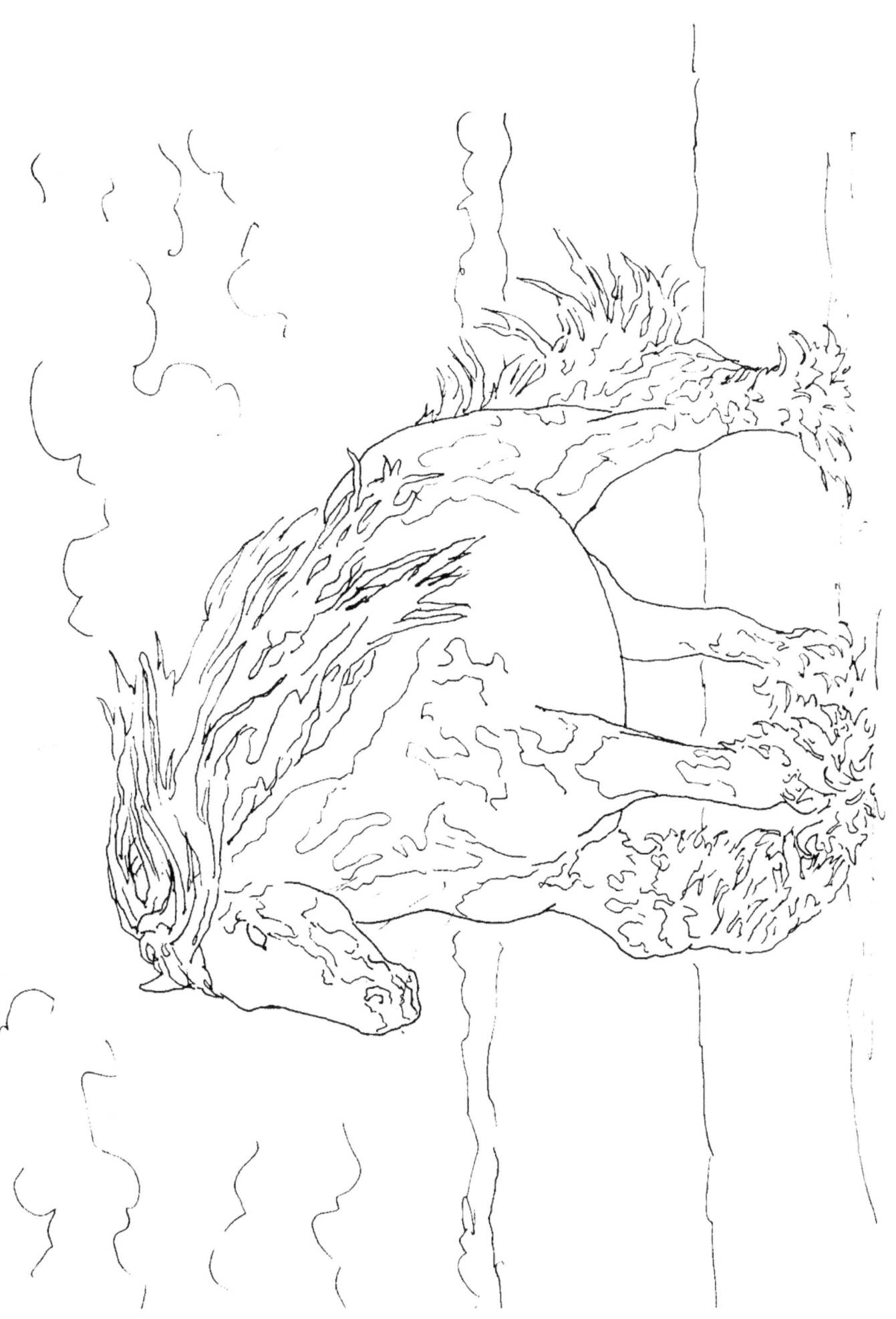

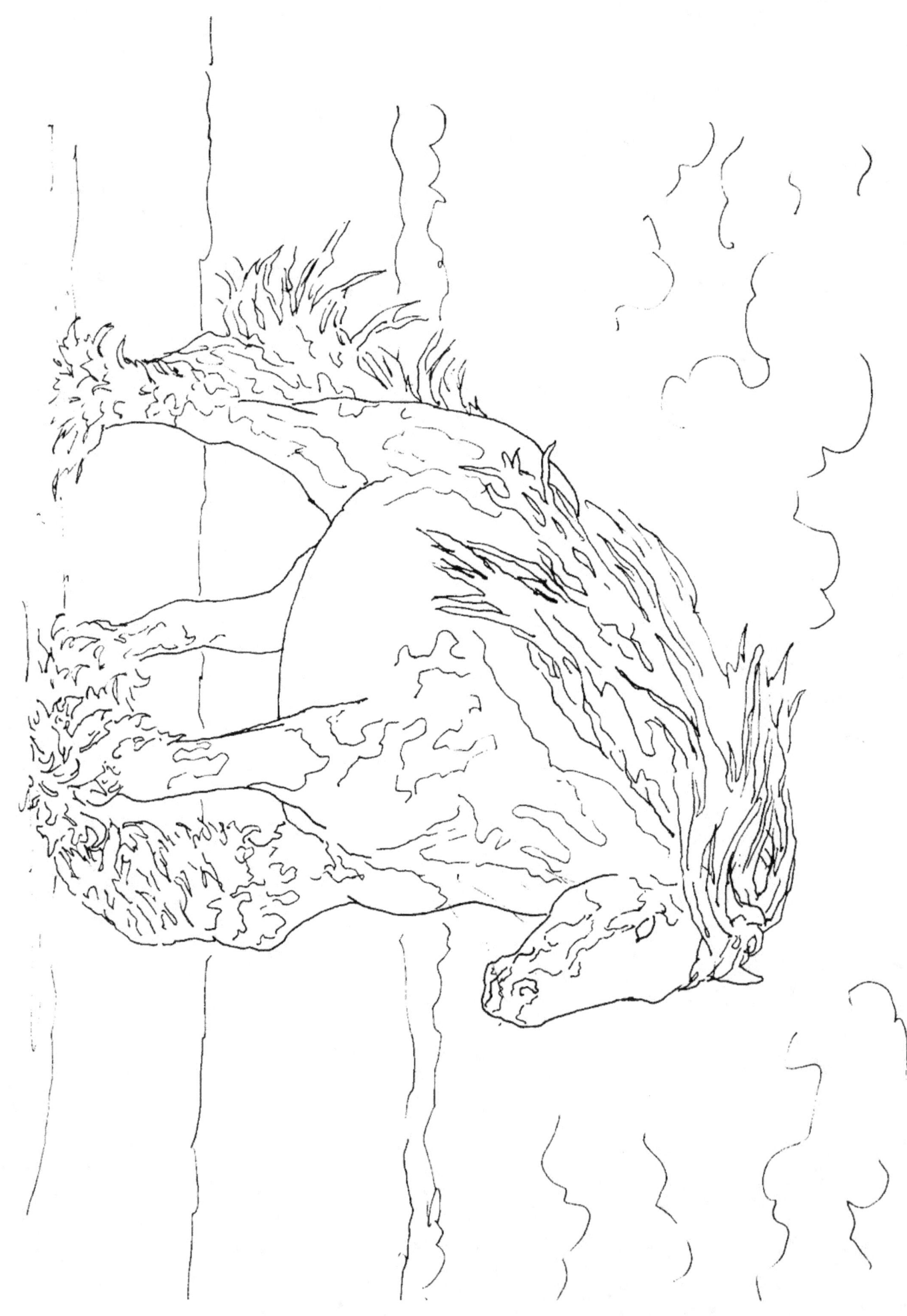

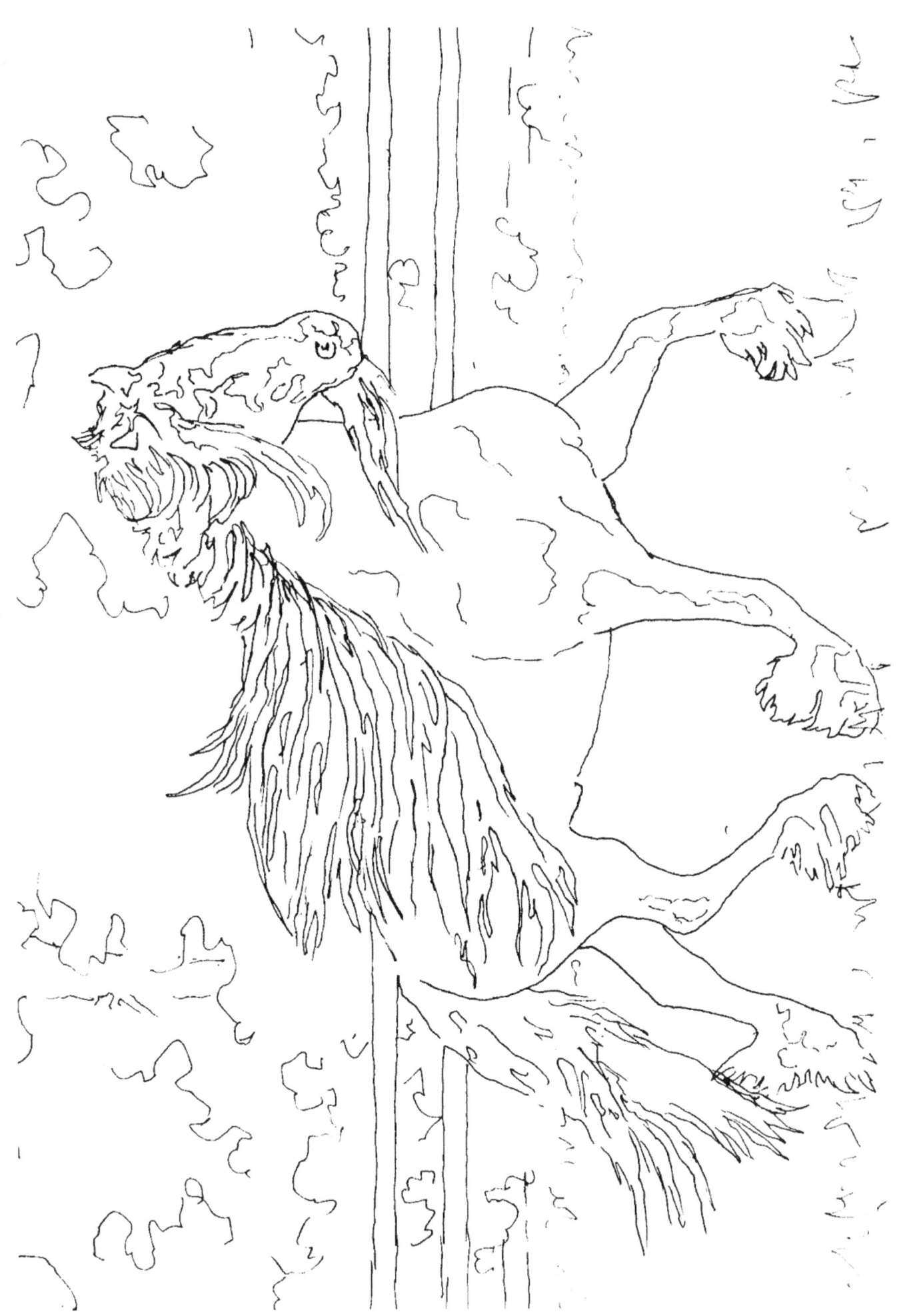

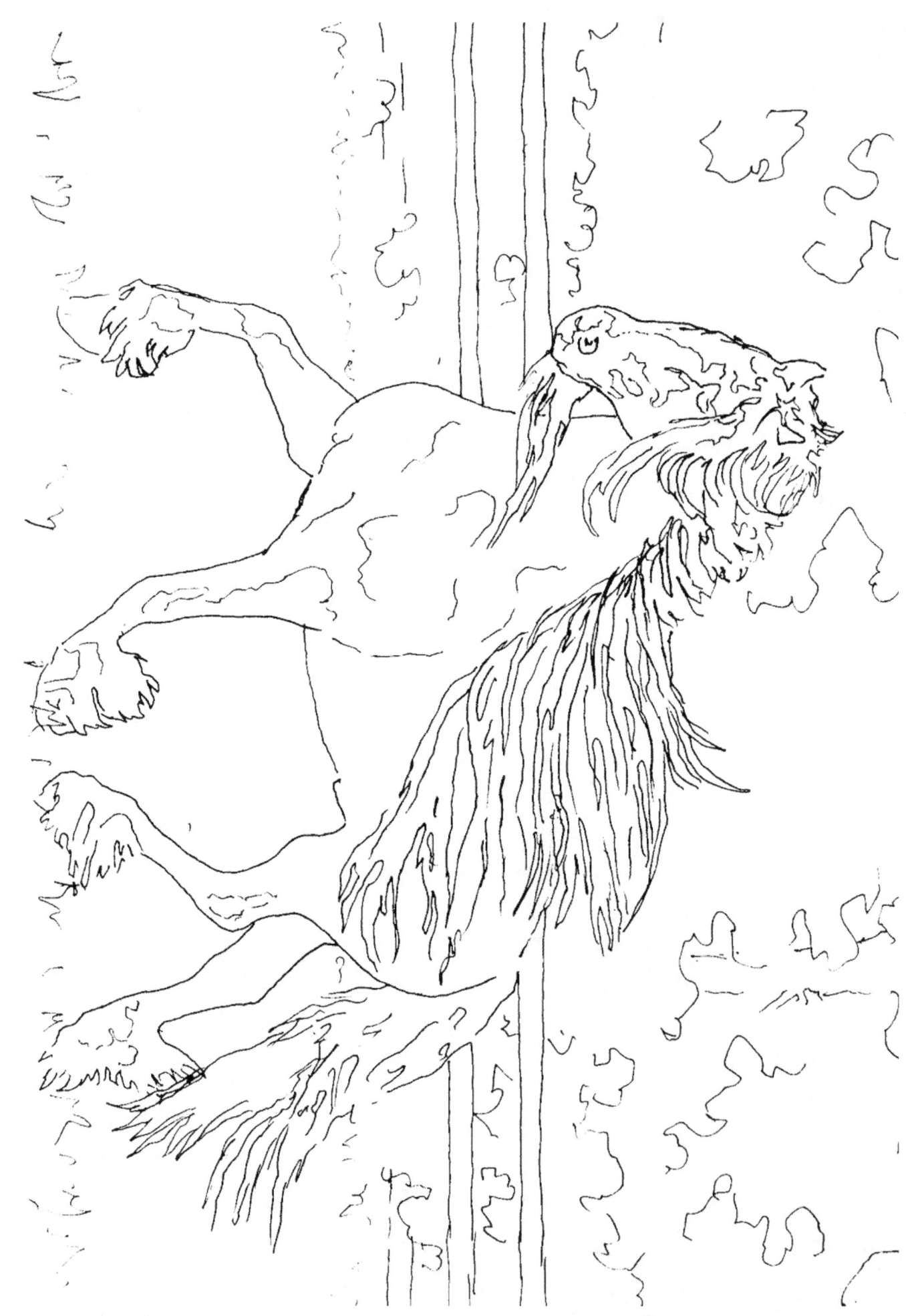

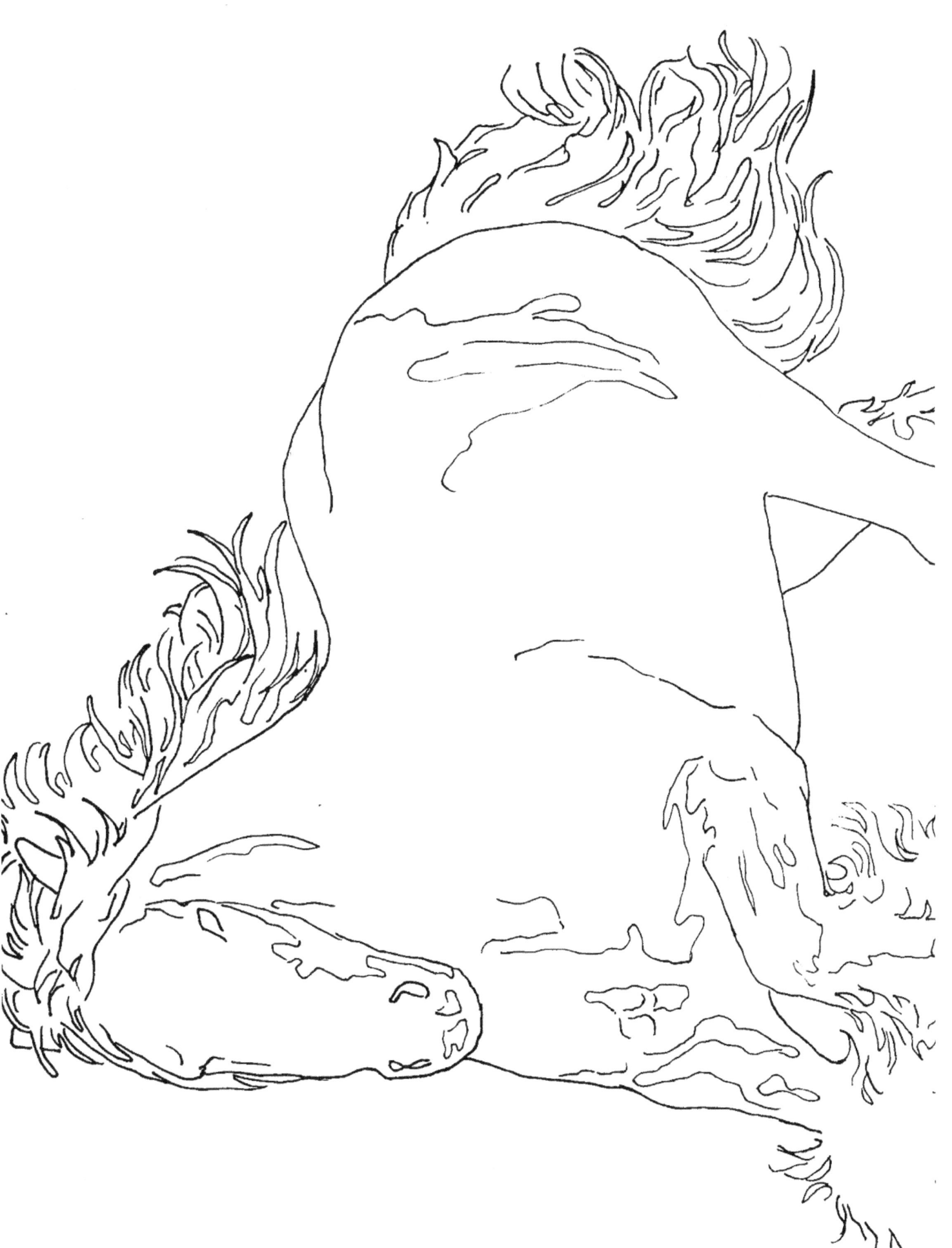

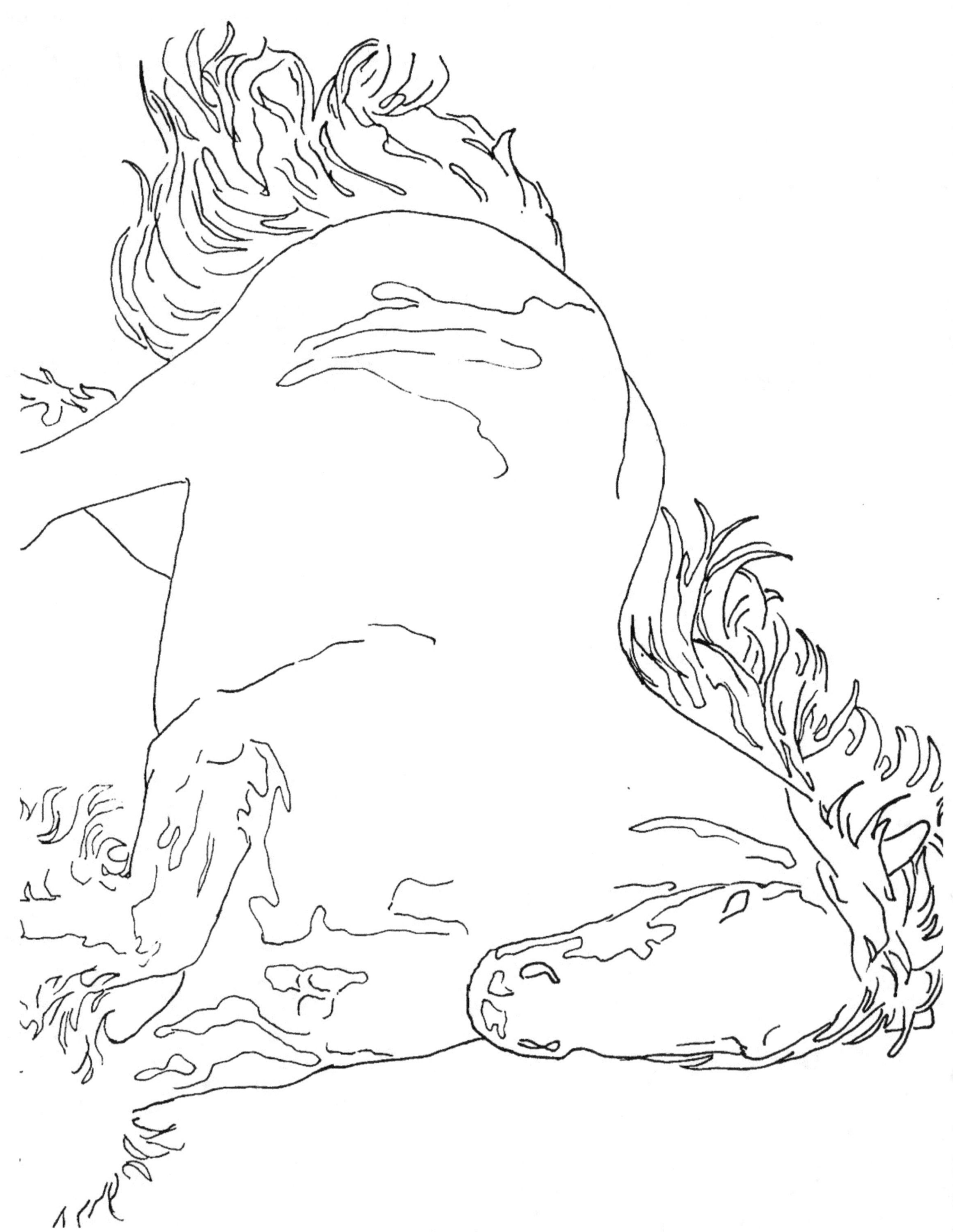

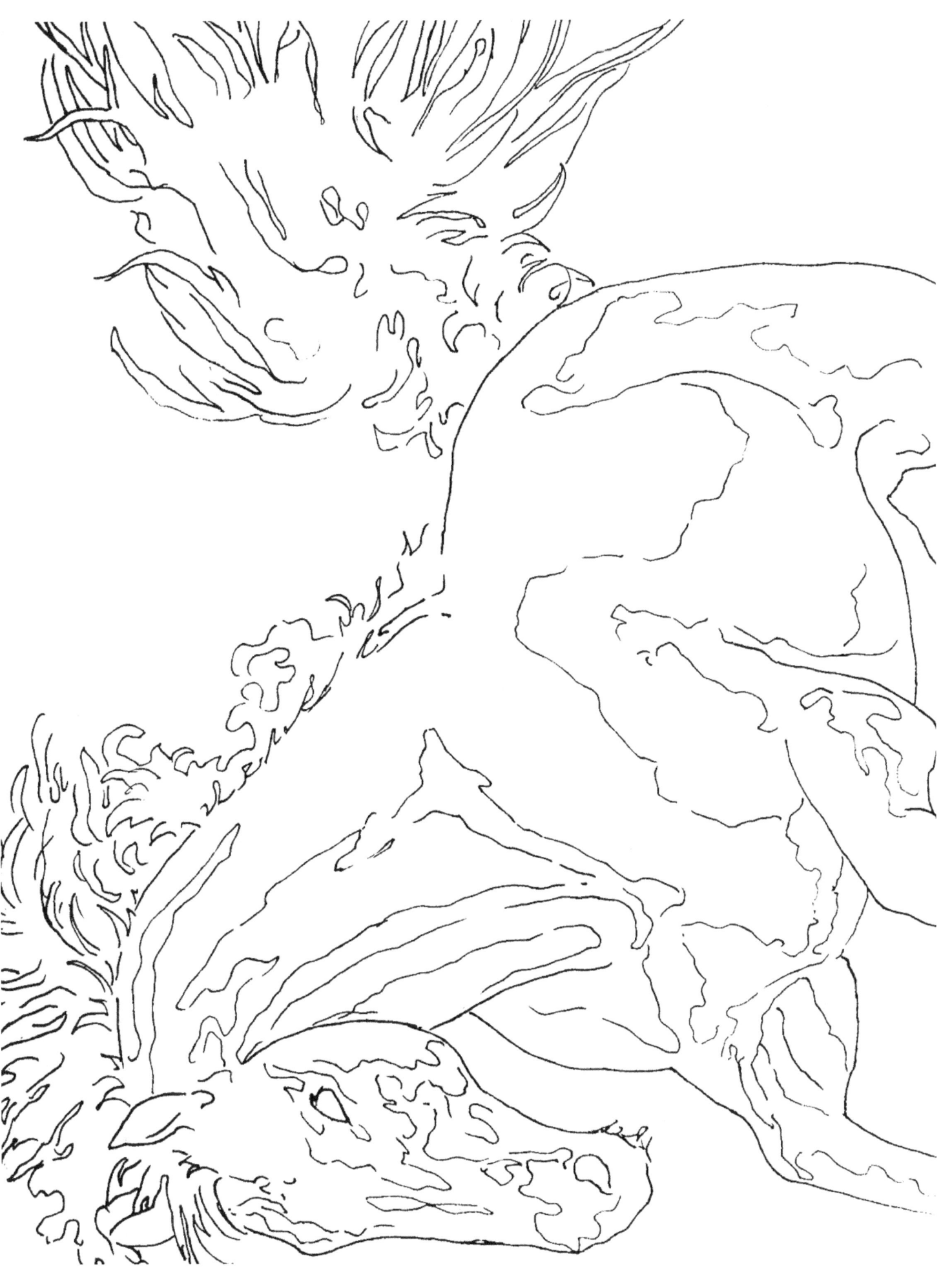

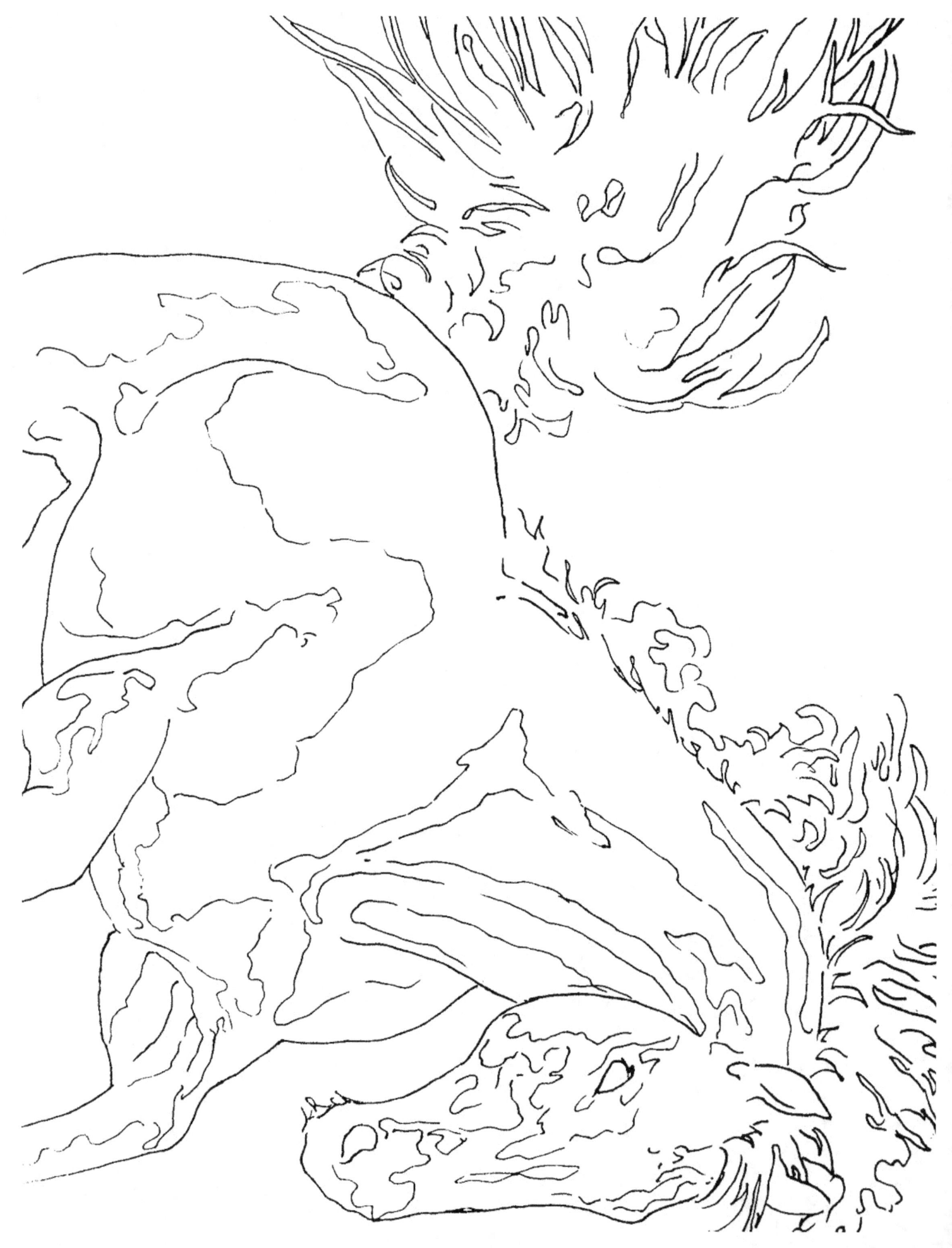

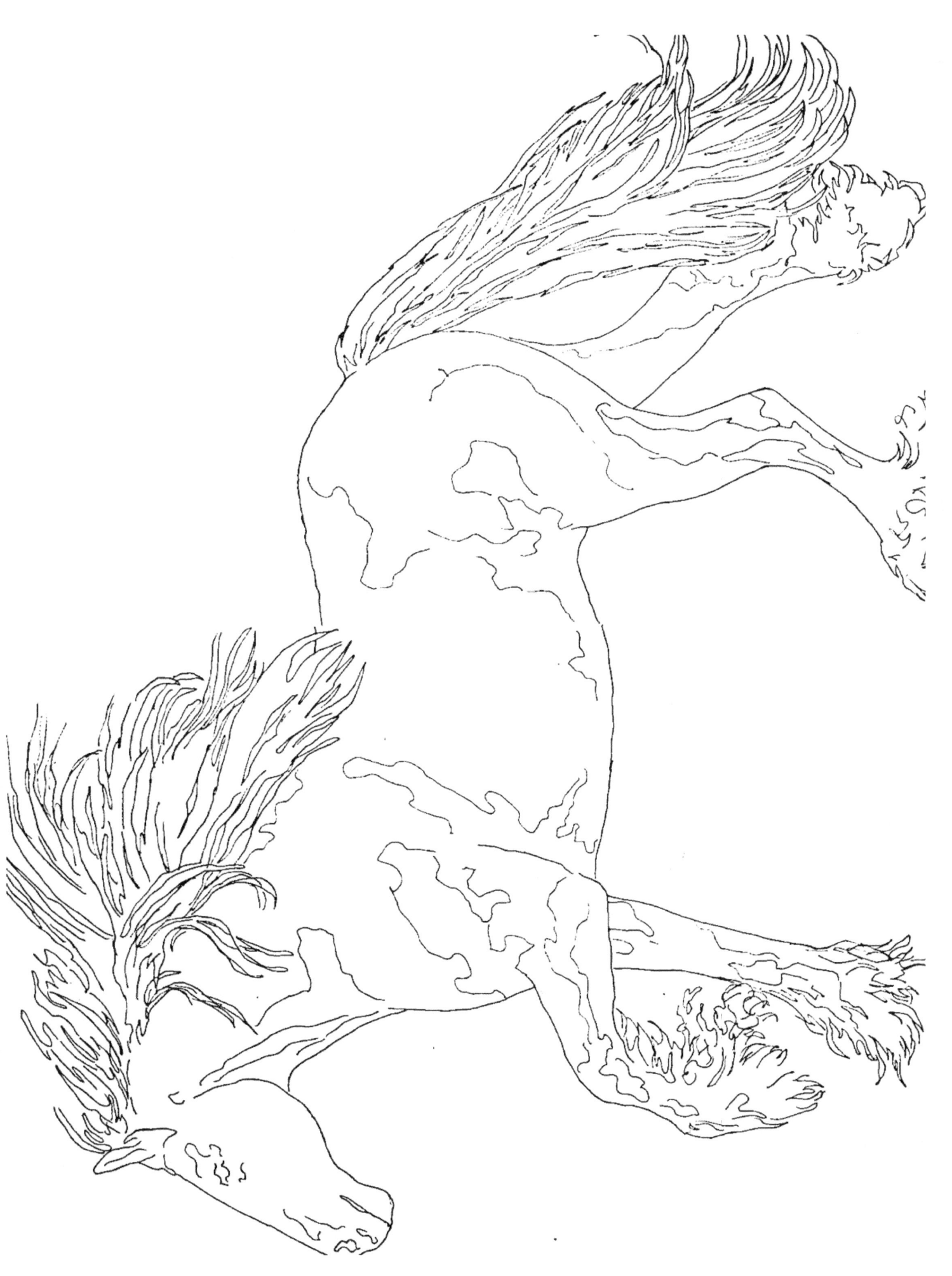

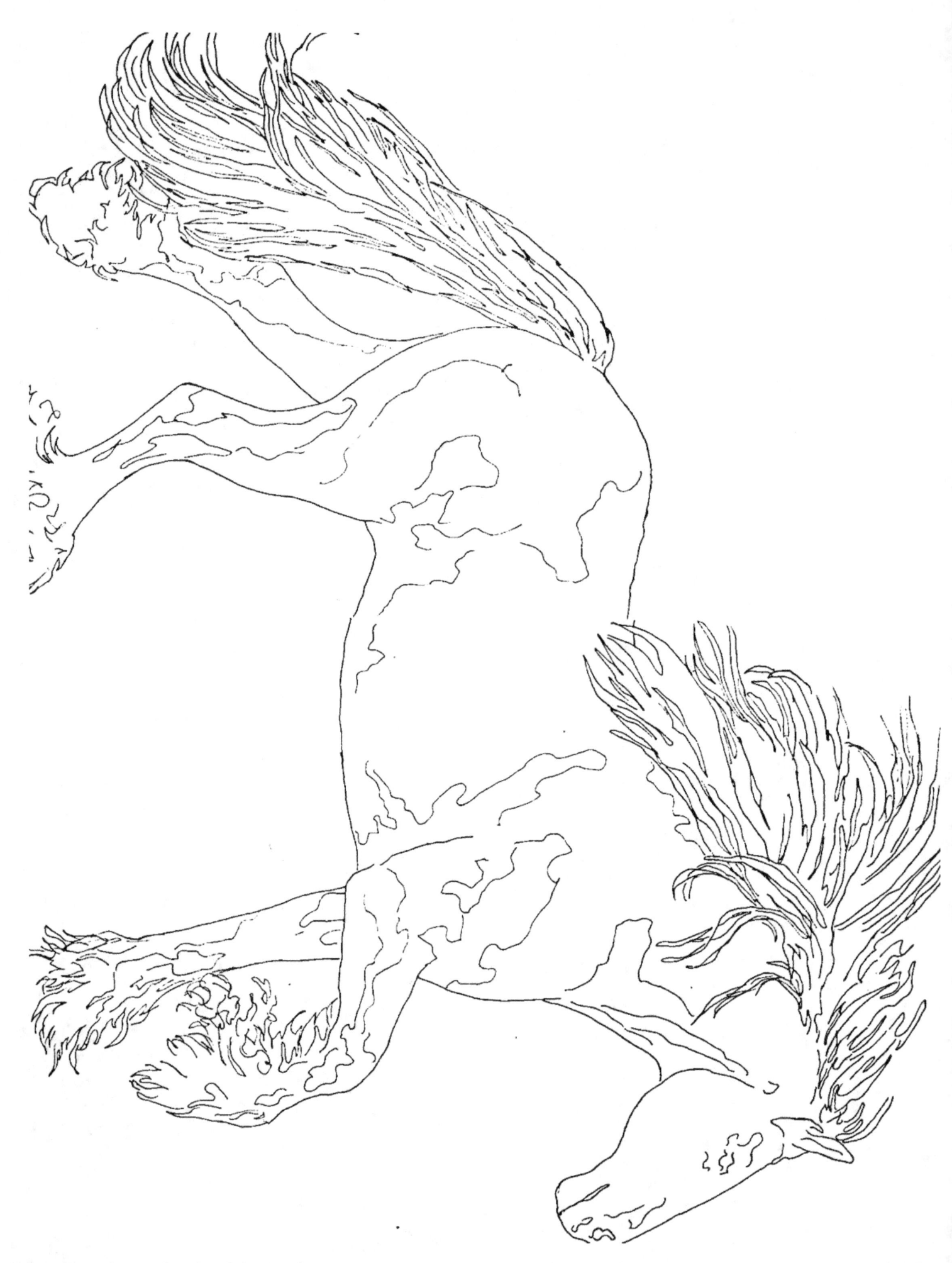

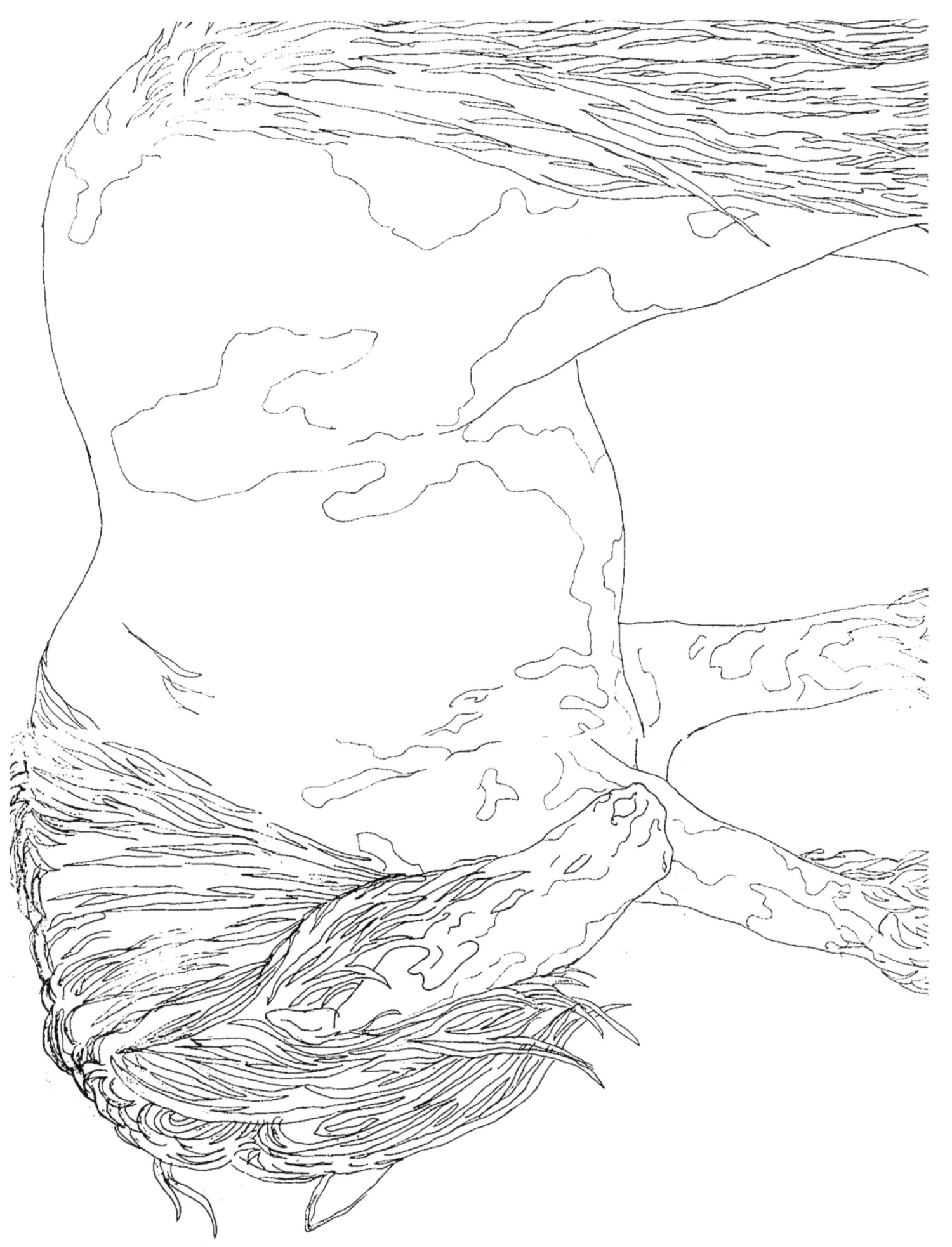

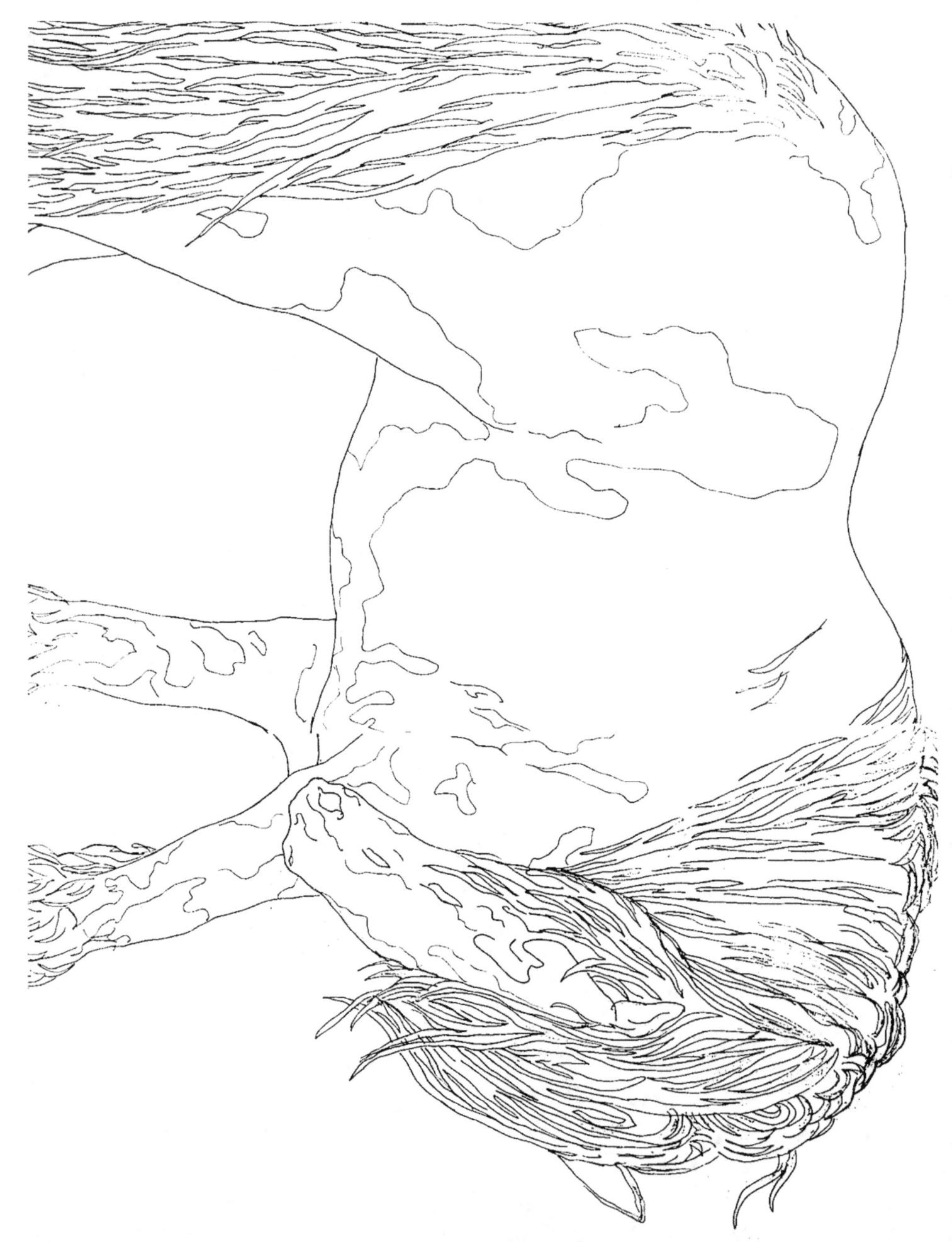

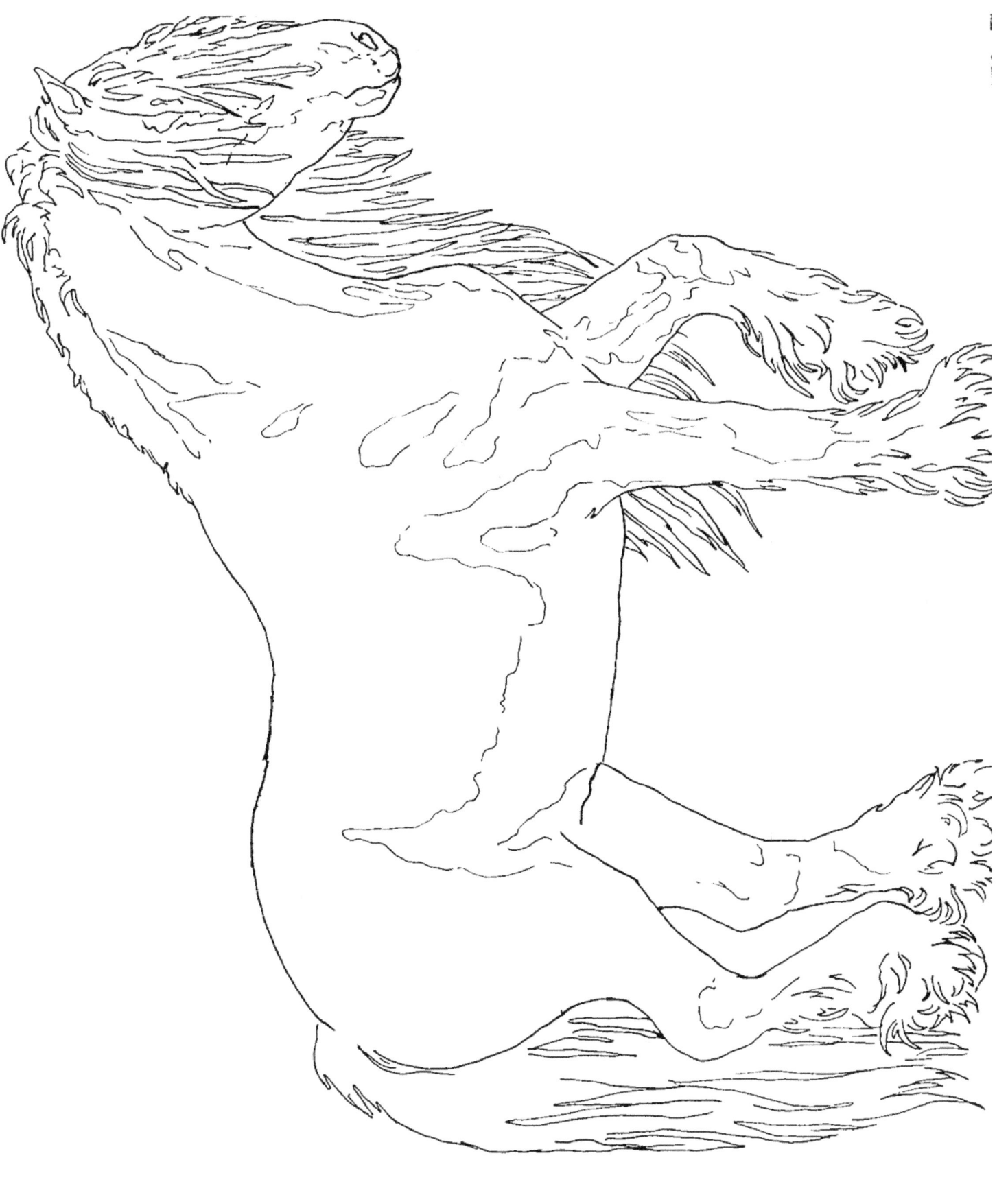

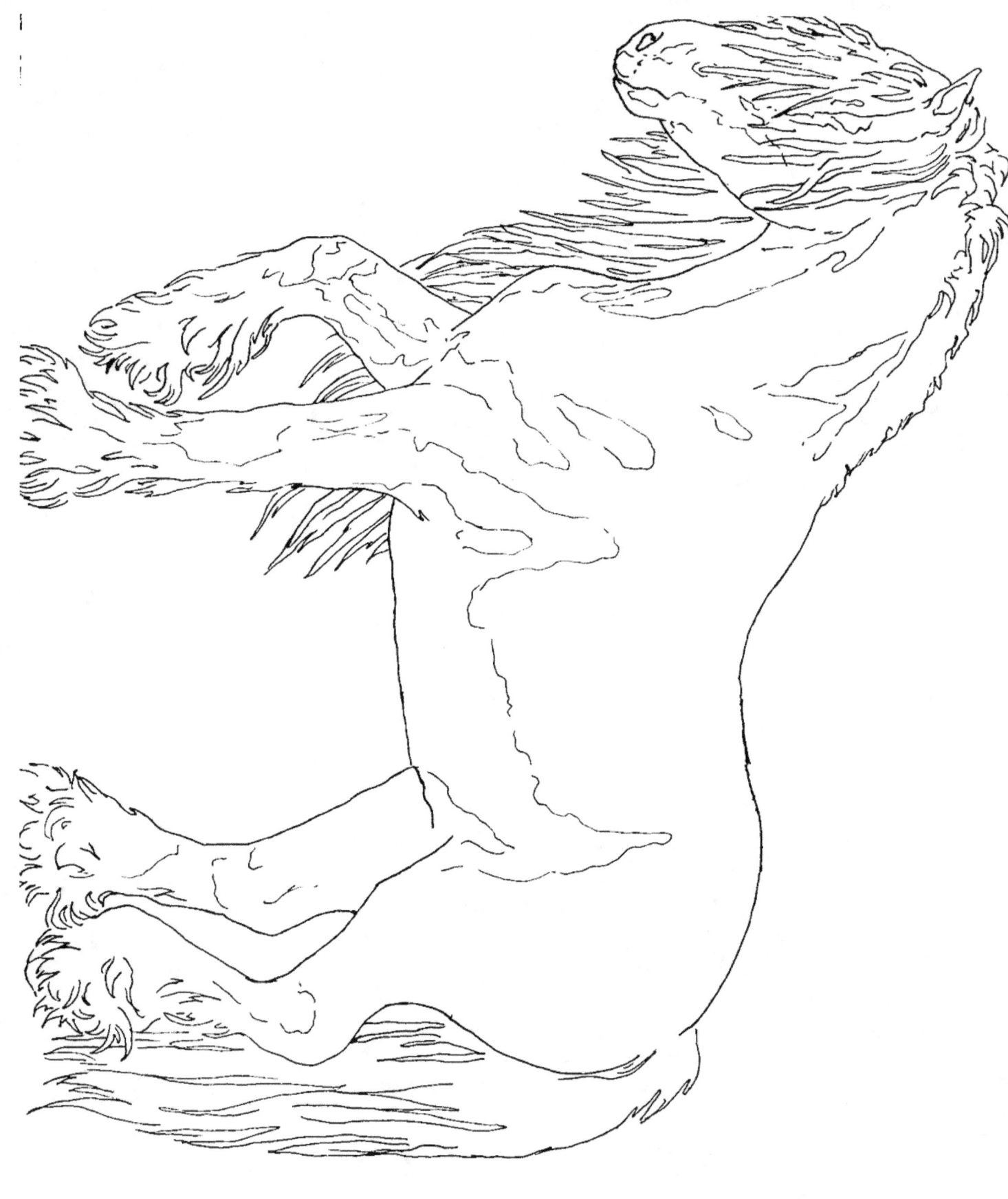

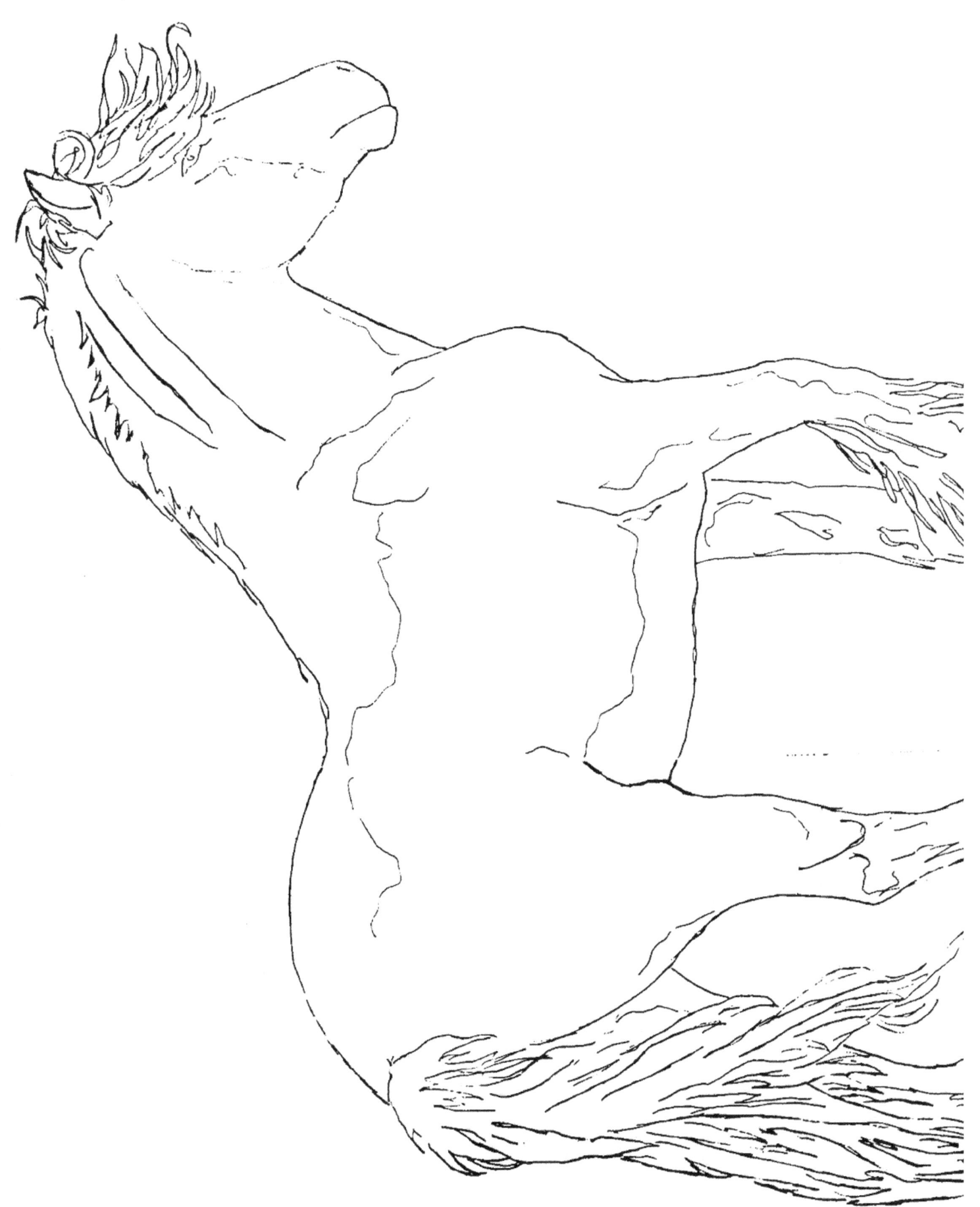

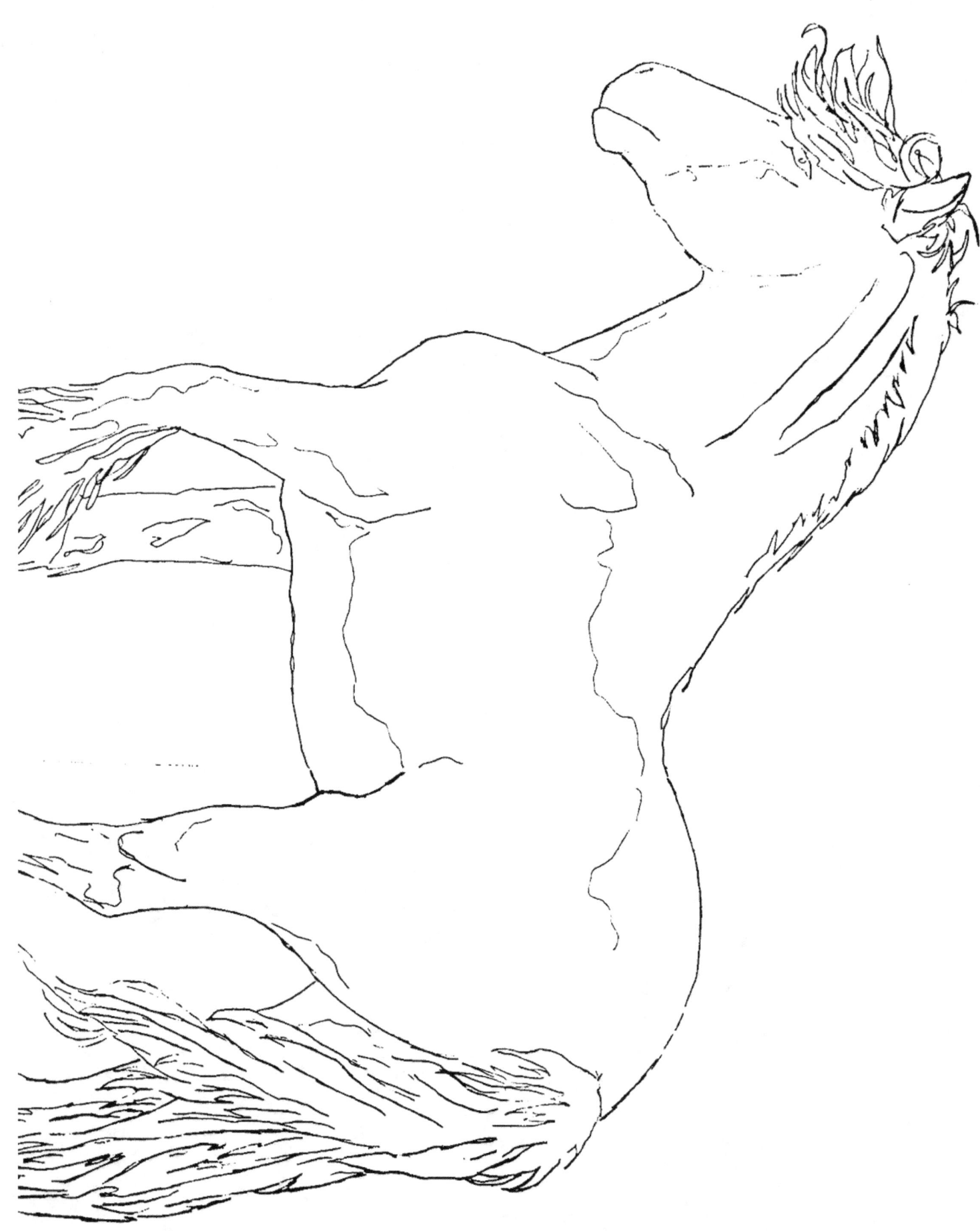

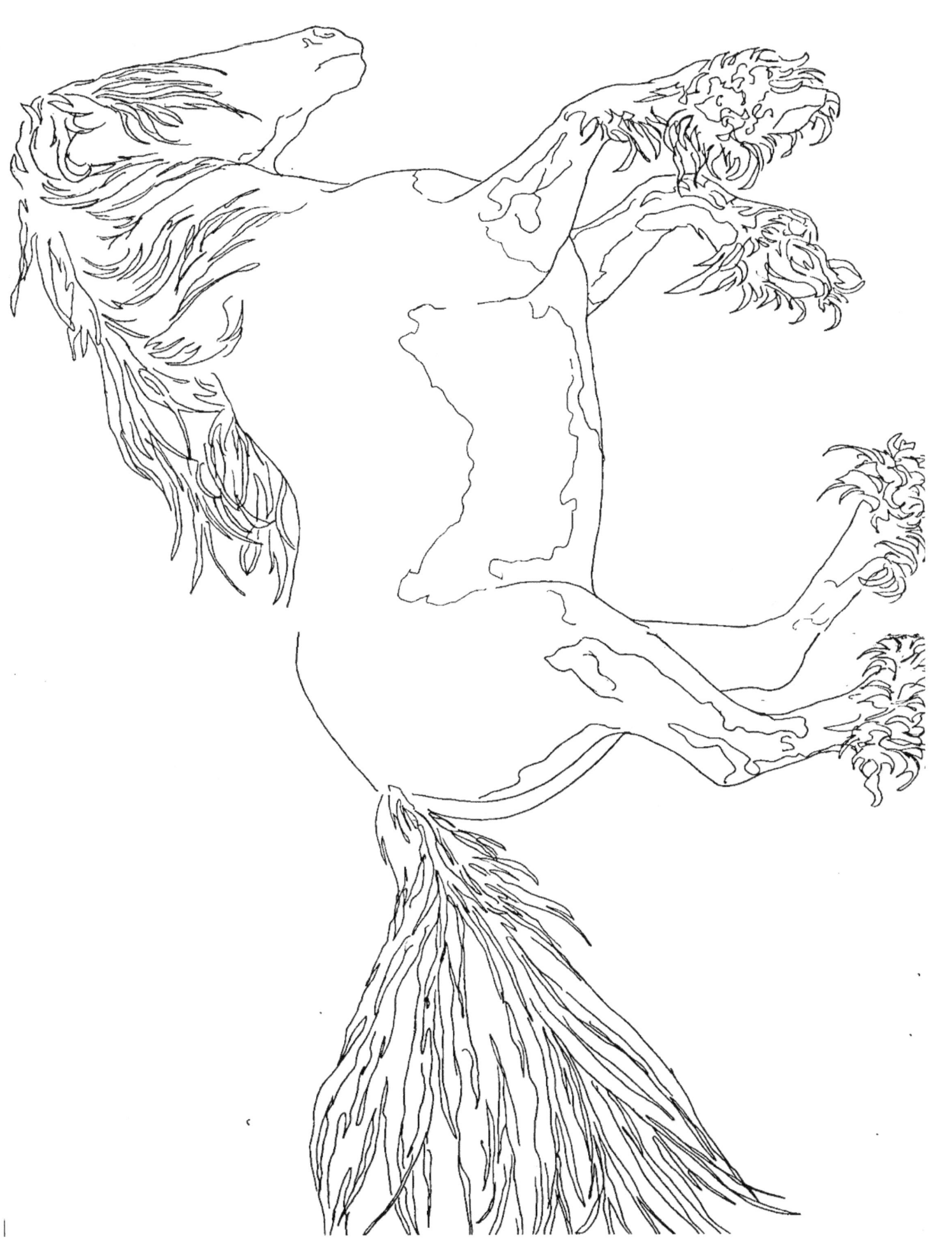

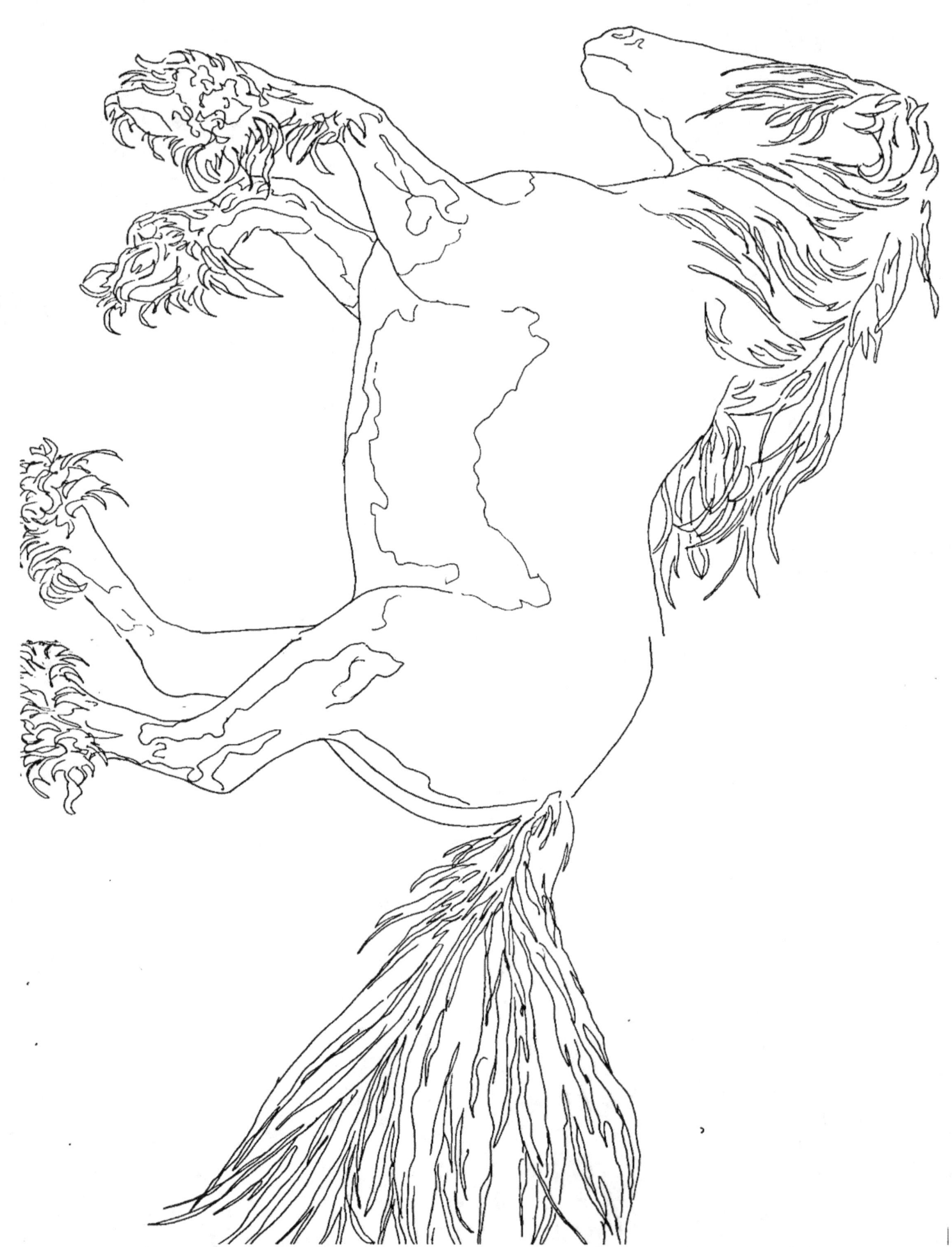

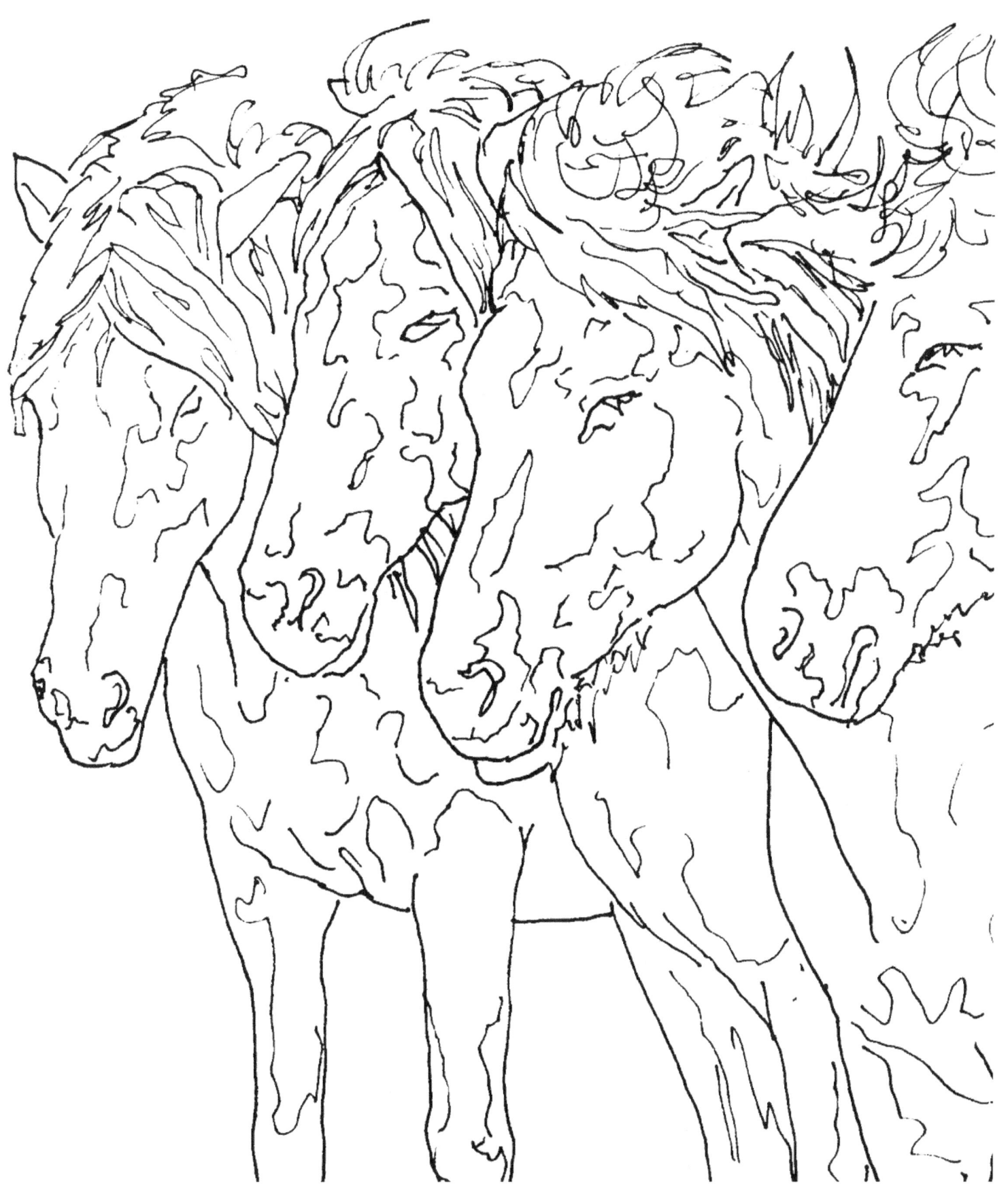

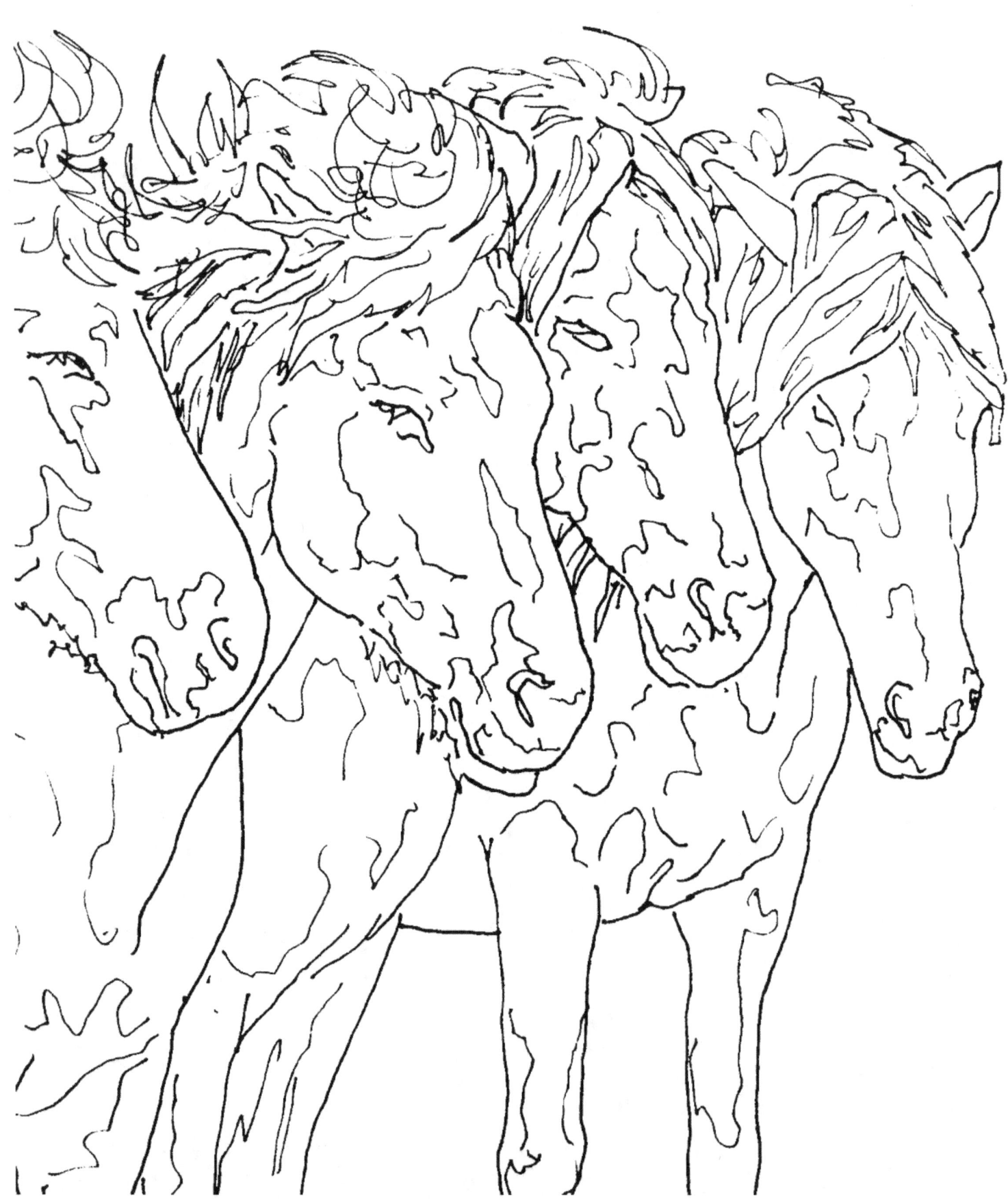

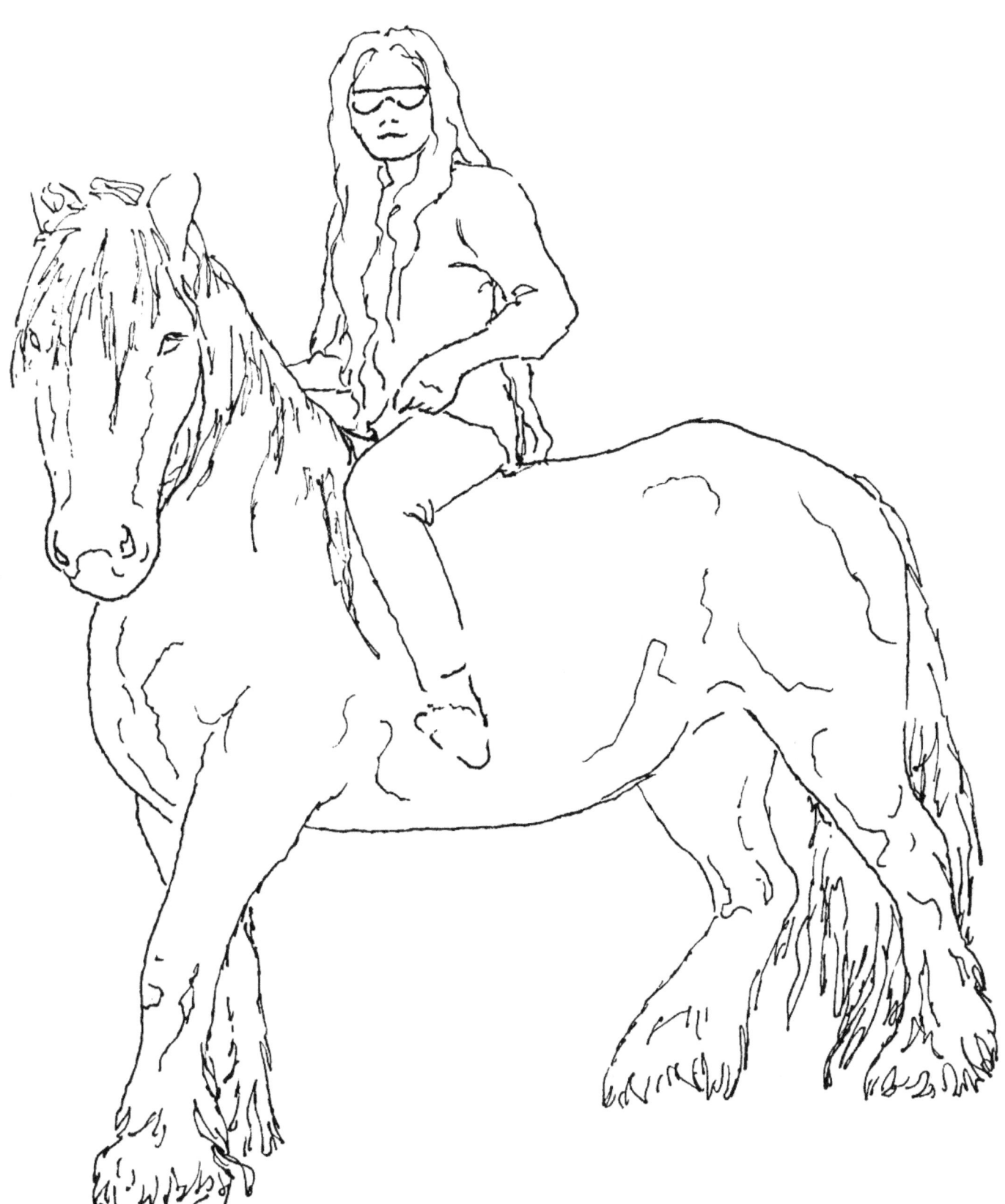

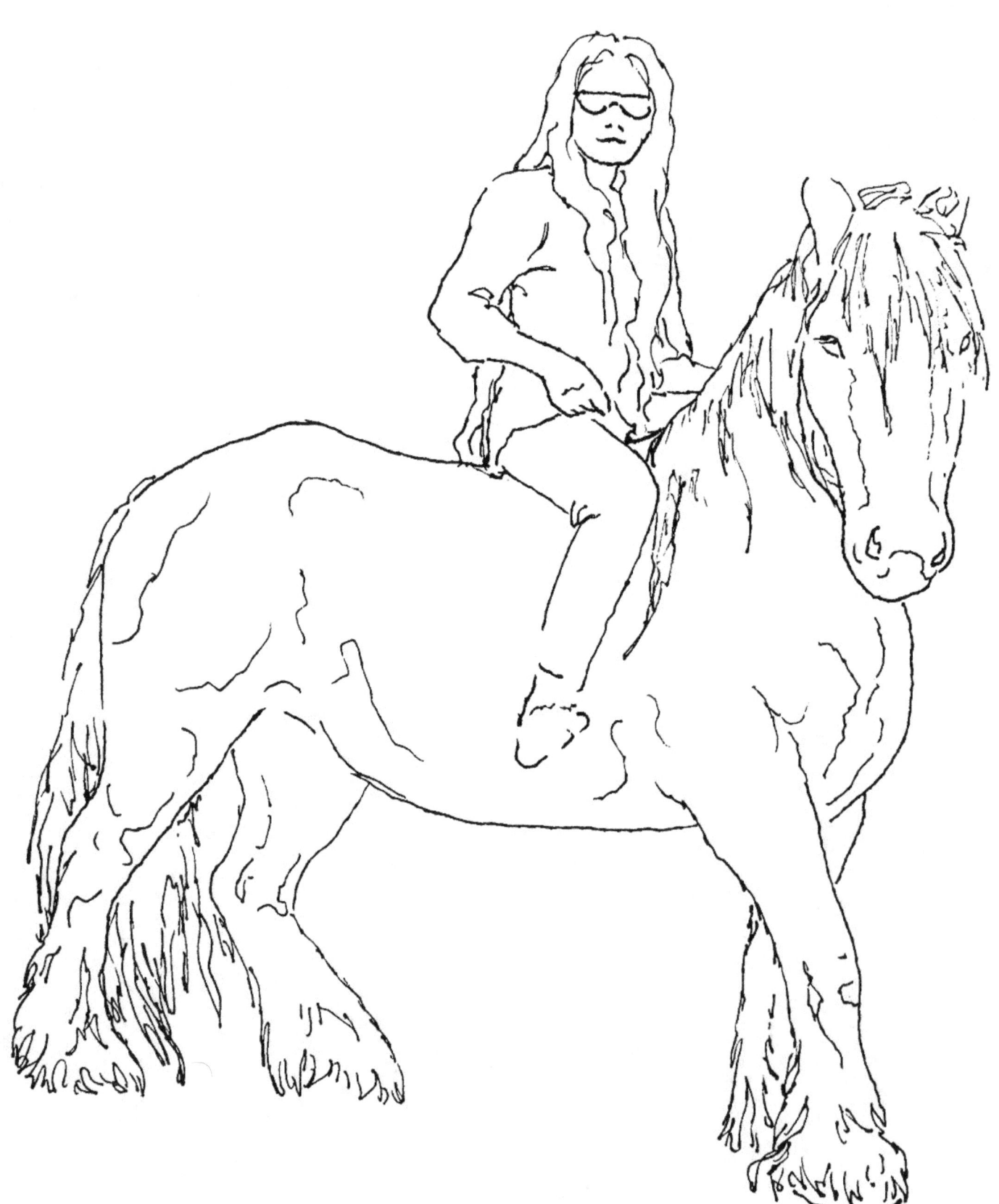

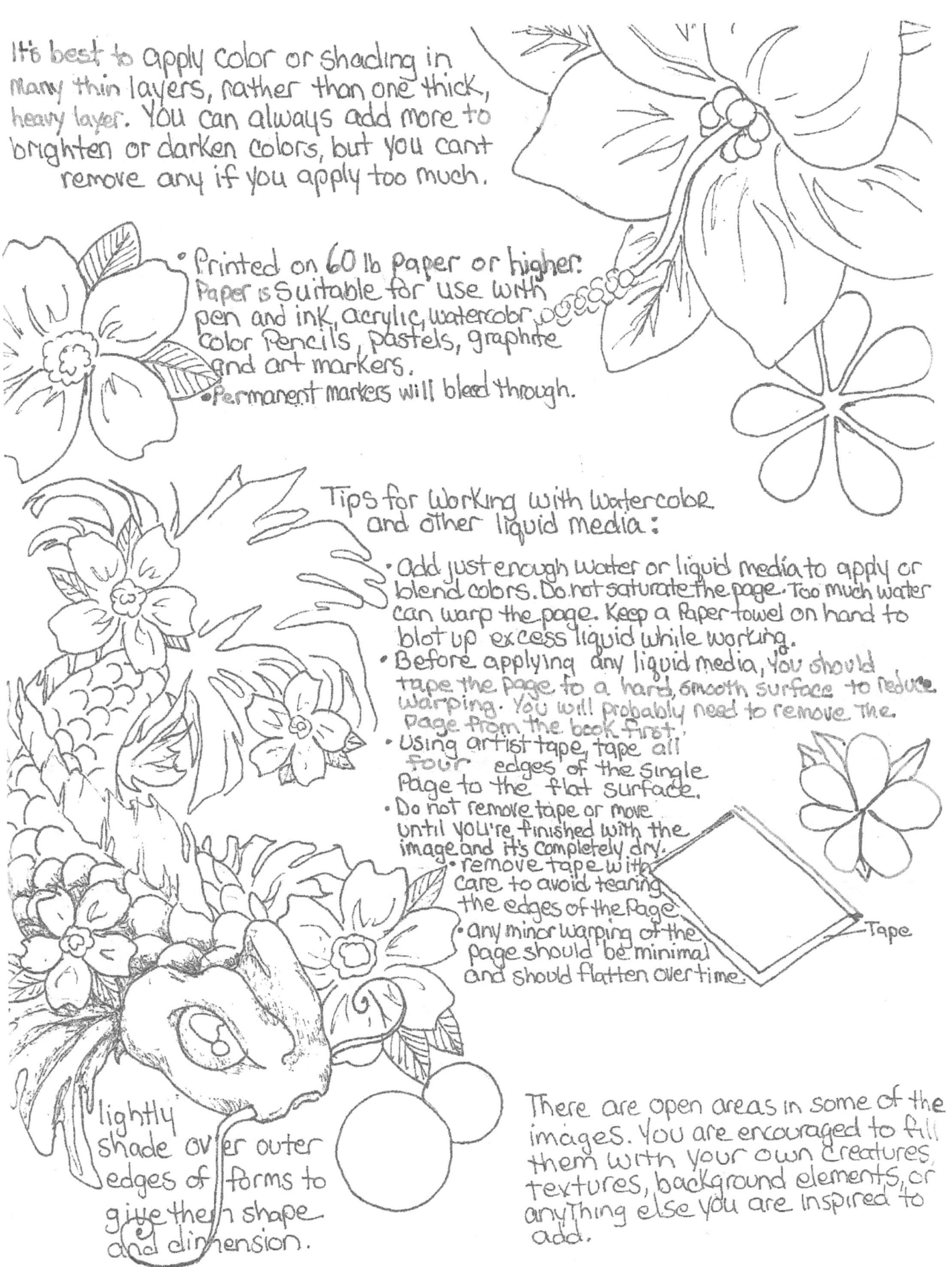

It's best to apply color or shading in many thin layers, rather than one thick, heavy layer. You can always add more to brighten or darken colors, but you can't remove any if you apply too much.

- Printed on 60 lb paper or higher. Paper is suitable for use with pen and ink, acrylic, watercolor, color pencils, pastels, graphite and art markers.
- Permanent markers will bleed through.

Tips for working with watercolor and other liquid media:

- Add just enough water or liquid media to apply or blend colors. Do not saturate the page. Too much water can warp the page. Keep a paper towel on hand to blot up excess liquid while working.
- Before applying any liquid media, you should tape the page to a hard, smooth surface to reduce warping. You will probably need to remove the page from the book first.
- Using artist tape, tape all four edges of the single page to the flat surface.
- Do not remove tape or move until you're finished with the image and it's completely dry.
- remove tape with care to avoid tearing the edges of the page.
- Any minor warping of the page should be minimal and should flatten over time.

Tape

lightly shade over outer edges of forms to give them shape and dimension.

There are open areas in some of the images. You are encouraged to fill them with your own creatures, textures, background elements, or anything else you are inspired to add.

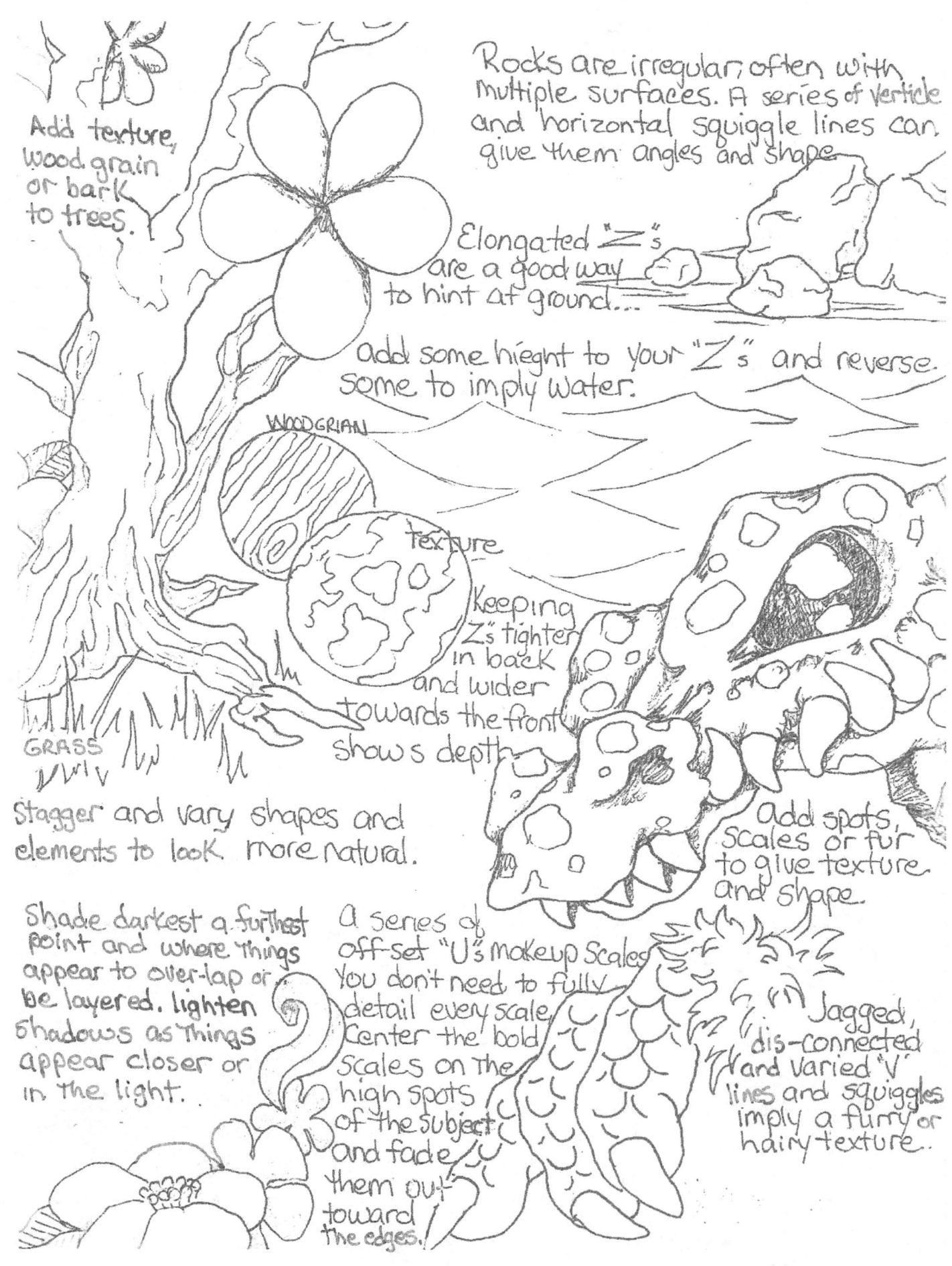

Add texture, wood grain or bark to trees.

Rocks are irregular, often with multiple surfaces. A series of verticle and horizontal squiggle lines can give them angles and shape.

Elongated "Z's are a good way to hint at ground...

Add some hieght to your "Z's and reverse some to imply water.

WOODGRIAN

texture

Keeping "Z's tighter in back and wider towards the front shows depth.

GRASS

Stagger and vary shapes and elements to look more natural.

Add spots, scales or fur to give texture and shape.

Shade darkest a furthest point and where things appear to over-lap or be layered. lighten shadows as things appear closer or in the light.

A series of off-set "U's makeup scales. You don't need to fully detail every scale. Center the bold scales on the high spots of the subject and fade them out toward the edges.

Jagged, dis-connected and varied "V" lines and squiggles imply a furry or hairy texture.

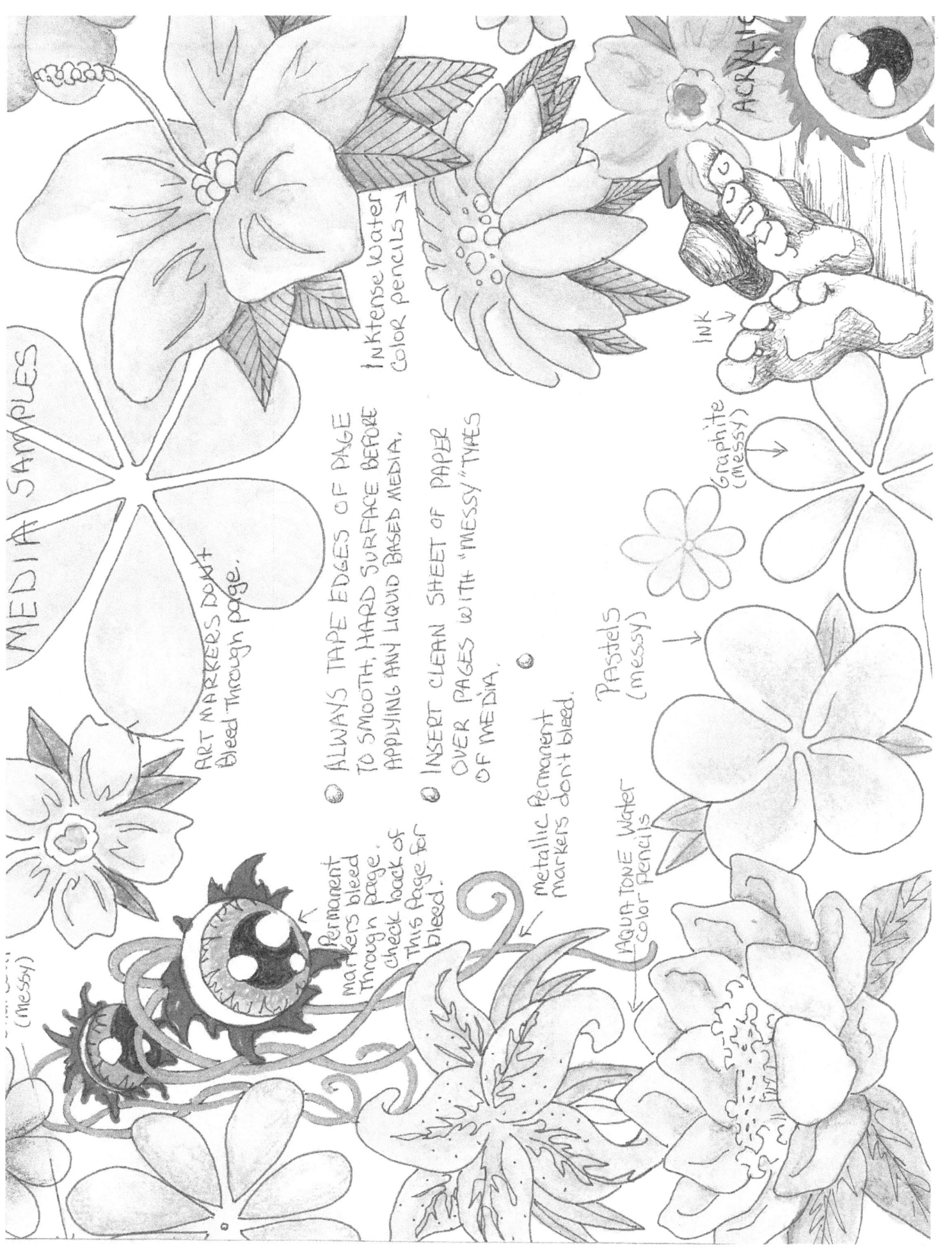

MEDIA SAMPLES

(messy)

ART MARKERS don't
Bleed Through page.

Inktense Water
Color Pencils →

ACRYLIC

Ink →

Graphite
(messy) →

• ALWAYS TAPE EDGES OF PAGE
  TO SMOOTH, HARD SURFACE BEFORE
  APPLYING ANY LIQUID BASED MEDIA.

• INSERT CLEAN SHEET OF PAPER
  OVER PAGES WITH "MESSY" TYPES
  OF MEDIA.

Pastels
(messy) →

Permanent
Markers bleed
Through page.
Check back of
This Page for
bleed.

Metallic Permanent
markers don't bleed.

AQUA-TONE Water
Color Pencils →

Place under the page
you are working on to
protect pages beneath.

Remove this page
from book and
laminate.

or it be even if single page is
taped to hard smooth surface.